PALMS
BENEATH THE

A Tempting Taste of Tropical Texas

Brownsville Junior Service League

BROWNSVILLE TEXAS

Illustrated by **Don Breeden**, a Brownsville native. He recieved his degree in Art from the University of Houston, and is the President and founding partner of Breeden McCumber Gonzalez, Inc., a South Texas advertising agency. As an avid hunter and fisherman, he translates his love for the outdoors into his paintings of local flora and fauna.

Any inquiries about the book or additional copies ahould be directed to::

Brownsville Junior Service League, Inc.

P.O. Box 3151
Brownsville, Texas 78523-3151

International Standard Book Number
0-9653293-0-5

Printed in the USA by

WIMMER

The Wimmer Companies, Inc.

Memphis

Now a peaceful city on the Rio Grande River, Brownsville, Texas was born in conflict — conflict between the United States and Mexico as to the boundary of these two nations. From that adversarial beginning, Brownsville now enjoys a harmonious existence with its Mexican sister city, Matamoros.

When settlers arrived in South Texas following the Mexican-American War, they found palm trees swaying in the balmy breezes. Amid the lush semitropical vegetation, birds and animals of all types roamed freely about the land. There were beautiful bodies of water winding through the area. These small lakes, created by the former riverbed of the Rio Grande, are locally known as "resacas". They vary in width and depth providing additional color to the landscape. Many of these "resacas" are lined with tall palms that stand majestically as guardians of the shoreline.

In this wonderful setting, residents established their homes. The well-to-do constructed adobe brick homes. The less fortunate built "jacales" with tree limbs forming a frame and packed with mud to form the walls. The roofs were covered with multiple layers of palm fronds. The kitchens for these early structures were generally detached from the living quarters. This arrangement provided safety from kitchen fires in addition to keeping heat and odors away from the main house.

Cuisine of the early years of Brownsville soon became as interwoven as the cultures of the citizens themselves. The native Mexican population relied heavily on corn, tomatoes, onions, chili peppers and various spices. The French and Spaniards brought with them the recipes of their native countries and the settlers from the northern part of the United States added to the variety. Within a few years, a wide choice of foods and dining existed.

To purchase the ingredients for these tasty meals the City Market, established in 1862, was the central shopping center. Each morning a bell tolled, signaling the opening of the market for business. The vegetable stands were located on the west side of the market. Each stand had an extensive inventory of in-season produce. Shoppers moved from stand to stand inspecting the quality and selection. Prices were adjustable, settled after quotes and bids. Bakery products, brooms, cooking utensils and other household items such as lamps and coal oil were found on the east side of the market.

In the enclosed area of the building, the meat vendors were located. Fresh meats were brought in daily and displayed in show cases cooled by block ice. The butchers readily helped with the selection of purchases. Ground beef could be bought or ground from meat chosen for this purpose. Soup bones were generally thrown in as complimentary extras.Throughout the years, Mexican foods have remained very popular in our border culture. Tortillas, enchiladas, tacos, stuffed "relleno" peppers, spices, chili peppers, rice and beans are the mainstay of Mexican dishes. Freshly prepared salads, vegetables and fruits are enjoyed seasonally. Mesquite charcoal continues to be a favorite for grilling meats.

With the mildly tropical climate of the Rio Grande Valley, dining "al fresco" on the patio is enjoyed year round. The beauty of the outdoors gives an extra flavor to foods. The aroma of spicy dishes, grilled meats and the landscape of lush tropical plants with record height palms in the background provides for colorful dining.

The culture of this unique community has enjoyed both Anglo and Mexican influence throughout its near 150 years existence. This mingling, felt in almost every aspect of daily life, gives Brownsville a beauty unique in this nation. Foods often connect us to our heritage, family and community. "Beneath the Palms" offers you a wide choice of favorite dishes from the kitchens of Brownsville's best culinary citizens. This collection reflects American, Mexican, Texan, contemporary and treasured family recipes that are shared in our homes and social gatherings. As a historian, I am pleased to join with the Brownsville Junior Service League in offering this cookbook for all to enjoy!

Bruce Aiken is a former Chairman of the Cameron County Historical Commission and current Executive Director of the Historic Brownsville Museum. Mr. Aiken is known as a scholar on the history of Brownsville and South Texas. He is sought out frequently by researchers and authors for his historic expertise.

by Rita Tyler-Aguilar
and Rita Eckert

Brownsville Junior Service League

A History of Helping

In 1939, the palms, poinsettias, cacti and farm land of the Texas Rio Grande Valley city of Brownsville were featured in National Geographic magazine. The article featured tracts of land being cultivated for citrus and vegetable crops with palm trees planted to break the stark skyline and to serve as windbreaks. The homemakers of Brownsville routinely shopped open air markets for fresh flounder, redfish, crabs, and shrimp that were caught in local waters and a bounty of vegetables and citrus from surrounding fields to prepare meals. Texas Market and Grocery in the historic Market Square sold meats, including game and fowl. Neighborhood grocers offered breads, flour, sugar, spices, dried chilies and necessities to run a household. The bicultural blend of American and Mexican foods were served daily in homes.

Led by Gladys Sams Porter in May of that year, thirty-six women founded the Brownsville Junior Service League with the purpose of fostering the economic, cultural and educational conditions of their city. The first successful major fundraising effort in the Fall of 1941 was a Broadway-style "Follies" revue that continues today. Financial support has been generated through countless events over the years, from sock hops to gala balls, Sombrero Festival ticket sales to ice cream sales and craft bazaars to auctions. All proceeds from fundraising efforts, including those from the sale of this book, are reinvested in the community. Today, in 1996, the active and sustaining membership continues to share the beliefs of our charter members.

BJSL membership is composed of women of diverse backgrounds and careers who actively take part in community affairs. Members are volunteers who work with the knowledge that individual development is without meaning unless it results in a tangible contribution to the world in which we live. As our oldest project, Well Baby clinic, providing pediatric care of infants from birth to one year, has been continuously League supported for fifty-six years. Past and ongoing projects include providing meals for the needy, drug awareness programs in local elementary schools, aquatic exercise for the handicapped, diabetic screening, crippled children's clinic, nursing home visits, educational zoo classes, puppet shows targeting child abuse, dyslexia recording clinic, scoliosis examinations, children's reading and after-school tutoring programs. BJSL awards annual scholarships to local high school seniors and students enrolled in the community college nursing programs, as well as, annually contributes to a variety of charitable activities and organizations.

As a border city, our community culture and the foods we eat are often described as "Tex-Mex". "Beneath the Palms" represents the diverse recipes and culinary accomplishments of our area. Throughout this volume is a collection of healthy and lowfat recipes to improve nutrition, traditional American dishes and a special section of Mexican recipes to delight the appetite. As we relax under the swaying palms of the gentle Gulf breeze, we wish for our readers to enjoy good food, good health and joy in sharing meals with your family and friends. ¡Salud!

All proceeds from the sale of this cookbook are reinvested in projects targeted at helping the women and children of Brownsville.

Contents

 This symbol indicates a low-fat healthy recipe.

Acknowledgments

Cookbook Committee:
Chair: Connie W. Fischer
Editors: Phyllis Bates/Monica Garza
Publishing: Liz Swantner
Marketing: Colleen Plitt

Committee Members:
Rita Tyler-Aguilar
April Buentello
Kristie Gehring
Katharine M. Guajardo
Bertha Janis
Carol Mark
Melanie Oliveira
Leslyn Petersen
Carmela Petraitis
Thelma Quintanilla
Tracey Zavaletta

Artwork: Don Breeden
Photography: Mike Krzywonski
Preface: Bruce Aiken
Cookbook Title: Mellena H. Conner
Creative Coordinator: Rita S. Eckert
Spanish Language Consultant:
Frances Pinkerton

Sustaining Advisors:
Mellena H. Conner
Rita S. Eckert
Kaye K. Kimberling
Ann O. Kveton
Molly M. Plitt
Eloise Ely Sweeney

Former Cookbook Committee Chairs:
Marilyn Nelson: Chair 1989 - 1990
Traci Wickett: Chair 1990 - 1991
Susan Walker: Co-Chair 1990 - 1991

Recipe Testing:
The Brownsville Junior Service League thanks the members of the testing committee and their families who have given generously of their time and talents to assure the quality of the recipes.

Rita Tyler-Aguilar
Phyllis Bates
Michelle Belila
Phyllis Blakemore
April Buentello
Lecia Chaney
Andrea Clements
Barbara Collins
Sheri Dittman
Dani Faulk
Connie Fischer
Buddy Fischer
Janeah Anderson-Garcia
Monica Garza
Victoria Gauvreau
Kristie Gehring
Norma Griffin
Mary Griswold
Katharine M. Guajardo
Lynne Hacker
Yolanda Hykes
Bertha Janis
Lourdes Kilgore
Lorraine Knoch
Darla Lapeyre
Tony Lolcoma
Carol Mark
Elizabeth Neally
Marilyn Nelson
Melanie Oliveira
Anna Owen
Cynthia Pashos
Michael Pashos
Leslyn Petersen

Carmela Petraitis
Colleen Plitt
Molly M. Plitt
Thelma Quintanilla
Vicki Santa Ana

Betsy Sheets
Beverly Speer
Patty Sutherland
Liz Swantner
Betty Swantner

Robert Swantner
Amy Tipton
Traci Wickett
Pat Young
Tracey Zavaletta

Recipe Contributors:

The Brownsville Junior Service League wishes to thank its members, families, and friends who have contributed recipes, for without your support this book could not have been possible. It is our sincere hope that no one has been inadvertently overlooked.

Rita Tyler-Aguilar
Elizabeth Anderson
Odessa Angilelle
Amanda Atkinson
Mary Ann Auforth
Patti Ayala
Liz Axon
Irene Banaszak
Gina Mayo Barrera
Eva Barron
Phyllis Bates
Michele Belila
Glenda Berger
Mary Carter Berrios
Nancy Blanco
Leatrice Bradford
Mary Bradford
Aileen Brittain
Barbara Brooks
Brownsville Chamber
   of Commerce
April Buentello
Margie Canfield
Irena Carling
Sandra Castañon
Martha Castro
Ginny Clearman
Andrea Clements
Barbara A. Collins
Mellena H. Conner
Marlys Cortinas
Cynthia Crane
Candy Crouch
Elizabeth Cummins
Kay Cunningham

Ray Cunningham
Mary Daniel
Pam Dawson
Kathryn Deibel
Jacqui H. Dempsey
Bobbie Dew
June Dittman
Sheri Dittman
Clifton Dixon
Gwen Drennan
Ann Sweeney Dunkin
Penny Durham
Ann Earley
Rita S. Eckert
Lilia Esteve
Dani Faulk
Norma Ferguson
Bill Fischer
Buddy Fischer
Connie Fischer
Barbara Frank
Phyllis Frapart
Diamond Freeburg
Janeah Anderson-
   Garcia
Mary Irene Garcia
Bertha Champion
   Garza
Marla Garza
Mary Helen Garza
Norma Garza
Victoria Gauvreau
Roger Gauvreau
Judy Gavito
Jane Giese

Joni Gillis
Brenda Gloor
Catherine Gloor
June Gloor
Carlos Gomez
Ginger Grau
Chula Griffin
Judy Griffin
Sally Graham
Jay Griswold
Laurie Grubb
Katharine M. Guajardo
Emily Guminski
Fran Guminski
Sandra Guthrie
Lynne Hacker
Cynthia Hamilton
Elaine Hannon
Susan Hanson
Kathy Harding
Jan Hardman
Kathy Harlan
Laura Harse
Elaine Hatch
Rose Mary Head
Glenda Heaner
Marna Herman
Lana Hertel
Claire Hines
Lil Hodgson
Nellie D. Huffaker
Lindsay Irwin
Pat John
Catherine Johnson
Kaye K. Kimberling

Geralyn Kirkpatrick
Ann Kveton
Lizette Lacombe
Darla Lapeyre
David Lapeyre
Debbie Loff
Rose Lorenz
Mary Mann
Carol Mark
Marie A. Mark
Dorothy H. Martin
Helen Martinez
Margaret H. McAllen
Jane McKinney
Ivianne Merrill
Marylin Meyers
Patti Meyers
Bessie Kate Moore
Gloria Moore
Elizabeth Neally
Jane Neally
Marilyn Nelson
Anna Owen
Mary Jo Pace
Sherry Party
Cynthia Pashos
Lita Pashos
Michael Pashos
Margaret Pate
Betsy Peerman
Christy Peterson
David Pfurr

Karen Philipps
Diane Pineda
Patty Planters
Colleen Plitt
Molly M. Plitt
Betty Poe
Noralee Pope
Judy Powell
Lisa Proctor
Sallie Rainey
Susan Rieder
Teddy Renfrow
Nancy Reynolds
Daisy Richardson
Nelda Richardson
Diane Rickenbach
Nena Roser
Rachel Roser
Roslyn Roser
Margaret Ross
Else Hofmokel Roth
John Sahadi
Norma Sanchez
Susan
    Schmatchenberger
Mary Jane Shands
Betsy Sheets
Dorothy Smithart
Beverly Speer
Debbie Stern
Patty Sutherland
Billie Sutter

Betty Swantner
Coleen Swantner
Elizabeth Swantner
Eloise Ely Sweeney
Beth Terrazas
Amy Tipton
Maggie Treu
Mrs. Reginald Trice
Melissa Tullos
Earl Tyler
Dean Tyler
Eric Valle
Margaret Valle
Susan Valle
Janet Vaughan
Ileana Vicinaiz
Susan Walker
Keith Wallace
Laura Wallace
Traci Wickett
Elaine Wiedermann
Elaine Willette
Cecily R. Wilson
Jo Ann Witmer
Carmen White
Marge Whittemore
Penny Wolfe
Yucca Wyatt
Vivian Zapata
Tracey Zavaletta
Dolly Zimmerman
Elena Zorola

Appetizers/Beverages

Beneath the Palms

🌴 Artichoke Heart Spread

Yield: 4 servings

- 1 (8 ounce) can artichoke hearts, drained and chopped
- 1 cup fat free Parmesan cheese
- ½ cup fat free sour cream
- ½ cup fat free mayonnaise
- 1 (8 ounce) package fat free cream cheese
- ¼ teaspoon minced garlic
- 2 jalapeño peppers, seeded and diced

Mix all ingredients in food processor until smooth. Put mixture in an oven-proof dish and bake at 325° for 30 to 45 minutes. Serve with fat free crackers or sourdough bread.

Can be served in artichoke halves for a pretty presentation.

Baked Spinach and Artichoke Hearts

Yield: 12 servings

- 1 (8 ounce) package cream cheese
- 1 stick butter
  Juice of one lemon
- 2 (10 ounce) packages frozen chopped spinach
- 1 (14 ounce) can artichoke hearts, drained and sliced

In top of a double boiler, soften cream cheese and butter with lemon juice. Add spinach and artichokes. Place in greased casserole dish, bake at 350° for 15 minutes.

Chili Beef Dip

Yield: 2 cups

1   **pound ground beef**
1   **small onion, chopped**
1   **(8 ounce) can tomato sauce**
1   **(8 ounce) jar picante sauce**
½   **cup taco sauce**
1   **tablespoon chili powder**
4   **ounces green chilies, chopped**
¼   **teaspoon salt**
1   **cup shredded cheddar cheese**

Sauté beef and onion in large skillet until beef is browned, stirring to crumble meat, drain grease. Stir in next 6 ingredients. Spoon mixture into chafing dish, sprinkle with cheese. Serve with tortilla chips.

If a spicier taste is desired, use hot picante sauce.

🌴 Creamy Spinach Dip

Yield: 2 cups

1   **(10 ounce) package frozen chopped spinach, thawed and squeezed dry**
1   **cup fat free sour cream**
2   **scallions, cut into chunks**
2   **teaspoons dried dill weed**
2-3   **teaspoons lemon juice**
½   **teaspoon salt**

Process all ingredients in a food processor or blender until smooth.

Beneath the Palms

🌴 Frijoles Negros con Salsa (Black Bean Dip)

Yield: 2 cups

2   **cups cooked and drained black beans**
4   **teaspoons tomato sauce**
1   **clove garlic, minced**
2   **teaspoons lemon juice**
2   **green onions, finely chopped**
⅓   **cup picante sauce (medium or hot)**
1   **tablespoon fat free sour cream**

Place beans, tomato sauce, garlic, and lemon juice in a food processor. Blend until the mixture forms a smooth paste, about 1 minute. Stir in green onions, picante sauce, and sour cream. Spoon into a serving bowl. Garnish with additional chopped green onions.

Serve with fat free crackers.

🌴 Cowboy Caviar

Yield: 6 servings

8   **ounces dried black-eyed peas**
1   **red pepper, diced**
2   **green scallions, diced**
2   **(6 ounce) bottles jalapeño peppers in vinegar, drained and minced**
2   **tablespoons lemon juice**
1   **tablespoon Dijon mustard**
2   **cloves garlic, minced**
1   **teaspoon salt**
1   **teaspoon thyme leaves**
1   **teaspoon sugar**
¼   **teaspoon Tabasco Sauce**
    Black pepper to taste
¼   **cup fat free Italian salad dressing**

Soak beans overnight. Put in a large pot, cover with water and boil. Reduce heat and simmer for 35 to 40 minutes. Drain and rinse in cold water. Place in a large serving bowl; add all remaining ingredients. Toss to mix.

Serve at room temperature.

Lower Valley Vegetable Dip

Yield: 1½ cups

1½ **cups mayonnaise**
 Juice of one lemon
1 **tablespoon mustard**
1 **large onion, grated**
3 **shakes Worcestershire sauce**
½ **teaspoon salt**
 Celery salt to taste

Mix ingredients together in blender until smooth.

Serve with raw vegetables.

Smoked Salmon Paté

Yield: 2 cups

1 **can smoked salmon**
1¼ **sticks butter, softened**
½ **cup mayonnaise**
1 **tablespoon Worcestershire sauce**
1 **tablespoon lemon juice**
½ **teaspoon salt**
¼ **teaspoon Tabasco Sauce**
1 **dash cayenne pepper**
 Parsley or watercress

In large bowl, combine all ingredients, except parsley or watercress. With wooden spoon, beat mixture into smooth paste. Press half into 1-quart mold, add other half. Cover and refrigerate at least 8 hours or overnight. Turn onto serving dish. Garnish with parsley or watercress.

Serve with melba toast.

15

Beneath the Palms

Smoky Salmon Spread

Yield: 16 servings

1 (3 ounce) package cream cheese, room temperature
½ tablespoon lemon juice
½ teaspoon horseradish
1 tablespoon chopped fresh green onions
½ teaspoon salt
⅛ teaspoon black pepper
⅛ teaspoon Liquid Smoke seasoning
1 (7 ¾ ounce) can smoked salmon
1 tablespoon lemon juice
2 tablespoons finely chopped parsley

In a medium bowl, combine cream cheese and next 6 ingredients. Thoroughly drain salmon, remove and discard bones. Use two forks to flake salmon; stir into cream cheese mixture along with lemon juice. Refrigerate at least one hour. Shape into 8-inch by 2½-inch roll. Sprinkle with parsley, lightly pressing into roll; wrap in plastic wrap or foil. Refrigerate 6 hours or overnight. Spread on crackers.

Clifton's Coyote Cheese

Yield: 4 cups

1 pound processed cheese loaf
10 ounces cheddar cheese
1 stick butter
3 eggs
8 ounces mayonnaise
1 (7 ounce) jar pimentos
Jalapeño peppers to taste
Cayenne pepper to taste

Melt cheeses in double boiler. Melt butter in microwave, add eggs, mayonnaise, pimentos, and peppers, stir. Add to melted cheese, beat with electric mixer until smooth. Chill.

Padre Island Crab Dip

Yield: 2 cups

8   ounces crabmeat,
     picked clean
1   cup sour cream
3   tablespoons chili sauce
¼   cup chopped green
     onions
2   teaspoons horseradish
     Crackers
     Celery sticks

Drain and flake crabmeat. Mix with next 4 ingredients. Chill for several hours to blend flavors. Serve with crackers and celery sticks.

Light or fat free sour cream can be substituted to reduce the fat in this recipe.

Chicken Liver Paté

Yield: 2 cups

2   sticks butter
1   pound chicken livers
¼   cup Cognac
½   teaspoon salt
2   shallots
     Freshly ground pepper
     Dash of nutmeg

Melt butter in skillet, add livers and sauté until done. Put in blender with next 5 ingredients and blend well. Spoon into a glass bowl and refrigerate for 1½ days before serving.

Jalapeño Cheese Spread

Yield: 2 cups

4   jalapeño peppers,
     seeded
1   pound sharp cheddar
     cheese, cubed
1   large onion, sliced
4   cloves garlic, minced
¼   cup mayonnaise

In food processor fitted with metal blade, grind first 4 ingredients. Add mayonnaise and process until mixture is spreading consistency. Cover and chill.

Serve with crackers or celery sticks

Beneath the Palms

Brandied Chicken Liver Paté

Yield: 3 cups

2   **pounds chicken livers, chopped**
1   **stick butter**
2   **medium onions, chopped**
1   **teaspoon paprika**
1   **teaspoon curry powder**
¼   **teaspoon salt**
¼   **teaspoon black pepper**
2   **sticks butter, softened**
¼   **cup brandy**

In a saucepan, combine first 7 ingredients. Cover and cook over low heat 10 minutes. Force through a sieve or purée in a blender. Stir in softened butter and brandy; mound paté in covered dish. Refrigerate and chill until firm. Serve with crackers or melba toast.

Boursin Cheese Spread

Yield: 2 cups

1   **clove garlic**
2   **(8 ounce) packages cream cheese, softened**
2   **sticks butter or margarine, softened**
1   **teaspoon dried oregano**
¼   **teaspoon dried basil**
¼   **teaspoon dried dill weed**
¼   **teaspoon dried marjoram**
¼   **teaspoon dried thyme**
¼   **teaspoon black pepper**

Position knife blade in food processor bowl; add garlic. Process until finely chopped, stopping once to scrape down sides. Add cream cheese and remaining ingredients; process until smooth; stopping twice to scrape down sides. May be refrigerated up to 1 week or frozen up to 3 months.

Million Dollar Cheeseball

Yield: 1 cheese ball

¼ pound Roquefort cheese, at room temperature
½ pound Old English cheese, at room temperature
2 (8 ounce) packages cream cheese, at room temperature
¼ cup chopped pecans
¼ cup chopped parsley
1 small onion, chopped fine
1 clove garlic, minced
¼ cup chopped parsley
¼ cup chopped pecans

Combine cheeses with next 4 ingredients. Roll into a ball on wax paper; wrap and place in the refrigerator until firm. When ready to serve, roll ball in remaining parsley and pecans. Serve with assorted crackers.

Devilicious Cheese Ball

Yield: 10 servings

2 (4.5 ounce) cans deviled ham
1 (8 ounce) package cream cheese
1 (4 ounce) package dry ranch salad dressing
½ cup finely chopped tomatoes
½ cup diced bell pepper
2 cups shredded cheddar cheese
½ cup roasted sunflower seeds

In medium bowl, combine all ingredients except sunflower seeds; refrigerate until firm enough to handle. Form into a ball and roll in the seeds. Refrigerate until ready to serve with crackers of your choice.

Beneath the Palms

Black Olive Cheese Ball

Yield: 1 cheese ball

1 (8 ounce) package cream cheese, softened
8 ounces blue cheese, crumbled
½ stick butter, softened
⅔ cup drained and chopped black olives
1 tablespoon minced chives
⅓ cup chopped walnuts or almonds
Parsley

Blend cheeses and butter, stir in olives and chives. Form into ball and chill thoroughly on serving dish. Press nuts over ball and trim with parsley.

Amaretto Cheese Ball

Yield: 1 cup

1 (8 ounce) package cream cheese, softened
2 tablespoons Amaretto
2 tablespoons chopped walnuts
1 (2 ounce) package sliced almonds

Combine cream cheese and Amaretto. Beat at medium speed with electric mixer until well blended. Stir in chopped walnuts. Shape as desired. Cover and chill until hardened. Remove from refrigerator and place sliced almonds, beginning at the bottom, all around until covered. Serve with homemade gingersnaps.

Gingersnaps

Yield: 4 dozen cookies

2½ cups all-purpose flour
2 teaspoons baking soda
1 teaspoon ground ginger
1 teaspoon ground cinnamon
½ teaspoon ground cloves
¼ teaspoon salt
1 cup packed brown sugar
¾ cup shortening
¼ cup molasses
1 egg

Stir together all dry ingredients. Add brown sugar and next 3 ingredients; beat well. Form into 1-inch balls, roll in sugar. Place 2 inches apart on an ungreased cookie sheet. Bake at 375° for about 10 minutes.

Kahlúa Brie

Yield: 12 servings

¾ cup chopped pecans
¼ cup Kahlúa
3 tablespoons brown sugar
1 (14 ounce) mini Brie

Spread pecans on 9-inch plate; microwave on high 4 to 6 minutes. Stir every 2 minutes. Add Kahlúa and sugar, stir well. Remove rind from top of Brie, place in microwave safe dish. Spoon pecan mixture on top. Microwave uncovered on high for 1½ to 2 minutes.

Baked Brie in Phyllo

Yield: 12 servings

¼ **cup apricot preserves**
1 **(2 pound) wheel Brie**
½ **pound frozen phyllo dough (10 - 12 leaves), thawed**
½ **cup butter or margarine, melted**

Spread preserves on top of Brie. Wrap Brie in thawed phyllo dough brushing each sheet with melted butter. Keep unused phyllo covered with a damp cloth while wrapping Brie. For even distribution, turn cheese over after applying a sheet of phyllo. Brush phyllo wrapped Brie with remaining melted butter. Cover and refrigerate. Before serving, place phyllo wrapped cheese in a shallow baking pan. Bake at 425° for 8 to 12 minutes or until golden.

As a variation, brush cheese and preserves with an egg wash; sprinkle with seasoned bread crumbs; bake as above. Another variation is to cut an x into top of cheese, pour 4 ounces of champagne over top and bake 4 minutes before serving.

Blue Cheese Stuffed Mushrooms

Yield: 12 servings

2	pounds large mushrooms
¼	cup butter
4	large green onions
½	teaspoon garlic salt
¼	teaspoon dry mustard
1	(8 ounce) package cream cheese, cut into cubes
½	cup blue cheese, crumbled
1	teaspoon soy sauce
⅛	teaspoon oregano
3	tablespoons Parmesan cheese
3	tablespoons bread crumbs
1	(7 ½ ounce) can minced clams, drained

Rinse mushrooms and remove stems. Finely chop half the stems. In a skillet, melt butter; add green onion, stems, garlic salt, and dry mustard. Cook on high heat for 2 minutes. Stir in remaining ingredients and cook on high for 1 minute. Stuff mushroom caps and place in buttered glass dish. Sprinkle with additional Parmesan cheese and cover. When ready to serve, microwave on high for 3 minutes.

Pickle Sandwich

Yield: 12 servings

1	(16 ounce) jar baby dill pickles
1	loaf brown bread
1	teaspoon minced onion
1	(8 ounce) package cream cheese, room temperature
1	tablespoon mayonnaise
1	teaspoon lemon juice

Drain pickles, set aside. Cut crust from bread slices. Mix together remaining ingredients. Spread mixture on bread slices; add one pickle to each and roll. Chill 2 hours and slice.

Greek Feta Cheese Triangles

Yield: 4 dozen

1 **(17 ¼ ounce) box frozen puff pastry**
¾ **pound Feta cheese, crumbled**
2 **eggs**
¼ **cup chopped fresh parsley**
  Flour

Thaw puff pastry for 20 minutes. In bowl, mix cheese, eggs, and parsley until well blended. Unfold one pastry sheet; on a lightly floured surface, roll to a 9x12-inch rectangle; cut into 3-inch squares. Put one tablespoon cheese filling in the center of each square, moisten edges with water and fold pastry in half forming a triangle. Press edges together firmly with tines of fork to seal. Chill. Repeat with remaining pastry sheets and cheese mixture. Place triangles on ungreased cookie sheet; bake at 425° for 8 to 10 minutes or until puffed and golden brown.

Unbaked triangles may be wrapped tightly in plastic wrap and frozen until ready to use. No need to thaw prior to baking.

Serve warm or at room temperature.

Spinach Cheese Puffs

Yield: 5 dozen

- 2 **eggs**
- 1 **medium onion, chopped**
- ½ **pound Feta cheese, crumbled**
- 1 **(8 ounce) package cream cheese**
- 1 **(10 ounce) package frozen chopped spinach**
- 2 **tablespoons chopped parsley**
- ¼ **teaspoon black pepper**
- 1 **tablespoon dill weed**
- 1 **package phyllo leaves**
- 2 **sticks butter, melted**

Combine eggs, onion, and Feta cheese in blender until smooth; add cream cheese and blend until smooth. Squeeze spinach to remove as much liquid as possible. Add to cheese mixture with parsley, pepper, and dill weed. Refrigerate at least one hour. Cut phyllo leaves into lengthwise strips, 2-inches wide. Keep leaves covered with a damp cloth, work with only a few strips at a time. Brush strips with melted butter. Place rounded teaspoon of filling on one end of strip; take one corner of dough and fold to opposite side to form triangle. Continue folding this way to end of strip. Repeat with remaining leaves and filling. Place on ungreased cookie sheet, bake at 375° for 20 minutes. Serve hot.

Pastries may be frozen, unbaked, up to 3 weeks

Beneath the Palms

Confederate Air Force Wings

Yield: 25 wings

25 chicken wings
3 tablespoons honey
½ cup pineapple juice
⅔ cup soy sauce
½ teaspoon ginger
2 cloves garlic, chopped

Split wings, discard tips. Mix remaining ingredients together. Pour over chicken and marinate overnight. Bake on cookie sheet at 350° for 1 hour, turning 2 to 3 times.

Bagdad Stuffed Shrimp

Yield: 40 shrimp

6 cups water
2 pounds large fresh shrimp
¼ cup blue cheese, softened
4 ounces cream cheese
1 tablespoon mayonnaise
1 teaspoon paprika
1 teaspoon dried basil
1 teaspoon lemon juice

Bring water to boil over medium flame; add shrimp, cook for 3 to 5 minutes. Remove from heat; drain and rinse with cold water. Chill. Peel and devein shrimp. Combine cheeses and next 4 ingredients, mix until well blended. Butterfly each shrimp in half, lengthwise, and spread about ½ teaspoon filling between halves. Chill, covered, until ready to serve.

Border Bandits

Yield: 24 peppers

24 jalapeño peppers
½ cup red wine vinegar
½ cup tarragon vinegar
12 ounces tuna fish
8 ounces mayonnaise
4 ounces cheddar cheese, grated
4 ounces Monterey Jack cheese, grated

Two days prior to serving, seed and devein jalapeños. Mix vinegars in zip-top plastic bag, add jalapeños and marinate two days turning several times. The night before serving, mix remaining ingredients. Drain jalapeños well. Spoon mixture into each jalapeño.

Mushroom Turnovers

Yield: 48 turnovers

1 cup flour
1 stick butter
1 (8 ounce) package
    cream cheese
2 cups chopped cooked
    mushrooms
1 onion, chopped
1½ cups sour cream
    Salt and pepper to taste
    Cayenne pepper to taste
    Italian seasoning to
        taste

Using food processor, combine flour, butter, and cream cheese to form pastry. Place in freezer while preparing filling. Combine mushrooms and remaining ingredients in 10-inch skillet; cook until onions are translucent. Set aside. Remove dough from freezer, roll out and cut into 4-inch circles. Place one teaspoonful of mushroom mixture in center of each circle. Fold in half and seal edges with tines of fork. Be sure to seal well or mixture will bake out of turnovers. Bake at 425° for 12 to 15 minutes.

Cheese Wrapped Olives

Yield: 3 dozen puffs

1 cup shredded cheddar
    cheese
½ cup all-purpose flour
½ stick butter, softened
½ teaspoon paprika
¼ teaspoon salt
3 dozen pimento stuffed
    olives

Combine first 5 ingredients; mix well with fork. Drain olives on paper towels. Shape a thin layer of cheese mixture around each olive. Place on ungreased cookie sheet. Bake at 425° for 8 to 10 minutes.

May be frozen, bake as directed

In November 1892, the first Post Office and Customs House in Brownsville was built on the corner of Tenth and Elizabeth streets. The structure was demolished in 1931 and replaced by the current Federal Building in 1932.

Beneath the Palms

Grapes Exquisa

Yield: 24 grapes

1 (8 ounce) package
   cream cheese, softened
3 tablespoons
   horseradish
   Toasted almonds or
   pecans, crushed
24 fresh green grapes
   Grape leaves

With a wooden spoon, blend cream cheese and horseradish together until smooth. Refrigerate 15 to 20 minutes. Toast nuts and grind coarsely in a food processor. Encase each grape in mixture; roll in nuts. Refrigerate for a short time before shaping on tray as a bunch of grapes. Garnish with grape leaves.

Pecan Cheese Crisps

Yield: 4 dozen

2 sticks butter, softened
4 cups shredded sharp
   cheddar cheese
2 cups all-purpose flour
2 cups chopped pecans
¼ teaspoon cayenne
   pepper
1 teaspoon salt

Thoroughly cream butter and cheese together; add remaining ingredients and mix well. Roll into long rolls and refrigerate several hours. Slice into ¼-inch thick rounds. Place on lightly greased cookie sheet and bake at 325° for 20 minutes or until edges brown.

The long rounds may be frozen and baked months later. The sliced rounds may be baked, then frozen.

Fiesta Fruit Dip

Yield: 2 cups

7 ounces marshmallow
   cream
1 (8 ounce) container
   whipped cream cheese

In food processor or blender, beat ingredients together until well blended. Serve with fresh fruit slices such as apples, peaches, kiwi, papayas, mangoes, or strawberries.

🌴 Pineapple Shake

Yield: 1 serving

1 cup skim milk
½ cup crushed pineapple in juice, chilled
½ teaspoon coconut or rum extract
Sugar substitute (optional)
Crushed ice (optional)

In a blender, combine milk, pineapple, extract, and sugar substitute (if desired). Process until smooth. Add crushed ice.

One cup frozen strawberries (no sugar added) may be substituted for the pineapple.

🌴 Banana Coffee Shake

Yield: 3 servings

2 cups skim milk
1 large ripe banana, mashed
3 tablespoons nonfat dry milk
1 tablespoon sugar
1½ teaspoons instant coffee granules
½ teaspoon vanilla extract

In a 1-quart saucepan over medium heat, heat all ingredients, except vanilla, until tiny bubbles form around edge, stirring occasionally. Remove from heat; stir in vanilla. Pour half the milk mixture into a blender; cover and blend at low speed until smooth. Pour into bowl, repeat with remaining mixture. Pour into frosted glasses and serve.

Beneath the Palms

Patio Bloody Mary Mix

Yield: 8 servings

1 (23 ounce) can tomato juice
1 (10 ounce) can beef broth
1 (16 ounce) can orange juice
¼ cup lemon juice
¼ cup Worcestershire sauce
 Salt
 Dash of Tabasco Sauce
 Vodka
 Celery ribs

Mix all ingredients well. Use 1½ ounce vodka and ice for each serving. Serve with a celery rib for a swizzle stick.

Vodka Slush

Yield: 16 ounces

1 (6 ounce) can frozen orange juice concentrate, thawed
2 (6 ounce) cans frozen lemonade concentrate, thawed
2 (6 ounce) cans frozen limeade concentrate, thawed
1 cup sugar
3½ cups water
2 cups vodka
2 (28 ounce) bottles lemon-lime soda, chilled

Combine first 6 ingredients, mixing well. Freeze 48 hours, stirring occasionally. For each serving, spoon ¾ cup frozen mixture into a tall glass; fill with soda. Serve at once.

Great for lunch or brunch.

South Texas Sangrîa

Yield: 18 servings

3 **lemons, cut into ¼-inch slices**
6 **oranges, cut into ¼-inch slices**
2 **apples, cut into thin slices**
1 **lime, cut into ¼-inch slices**
1 **cup sugar, more to taste**
1 **gallon dry red wine**
8 **ounces brandy**
   Chilled club soda to taste

Combine lemons, oranges, apples, lime, and sugar in a large pitcher. Pour in wine and brandy; stir well. Refrigerate for at least 1 hour. Add chilled club soda to taste.

Rio Grande Tea

Yield: 4 servings

2 **cups brewed tea**
1½ **cups unsweetened orange juice**
¾ **cup unsweetened pineapple juice**
5 **whole cloves**
1 **(3-inch) stick cinnamon**
¼ **teaspoon whole allspice**
   Orange slices (optional)

Combine first 6 ingredients in a medium saucepan. Bring to a boil. Remove from heat; cover and let stand 20 minutes. Remove and discard spices using a slotted spoon. Cover and chill. Serve over ice, garnish with orange slices, if desired.

Beneath the Palms

Frozen Margaritas

Yield: 5 servings

1 (6 ounce) can frozen
  limeade
1 (6 ounce) can tequila
6 ounces Grand Marnier
5 lime wedges
  Coarse salt

Place first 3 ingredients in a blender. Fill with ice, purée until smooth. Run a lime wedge around rim of glasses, dip in coarse salt. Fill with mixture and garnish each glass with a lime wedge.

Wine Slush

Yield: 4 servings

1½ cups chilled sweet,
   fruity wine
2-3 cups melon cubes or
   peach slices

Pour wine into container of a 2-cup or larger ice cream maker. Freeze according to manufacturer's directions until softly frozen. Divide melon among 4 chilled bowls; top with wine slush.

By the Sea Mimosas

Yield: 4 servings

2 cups orange juice
2 cups champagne
4 strawberries
  Mint leaves

Mix together the orange juice and champagne. Chill. Pour into champagne flutes; garnish with a strawberry or fresh mint leaves.

Fresh mango can be substituted for the strawberries.

Hot Buttered Rum

Yield: 25 to 30 servings

1 **pound butter, softened**
1 **pound brown sugar**
1 **pound powdered sugar**
1 **quart softened vanilla ice cream**
2 **teaspoons cinnamon**
1 **teaspoon nutmeg**
 Rum
 Stick cinnamon
 Boiling water

In a large mixing bowl, cream butter and sugars together. Blend in ice cream, cinnamon and nutmeg. Store in freezer. When ready to serve, mix one jigger of rum and 2 tablespoons of frozen mixture in a mug. Fill with boiling water. Garnish with a cinnamon stick.

This is so good, it should be called dessert!

Irish Cream

Yield: 10 to 12 servings

3 **eggs**
1 **(14 ounce) can sweetened condensed milk**
½ **pint heavy cream**
12 **ounces half and half**
4 **tablespoons chocolate syrup**
1 **teaspoon vanilla**
14 **ounces whiskey**

Blend all ingredients, except whiskey, in a blender. Pour into large bowl, add whiskey, mix well. Bottle and refrigerate 24 hours. To serve pour over ice.

Must be used within 30 days.

Beneath the Palms

Kahlúa

1 vanilla bean
3½ cups sugar
4 cups water
¾ cup instant coffee
    powder
4 cups vodka

In a small saucepan, boil vanilla bean, sugar, and water for 5 minutes. Add coffee and boil 2 minutes longer, stirring constantly. Cool for 30 minutes, add 4 cups vodka. Store in covered bottle and shake daily for 3 weeks before drinking.

Spiced Tea

Yield: 16 servings

2 cups boiling water
6 teaspoons tea leaves
1 (6 ounce) can frozen
    lemon juice concentrate
1 (6 ounce) can frozen
    orange juice
    concentrate
1½ cups sugar
8 cups water
1 stick cinnamon
    Sugar to taste

Pour boiling water over tea leaves and let cool. Strain; add remaining ingredients. Simmer mixture for 20 minutes. If tea is too strong, dilute with more water. Add extra sugar to taste.

This was Mrs. Lyndon B. Johnson's recipe.

Orange Blush

Yield: 10 servings

1 (6 ounce) can frozen
    orange juice
    concentrate
2 quarts cranberry juice
1 (12 ounce) can lemon-
    lime soda, chilled

Thaw orange juice and mix with cranberry juice, add soda just prior to serving.

Iced Tea Punch

Yield: 50 servings

4   **family-size tea bags**
4   **cups boiling water**
2   **cups sugar**
1   **cup lemon juice**
1   **quart cold water**
2   **(46 ounce) cans
      pineapple juice**
2   **(32 ounce) bottles
      ginger ale**
    Ice

Steep tea bags in boiling water for 10 to 15 minutes. Add sugar and lemon juice; divide into 2 quart jars (not full) and store in refrigerator. To serve, mix 1 jar tea base, 1 quart cold water, pineapple juice, ginger ale, and ice.

Kir Royale

Yield: 1 serving

1   **tablespoon creme de
      cassis**
8   **ounces champagne
      Lime wedges**

Pour creme de cassis into champagne flute. Fill with champagne. Garnish with lime wedge.

White wine may be substituted for the champagne.

Shanti

Yield: 1 serving

6   **ounces lemonade, cold**
16 **ounces Bass Ale, cold**

Pour lemonade into a tall frosty glass. Pour ale on top and serve.

Beneath the Palms

Italian Margaritas

Yield: 4 servings

6 ounces Tequila
6 ounces Triple Sec
3 ounces Amaretto
1 (6 ounce) can frozen
   lime concentrate
Ice
Lime slices
Salt

Combine all ingredients in a blender. Purée until smooth. Rub lime on edge of glasses then dip into salt. Pour mixture into glasses.

Border Buttermilk

Yield: 4 servings

1 (6 ounce) can pink
   lemonade concentrate
3-4 ounces light rum
1 blender crushed ice

Place all ingredients in a blender. Fill with crushed ice. Blend until smooth. Serve and sip slowly.

This is the Chamber of Commerce's welcome to Brownsville drink!

Cranberry Sparkle

Yield: 20 servings

¼ teaspoon cinnamon
¼ teaspoon nutmeg
⅛ teaspoon allspice
4 pints cranberry juice
   cocktail
1 quart orange juice
1 liter lemon-lime soda

Combine first 5 ingredients. Strain through a cheese cloth. Chill in refrigerator. Chill soda; add to mixture just prior to serving.

Soups/Stews/Chilis

Beneath the Palms

Chilled Avocado Soup

Yield: 6 servings

3 ripe avocados
1 cup chicken broth
1 cup light cream
1 teaspoon salt
¼ teaspoon onion salt
1 teaspoon lemon juice
   Pinch of white pepper
   Lemon slices

Half avocados lengthwise, remove pits and peel. In a blender, mix with chicken broth until smooth. Add cream and seasonings; mix well. Pour into glass container, cover and refrigerate for three hours or overnight. Stir in lemon juice, garnish with lemon slices and serve chilled.

This is a very rich soup. Small servings are recommended.

Chilled Parsley and Tarragon Soup

Yield: 4 servings

3 tablespoons unsalted butter
1 cup chopped onion
4 cups chicken stock or low salt broth
1 bunch fresh parsley, trimmed and chopped
1 large russet potato, peeled and chopped
3 tablespoons chopped fresh tarragon
¼ cup half and half
   Salt and pepper to taste
   Parsley sprigs

Melt butter in heavy large saucepan over medium heat. Add onion and sauté 5 minutes. Add stock, parsley and potato; bring to a boil. Reduce heat; simmer until potato is tender, about 10 minutes. Mix in tarragon. Puree mixture in blender in batches, and transfer to bowl. Mix in half and half. Chill at least 3 hours. Season soup to taste with salt and pepper. Ladle into bowls; sprinkle with parsley and serve.

Can be made 1 day ahead. Cover; keep refrigerated.

🌴 Tropical Texas Melon Soup

Yield: 9 cups

6½	**cups coarsely chopped cantaloupe**
¼	**cup sugar**
¼	**cup dry sherry**
¼	**cup orange juice**
6½	**cups coarsely chopped honeydew melon**
	Fresh mint sprigs

Place cantaloupe in container of an electric blender; add half each of sugar, sherry, and orange juice. Process until very smooth. Spoon mixture into an airtight container, and chill at least 3 hours.

Place honeydew in container of an electric blender; add remaining sugar, sherry, and orange juice. Process until very smooth. Spoon mixture into an airtight container, and chill at least 3 hours.

For each serving, pour equal amounts of both mixtures into individual bowls, pouring both at the same time. Garnish with a mint sprig.

Mustard Soup

Yield: 4 servings

2	**tablespoons butter**
⅓	**cup flour**
3	**(14.5 ounce) cans chicken broth**
¼	**cup hot spicy mustard**
¼	**cup heavy cream, whipped**

In a large saucepan, melt butter; add flour, cooking for 5 minutes without coloring. Let mixture cool down. Heat chicken broth and add to flour mixture, stirring constantly. Spoon mustard through mixture. Prepare whipped cream and spoon through soup just prior to serving.

Great with poached fish.

Beneath the Palms

🌴 Mission Gazpacho

Yield: 12 servings

3 pounds ripe tomatoes, peeled and diced
1 clove garlic, minced
2 medium cucumbers, peeled and diced
1 medium onion, diced
¼ bell pepper, diced
1 clove garlic, minced
2 cups tomato juice
3 tablespoons tarragon vinegar
¼ cup olive oil
½ teaspoon dried basil
½ teaspoon dried chervil
½ teaspoon dried tarragon
3 tablespoons chopped parsley
1 tablespoon chopped chives
3 tablespoons lemon juice
1 teaspoon paprika
Tabasco Sauce to taste
Salt and pepper to taste

Peel and dice tomatoes without losing any juice. Rub a large bowl with garlic clove. Add all ingredients. Stir well and chill.

Potato Soup

Yield: 8 servings

8 medium potatoes, sliced
3 medium onions, sliced
4 cups cold water
6 cups milk, scalded
½ stick butter
1½ teaspoons salt
Black pepper to taste
2 tablespoons chopped parsley

Place potatoes and onions in a Dutch oven; cover with 4 cups of cold water. Bring to a boil, cover and cook for 20 minutes. Transfer to a blender and purée with liquid. Melt butter in milk and add to potato mixture. Season to taste with plenty of salt and pepper. Garnish with parsley.

🌴 *Peppery Pumpkin Soup*

Yield: 4 servings

1 (16 ounce) can pumpkin
1 (10 ounce) can low-sodium chicken broth
¼ teaspoon salt
¼ teaspoon onion powder
¼ teaspoon black pepper
⅛ teaspoon ground nutmeg
1 (12 ounce) can evaporated skim milk
¼ cup fat free sour cream
1 tablespoon unsalted pumpkin seeds (optional)

In a medium saucepan, combine first 6 ingredients. Cook over medium-high heat until bubbly, about 10 minutes, stirring occasionally. Stir in evaporated skim milk. Heat thoroughly, about 5 minutes, but do not boil. Spoon into 4 bowls and top each with a dollop of sour cream. Garnish with pumpkin seeds if desired.

To defat canned broth, store the can in the refrigerator. When ready to use, open the can and skim off solidified fat accumulated on top.

Pioneer Stew

Yield: 6 servings

Olive oil
2 pounds stew meat, cubed
1 (14 ounce) can beef broth
1 (14 ounce) can chicken broth
8 small potatoes, cubed
8 carrots, cut into 1-inch pieces
2 bunches green onions, chopped
2 bell peppers, chopped
Salt and pepper to taste
1 bay leaf
1 clove garlic, crushed

Brown meat in olive oil, drain well. Add to large pot with broths; stir. Add remaining ingredients. Cook on medium heat until meat is done and vegetables are tender, about 2 to 3 hours.

May also add celery, fresh corn kernels, squash, or tomatoes.

Beneath the Palms

Spinach Soup

Yield: 6 servings

2 **tablespoons butter**
1 **small onion, chopped**
5 **ounces fresh spinach,**
    cleaned
4 **cups chicken broth**
1 **cup diced potatoes**
1 **cup 2% milk**
    Salt and pepper to taste
    Pinch of nutmeg

In a 4-quart saucepan, heat butter in saucepan and sauté onion until translucent. Add spinach and sauté until spinach wilts. Pour in broth and potatoes. Boil gently for 30 minutes. Place mixture in blender or food processor and blend to coarse texture. Return mixture to saucepan and bring to a boil. Stir in milk and adjust seasoning with salt, pepper, and nutmeg.

Croutons:
Cut 2 slices of white bread into 1-inch cubes. Brown in 1 tablespoon of butter until golden brown and season with salt and pepper.

Homestyle Chicken Broth

Yield: 4 quarts

5 **pounds chicken pieces**
    with bones
2 **large onions, cubed**
2 **large carrots, cubed**
6 **sprigs parsley**
½ **teaspoon whole black**
    peppercorns
3½ **quarts water**

Clean chicken and place in a 6 to 8-quart pan. Add remaining ingredients. Bring to a boil over high heat; reduce heat, cover, and simmer for three hours. Let cool. Strain broth into a bowl, discard residue. Cover and refrigerate for at least four hours or up to two days. Skim and discard fat.

Can be frozen.

French Onion Soup au Gratin

Yield: 6 servings

2   **medium onions, thinly sliced**
2   **tablespoons butter or margarine, melted**
4   **cups beef broth**
½   **cup water**
    Salt and pepper to taste
½   **cup Madeira wine (optional)**
½   **cup shredded Swiss cheese**
    Parmesan croutons

In a large covered skillet, cook onions in butter, until tender (about 5 minutes). Uncover skillet; continue cooking onions until well browned; stirring occasionally. Stir in broth and water; cover and simmer 30 minutes. Add salt and pepper; stir in wine, if desired. Ladle into individual oven proof dishes. Place a Parmesan crouton on each serving, and sprinkle with Swiss cheese. Bake at 400° for 15 minutes or until cheese is melted and golden brown.

New England Clam Chowder

Yield: 6 servings

4   **slices bacon, diced**
4   **medium onions, finely chopped**
2   **tablespoons flour**
¼   **teaspoon sage**
¼   **teaspoon thyme**
¼   **teaspoon paprika**
1   **quart milk**
4   **medium potatoes, diced**
4   **(7 ½ ounce) cans minced clams**
1   **dash cayenne pepper, generous**
    Salt and pepper to taste

Brown bacon until crisp; remove. Sauté onion in bacon grease, set aside. Drain all but 2 tablespoons of grease from pan. Add flour and seasonings. Make a roux, then slowly add 2 cups of milk. Cook and stir until thick and bubbly. In another saucepan, cover potatoes with water, cook until tender. Without draining water from potatoes, add clams, sauce, remaining milk, onion, and bacon. Season with salt and pepper to taste. Heat thoroughly, but do not boil.

Beneath the Palms

Pistou Savoyard

Yield: 6 servings

¼	cup olive oil
1	large onion, diced
3	cloves garlic, minced
4	large tomatoes, peeled, seeded, and chopped
½	pound green beans, diced
1	small zucchini, diced
1	medium potato, diced
1	cup diced leeks
1	cup diced celery
¼	pound spinach (or 1 cup), chopped
1½	quarts water
2	tablespoons salt
1	tablespoon leaf basil
½	teaspoon leaf thyme
¼	pound spaghettini
1	pound pinto beans, cooked (canned may be used)
	Black pepper to taste
1	cup grated Gruyere cheese
	French bread slices, toasted

Heat oil in large kettle; add onions and garlic, sauté until tender. Stir in tomatoes and next 6 ingredients. Add water and seasonings. Heat to boiling; lower heat; cover and simmer 30 minutes. Break spaghettini into 2-inch pieces, add to soup. Add beans. Cook about 10 minutes, add pepper to taste. Serve soup topped with cheese and toasted French bread slices.

The City Market started operation in 1862. This center of commerce was located beneath the Brownsville City Hall. It sustained severe damage during the October 1867 hurricane. Today, the entire structure continues to house City offices.

Split Pea Soup

Yield: 6 servings

1	pound dried split peas
1	cup chopped onion
1	cup chopped carrot
1	cup chopped celery and leaves
1	tablespoon olive oil
	Ham bone and left over ham scraps
1	clove garlic, minced
1	bay leaf
	Tabasco Sauce
	Dash of marjoram
	Dash of thyme
	Dash of ginger
	Dash of white pepper
8	cups water or ham broth or combination
1	pound smoked sausage

Wash and pick over peas; drain in colander. Wilt chopped vegetables in 1 tablespoon oil; add bones, meat scraps, all seasonings and liquid. Bring to boil; lower heat and simmer 4 hours. Remove bones and meat; chop up meat and return to pot. Brown sausage and cut into bite size pieces. Add to soup, taste for seasoning.

Great soup to make after a ham dinner.

Serve with hot mustard and dark rye bread.

🌴 Quick and Easy Beef Soup

Yield: 4 to 6 servings

1½	pounds stew meat
1	cup chopped celery
1	cup chopped onion
1	(28 ounce) can crushed tomatoes
1	(10 ounce) package mixed frozen vegetables
2-3	cups water
1	tablespoon chopped parsley
½	teaspoon dried thyme
½	teaspoon dried marjoram
	Salt and pepper to taste

In a nonstick skillet, brown meat on all sides. Remove meat; sauté celery and onions in the skillet. Place all ingredients in a large soup pot. Simmer forever or at least 2 hours. The longer the better.

Oyster Rockefeller Soup

Yield: 8 servings

2 pints oysters, strained and puréed
1 (750 ml) bottle white wine
1 pint clam juice
2 white onions, diced
½ rib celery, diced
3 tablespoons chicken bouillon granules
4 tablespoons "Paul Purdomme Seafood Seasoning"
1 quart heavy whipping cream
2 (10 ounce) bags spinach, cleaned and chopped
   Pernod to taste (optional)
   Salt and pepper to taste

Strain oysters from liquid, reserving liquid, and purée in a food processor. In a large saucepan, add white wine, puréed oysters, oyster liquid, clam juice, onions, and celery. Cook for 10 minutes on medium heat. Add chicken bouillon, seafood seasoning, and heavy cream. With a whisk, blend thoroughly. Let cook 10 minutes on low heat, add spinach. Add Pernod, if desired, salt, and pepper. Serve.

This is a favorite for Christmas Eve.

Vegetable Soup

Yield: 9 servings

2 cups potatoes, peeled and diced
1 cup diced carrots
1 cup diced celery
1 cup chopped onion
3 cups shredded cabbage
1 (6 ounce) can no salt added tomato paste
1 teaspoon thyme
¼ teaspoon freshly ground black pepper
6 cups low sodium beef broth
⅓ cup chopped fresh parsley

Combine all ingredients, except parsley, in a large stockpot. Bring to boil, reduce heat and simmer 20 minutes, or until vegetables are tender. Remove 3 cups vegetables and broth and purée in a blender or food processor. Return purée to pot, add parsley and reheat. Serve hot.

Black Bean Soup

Yield: 8 servings

1 **pound dried black beans (2 cups)**
1 **quart water**
1 **tablespoon salt**
3 **cups chicken broth**
2 **tablespoons olive oil**
1 **large onion, finely chopped**
2 **cloves garlic, minced**
½ **cup canned tomatoes, chopped**
2 **tablespoons vinegar**
1 **teaspoon freshly ground black pepper**
¾ **teaspoon ground cumin**
½ **pound cooked ham, cut into 1-inch pieces**
3-4 **cups cooked rice**
Chopped raw onion

Rinse beans well and put into large cooking pot. Add 1 quart water or enough to cover beans by 2 to 3 inches. Bring to a boil, lower heat, cover with a lid but leave a little air space. Simmer slowly for 2 hours and 30 minutes or until beans can be mashed softly against the sides of the pot with a spoon. Beans burn easily so make sure there is enough water. Stir in salt. Drain beans but save juice. Add enough chicken broth to juice to make 6 cups. Put 1 cup beans and 1 cup juice into a blender and blend into a coarse pureé. Repeat with the rest of beans and juice. Place in a large bowl. Heat olive oil in a large pot. Add onions and garlic; sauté over low heat, stirring frequently for about 10 minutes or until limp and transparent. Do not brown. Stir in tomatoes, vinegar, pepper, cumin, and ham; cook for a few more minutes. Add black bean puree and slowly bring to a boil. Stir frequently to prevent sticking. Serve in soup bowls with cooked rice and raw onion.

Serve with French bread for a complete meal.

Beneath the Palms

Moroccan Beef and Vegetable Stew

Yield: 8 servings

- 2 acorn squash, halved and seeded
- 1 tablespoon vegetable oil
- Salt and pepper to taste
- 1 cup chopped celery with leaves
- 2 onions, chopped
- 2 pounds boneless beef chuck, cut into 2-inch cubes
- 1 stick unsalted butter
- 3 coriander sprigs
- 3 parsley sprigs
- 1 stick cinnamon
- 1 (35 ounce) can plum tomatoes with juice
- 4 cups water
- 6 carrots, cut into 1-inch pieces
- ¾ cup raisins
- 2 red bell peppers, seeded and chopped
- 4 small zucchini, cut crosswise into ¾-inch pieces
- 3 tablespoons fresh minced parsley
- 1 tablespoon coriander

In a shallow pan, arrange acorn squash cut side up, drizzle with vegetable oil; sprinkle with salt and pepper. Bake squash at 400° for 40 minutes or until tender. Cool. Quarter squash, discard skin, reserve squash. In a saucepan, sauté celery, onions, and meat in butter over moderately low heat, stirring occasionally for 5 minutes. Add coriander, parsley sprigs, and cinnamon; cook for 10 minutes. Add tomatoes with juice and 4 cups of water; bring to a boil and simmer, covered, for 1 hour. Add carrots and simmer 30 minutes until chuck is tender. Bring mixture to a boil, skim off 1¾ cups cooking liquid; (if desired) reserve for couscous or rice. Stir in raisins and bell pepper; simmer for 5 minutes. Stir in zucchini and simmer for 5 minutes. Stir in minced parsley, coriander, and acorn squash; simmer until heated through discard cinnamon stick.

Black Bean Chili

Yield: 6 servings

1½	pounds black beans
8	cups water
1	tablespoon vegetable oil
3	large onions
3	cloves garlic, minced
1	bay leaf
4	teaspoons cumin
1	tablespoon paprika
½	teaspoon cayenne
2	tablespoons chili powder
2	teaspoons oregano
1	medium bell pepper, chopped
½	teaspoon sugar
1	tablespoon apple cider vinegar
8	small sun-dried tomatoes, chopped
1	(28 ounce) can chopped stewed tomatoes, with juice
	Crushed red pepper to taste
	Salt and pepper to taste
1	bunch cilantro, chopped

Cover beans with water and soak for 6 hours; drain. Place beans in heavy pan with 8 cups water, simmer 1 hour. In a small skillet, sauté onion and next 8 ingredients in oil; add to beans with sugar and cider vinegar. Add sun-dried tomatoes and chopped tomatoes with juice. Add red pepper, salt, and pepper to taste. Cook on medium heat until beans are done. Add chopped cilantro, and serve.

Beneath the Palms

John's Left Coast Chili

Yield: 6 servings

3½ **pounds beef chuck or rump roast**
2 **onions, diced**
3 **cloves garlic, minced**
1 **bell pepper, diced**
2 **teaspoons salt**
1 **(16 ounce) can tomato puree**
½ **teaspoon black pepper**
1 **(4 ounce) can diced green chilies**
3 **tablespoons mild chili powder**
1 **tablespoon hot red chili powder**
4 **tablespoons cumin**
1 **teaspoon oregano**
1 **teaspoon thyme**
½ **cup dry red wine**
½ **teaspoon cayenne pepper**

Trim and render fat from meat. Dice remainder of meat. Sauté onion, garlic, and bell pepper in rendered fat, then transfer mixture to a 4 to 5-quart pot. Brown beef in rendered fat and add to pot. Add remaining ingredients. Stir and simmer covered at least three hours, stirring occasionally. Taste for additional seasoning.

Add cayenne halfway through cooking, a little at a time. It's potent.

Lentil Soup Spanish Style

Yield: 6 servings

1 **pound lentils**
¼ **pound salt pork, diced**
½ **cup chopped parsley**
2 **bay leaves**
2 **carrots, chopped**
1 **large onion, chopped**
4 **cloves garlic, minced**
Salt and pepper to taste
2 **tablespoons wine vinegar**

Place lentils in a large pot and cover with water. Add salt pork, parsley, and bay leaves. Bring to a boil, cover and let simmer for 40 minutes. In a skillet, sauté the carrots, onion, and garlic. Add to lentils and season to taste. Add vinegar and cover. Simmer for 45 minutes more or until lentils are done.

Salads

Beneath the Palms

Kiwi and Orange Salad

Yield: 6 servings

- 1 head Boston lettuce
- 2 oranges, peeled and sectioned
- 2 kiwi fruit, peeled and sliced
- 1 cup oil
- ½ cup sugar
- ⅓ cup white wine vinegar
- 1½ tablespoons chopped green onions
- 1½ tablespoons poppy seeds
- 1 teaspoon salt
- 1 teaspoon dry mustard

Arrange lettuce leaves on a serving platter. Arrange fruit in a decorative pattern on lettuce. Mix all other ingredients together to make a dressing. Drizzle over salad.

Hearts of Palm and Tomato Salad

Yield: 6 servings

- 1 (12 ounce) container cherry tomatoes, sliced in half
- 1 (14 ounce) can hearts of palm, sliced ¼-inch thick
- 1 small red onion, thinly sliced
- 1 tablespoon chopped parsley

Vinaigrette:
- ½ cup balsamic vinegar
- ½ cup light olive oil
- 2 tablespoons brown sugar
- 1 clove garlic, minced
  Salt and pepper to taste

Mix all salad ingredients together. Prepare vinaigrette; toss with salad. Chill.

Cilantro may be substituted for parsley.

🌴 Green Papaya Salad

1 clove garlic
2 red chili peppers,
   seeded (more to taste)
½ pound green papaya,
   peeled, seeded, and
   grated
1 medium tomato, sliced
   into strips
2 tablespoons fish sauce
3 tablespoons lime juice
   Lettuce leaves

Grind garlic and peppers in a food processor. Mix together papaya, tomato, fish sauce, and lime juice. Add garlic mixture and toss lightly. Place a portion of papaya mixture onto a lettuce leaf. Fold leaf to form a packet to eat. Serve with lime wedges.

Antipasto Salad

Salad:
1 pound shell macaroni
¼ pound pepperoni
¼ pound hard salami
¼ pound mozzarella or
   provolone cheese
3 tomatoes
3 ribs celery
1 medium sweet onion
2 medium bell peppers
1 (6 ounce) can black
   olives, sliced
1 (5 ounce) can green
   olives
Dressing:
¾ cup oil
¼ cup vinegar
1 teaspoon oregano
½ teaspoon salt
   Black pepper to taste

Boil and drain macaroni according to package directions. Cut pepperoni, hard salami, and mozzarella into small pieces. Chop tomatoes, celery, onion, and peppers. Mix together, with olives and macaroni. Stir together all ingredients for dressing; toss with macaroni mixture. Marinate at room temperature for at least 3 hours before serving. After serving keep refrigerated.

Beneath the Palms

Sago Palm Chicken Salad

Yield: 12 servings

1 stick butter, melted and cooled
2 cups mayonnaise
¼ cup minced parsley
½ teaspoon curry powder
¼ teaspoon minced garlic
Pinch of marjoram
Salt and pepper to taste
4 cups chicken, cooked and shredded
2 cups seedless grapes
½ cup almonds, toasted and slivered

Combine butter, mayonnaise, and other seasonings. In a large bowl, toss chicken and grapes. To serve, line salad plates with greens and top with chicken and grape mixture. Top with dressing and sprinkle with almonds.

Festive Tomato Wedges

Yield: 8 servings

⅔ cup salad oil
¼ cup white wine vinegar
¼ cup chopped parsley
¼ cup thinly sliced green onion
2 tablespoons mayonnaise
1 clove garlic, minced
1 teaspoon salt
1 teaspoon dried dill weed
1 teaspoon dried basil
¼ teaspoon oregano
¼ teaspoon black pepper
6 medium tomatoes, cut into wedges

Mix all ingredients, except tomatoes, in a covered jar. Shake well and pour over tomato wedges.

This was one of the committee's favorites.

Fondulaha

- 1 **fresh pineapple**
- 1½ **cups cooked chicken, cubed**
- ½ **cup diced celery**
- ½ **cup sliced bananas**
- ¼ **cup salted Spanish peanuts**
- ½ **cup mayonnaise**
- 1 **tablespoon chopped chutney**
  Dash of salt
  Dash of curry powder
- ⅓ **cup shredded flaked coconut**
- 12 **orange sections**

Leaving green top on, cut pineapple into fourths lengthwise. Cut around edges with curved knife. Remove pineapple from the rind and cut into chunks. Mix pineapple, chicken, celery, bananas, and peanuts. Blend mayonnaise, chutney, salt, and curry powder. Mix all ingredients together. Fill each pineapple shell with mixture, sprinkle with coconut. Garnish each with 3 orange segments.

This makes an attractive lunch, or brunch dish. Additional seasonal fruit may be added.

Artichoke and Rice Salad

- 1 **(7 ounce) box chicken flavored rice vermicelli mix**
- 2 **(6 ounce) jars marinated artichokes, reserve liquid, chopped**
- ⅓ **cup mayonnaise**
- ¼ **cup chopped green onions**
- ½ **cup chopped black olives**
- ¼ **cup chopped green olives**
- ¼ **cup chopped bell pepper**
- ¾ **teaspoon curry powder**

Cook rice according to package instructions, omitting butter. Cool and set aside. Mix reserved artichoke liquid with mayonnaise; stir in all other ingredients. Combine this mixture with rice. Chill well before serving.

Layered Salad

Yield: 12 servings

Salad greens
1 bell pepper, chopped
2 ribs celery, chopped
1 bunch green onions, chopped
8 ounces fresh mushrooms, sliced
1 (8 ounce) can sliced water chestnuts
1 (6 ounce) can black olives, drained and chopped
1 (10 ounce) package frozen peas (up to 2 packages)
1 cup mayonnaise
1 (8 ounce) carton sour cream
1 tablespoon sugar, up to 2 tablespoons (optional)
1 package dry ranch dressing mix (optional)
2 cups grated cheddar or Swiss cheese
Parmesan cheese
10 slices bacon, cooked and crumbled

The first layer should be a mixture of several salad greens, such as spinach, romaine, bibb, or red leaf lettuce. Tear into bite size pieces. Greens should equal about 1½ heads. Place in a large straight sided, clear bowl. Next layer any combination of the following: green pepper, celery, onions, mushrooms, water chestnuts, and olives equal to 1½ to 2 cups. The third layer should be frozen peas. For the fourth layer, combine mayonnaise, sour cream and if a sweet dressing is desired, add sugar. If not, add dry ranch dressing mix. Spread dressing evenly on top, making sure edges are sealed. Next sprinkle cheese, cover generously with Parmesan and top with crumbled bacon. Do not mix. Cover tightly with plastic wrap. Refrigerate overnight.

Black Bean Salad

Yield: 8 servings

⅓ cup red wine vinegar
⅓ cup olive oil
¾ teaspoon salt
½ teaspoon freshly ground black pepper
3 cloves garlic, chopped
3 (15 ounce) cans black beans
1 (10 ounce) can shoepeg corn
1 large bell pepper, chopped
1 large red bell pepper, chopped
1 medium red onion, chopped

Combine first five ingredients. Drain, rinse, and add black beans to mixture. Stir well. Mix in all other ingredients, refrigerate 3 to 4 hours or overnight. Serve cold.

South Padre Island Salad

Yield: 6 servings

1 small head lettuce
1 small head cauliflower
½ cup diced celery
¼ cup diced onion
¼ cup diced bell pepper (optional)
1 cup crisp crumbled bacon
½ cup roasted sunflower seeds
4 ounces shredded cheddar cheese

Dressing
2 cups mayonnaise
¼ cup sugar
¼ cup Parmesan cheese

Toss together all salad ingredients. Set aside. Mix remaining ingredients together for salad dressing. Toss salad with dressing just before serving.

Beneath the Palms

🌴 Coastal Crab Salad

Yield: 4 to 6 servings

½ **cup low fat mayonnaise**
2 **teaspoons jalapeño
   juice**
1 **teaspoon dill weed**
1 **(3 ounce) jar capers**
½ **medium onion, chopped**
2 **pounds imitation crab
   meat**

In a bowl, mix mayonnaise and next 4 ingredients. Chop crab meat into small chunks. Add crab to mayonnaise mixture and refrigerate.

This salad can be served in an avocado half, tomato half, or as an appetizer with crackers. As a light meal it serves 4 to 6.

Cilantro Chicken Salad

Yield: 3 servings

3 **boneless, skinless
   chicken breasts**
1 **tablespoon vegetable oil**
3 **ribs celery, sliced**
2 **green onions, chopped**
3 **tablespoons chopped
   cilantro**
1 **tablespoon lemon juice**
2 **tablespoons chopped
   red bell pepper**
¼ **cup mayonnaise**
3 **tablespoons slivered
   almonds**
   Avocado slices
   Tomato wedges

Cook chicken in oil about 4 minutes per side or until well done. Cool and dice. Add celery and next 4 ingredients. Mix in mayonnaise, toss and chill. Sprinkle with almonds, garnish with avocado slices and tomato wedges.

Chicken may be grilled.

Sahadi Tabouli (Mid-Eastern Health Salad)

Yield: 6 to 8 servings

- 1 cup #2 bulghur (blanched, cracked wheat)
- ¾ cup lime juice
- 1 cucumber, minced
- 2 teaspoons salt
- ½ teaspoon ground cumin (optional)
- 2 tablespoons fresh mint (optional)
- 2 bunches green onions, minced
- 4 tomatoes, minced
- 4 bunches parsley, rinsed and minced
- ½ cup virgin olive oil

Layer ingredients in large glass container as follows: bulghur, lime juice, cucumber. Sprinkle salt over cucumber, add cumin or mint. Continue with onion, tomatoes, and parsley. Refrigerate 2 to 8 hours. Add oil, toss and serve.

Bulghur (or burghul) can be found in specialty food stores.

Corn Salad

Yield: 8 servings

- 2 (11 ounce) cans shoepeg corn
- 1 (2 ounce) jar pimento
- ½ cup chopped bell pepper
- ½ cup chopped onion
- 2 ribs celery, chopped
- ½ cup white vinegar
- ½ cup sugar
- ½ cup oil
- 1 teaspoon salt
- ½ teaspoon black pepper

Mix all ingredients together in a bowl. For best results, mix and let stand in refrigerator overnight before serving.

Beneath the Palms

Cilantro Vinaigrette

Yield: Enough for 1 salad

1 **bunch cilantro leaves, washed and dried**
2 **cloves garlic**
4 **tablespoons white wine vinegar**
1 **tablespoon chicken bouillon granules**
½ **cup olive oil**
1 **egg**
 Dash of salt
 Dash of black pepper
 Dash of sugar

Fit food processor with metal blade; process cilantro and garlic cloves until finely minced. Add all other ingredients through tube and process until well blended. Do not over process.

Fresh Parsley Dressing

Yield: 1 cup

½ **cup parsley sprigs**
1 **clove garlic, sliced**
3 **tablespoons red wine vinegar**
1 **teaspoon Dijon mustard**
¼ **teaspoon salt**
½ **cup olive oil**

With metal chopping blade in a food processor, mince parsley, remove to small bowl. With motor running, drop garlic through chute. Scrape sides of bowl; add vinegar, mustard, and salt. With motor running, pour in oil within 30 seconds. Return parsley and process to blend about 5 seconds.

> *A streetcar system in Brownsville first began in December of 1912 using motor cars. It was converted to an electric system in 1915 and served the population into the 1920's.*

Roquefort Dressing

3 (1½ ounce) **Roquefort cheese wedges, crumbled**
2 **tablespoons cream**
1 **pint mayonnaise (preferably homemade) Freshly ground black pepper**
1 **clove garlic, crushed**
¼ **onion (up to ½), squeezed**
1 **tablespoon Worcestershire sauce**
1 **lemon, juiced**
1½ **teaspoons mustard**

Mix cheese and cream together, add remaining ingredients. This is better if prepared one day in advance.

Raspberry Poppy Seed Dressing

1½ **cups sugar**
2 **teaspoons dry mustard**
2 **teaspoons salt**
⅔ **cup raspberry vinegar**
3 **tablespoons fresh onion juice**
2 **cups salad oil**
1 **tablespoon poppy seeds (up to 1½ tablespoons)**

Mix sugar, mustard, salt, and vinegar. Add onion juice. Stir thoroughly; add oil slowly using electric mixer and beating constantly, beat until thick. Add poppy seeds, beat for a few minutes. Use over fruit salad or grapefruit.

Beneath the Palms

Basic Imperial Dressing

Yield: 2 ¾ cups

½ **cup red wine vinegar**
⅓ **cup packed brown sugar**
1 **teaspoon salt**
1 **teaspoon onion salt**
1 **teaspoon celery seed**
1 **teaspoon paprika**
½ **teaspoon dill weed**
•¼ **teaspoon black pepper**
1 **(8 ounce) can tomato sauce**
1 **cup olive oil**
2 **tablespoons capers, with liquid**
1 **tablespoon Worcestershire sauce**
1 **clove garlic, minced**

Combine red wine vinegar and next 7 ingredients in a saucepan. Bring to boil; reduce heat and simmer 2 minutes. Pour into a quart jar, cool. Add remaining ingredients, cover tightly and shake to blend. Store in refrigerator until ready to use.

Greek Salad Dressing

Yield: 6 servings

4 **tablespoons olive oil**
2 **teaspoons fresh chopped chives**
½ **teaspoon tarragon**
½ **teaspoon salt**
1 **teaspoon sugar**
2 **tablespoons tarragon vinegar**
2 **tablespoons fresh chopped parsley**
½ **teaspoon dried chervil**
½ **teaspoon coarse French mustard**

Combine all ingredients in a covered container; shake. Allow to stand 1 hour before serving.

🌴 Cucumber Salad with Yogurt

Yield: 2 servings

1 medium cucumber, peeled, seeded, and thinly sliced
1 tablespoon lemon juice or vinegar
1 tablespoon chopped cilantro or parsley
2 tablespoons chopped scallions
1 cup plain fat free yogurt, drained
Salt and pepper to taste

Combine all ingredients and chill.

Good with dark rye bread.

🌴 Scallion Cucumbers

Yield: 4 servings

3 tablespoons rice wine vinegar or white wine vinegar
1 tablespoon water
1 teaspoon salt
2 teaspoons sugar
2 medium cucumbers, peeled and sliced
2 scallions, thinly sliced

In a shallow container, stir together vinegar, water, salt, and sugar. Mix in cucumbers; cover and chill. At serving time sprinkle with scallions.

Dill weed is good on this dish.

Hot German Potato Salad

Yield: 6 servings

1½ **tablespoons flour**
2 **tablespoons sugar**
2 **tablespoons bacon drippings**
1 **teaspoon salt**
½ **teaspoon black pepper**
½ **cup water**
⅓ **cup cider vinegar**
4 **teaspoons prepared mustard**
3 **tablespoons minced green onion**
4 **cups cooked potatoes, sliced**
½ **teaspoon celery seed**
¼ **cup chopped celery**
2 **tablespoons diced pimento**
2 **tablespoons diced bell pepper**
4 **slices bacon, cooked and crumbled**

Mix flour and sugar in a skillet. Add bacon drippings and next 4 ingredients. Stir and cook until thickened. Add mustard and next 6 ingredients; mix well but lightly. Sprinkle with bacon and serve hot.

Shredded Carrot Salad

Yield: 4 servings

6 **medium carrots**
1 **teaspoon salt**
6 **tablespoons olive oil**
1 **tablespoon lemon juice**

Peel and wash carrots, grate on largest holes of grater. When ready to serve, add salt, olive oil, and lemon juice. Toss and serve immediately.

Brunch/Breads

Beneath the Palms

Norwegian Torte

Yield: 12 servings

Pastry Dough:
- 1 stick butter
- 1 cup flour
- 2 tablespoons water

Filling:
- 1 cup water
- 1 stick butter
- 1 cup flour
- 3 eggs
- ½ teaspoon vanilla extract

Glaze:
- 1 cup powdered sugar
- 2 tablespoons butter
- Milk
- 1 cup almonds, toasted

Pastry Dough:
Cut butter into flour, toss with water. Spread in jelly-roll pan.

Filling:
Heat water with butter to boiling point. Remove from heat, add flour. Stir until smooth. Beat in eggs, one at a time, and vanilla. Spread filling on top of pastry. Bake at 375° for 45 minutes. Cool.

Glaze:
Mix powdered sugar and butter with just enough milk to spreading consistency. Using a pastry brush, spread glaze on top of filling. Sprinkle with toasted almonds.

Southwestern Quiche

Yield: 6 servings

- ¾ cup grated cheddar cheese
- ½ cup grated Monterey Jack cheese
- 1 (9-inch) pastry shell, unbaked
- 3 eggs, lightly beaten
- 2 tablespoons chopped green onions
- 1 (4 ounce) can diced green chilies
- 1 (2¼ ounce) can sliced ripe olives
- 1 teaspoon salt
- ¼ teaspoon white pepper
- 1½ cups half and half

In small bowl, mix cheeses; sprinkle in bottom of pastry shell. Combine remaining ingredients and pour over cheeses. Bake at 350° for 40 minutes or until tester inserted in center comes out clean.

Jam Kolaches

Yield: 2 dozen

½ **cup butter, softened**
3 **ounces cream cheese, softened**
1¼ **cups flour**
¼ **cup strawberry or raspberry jam**
¼ **cup powdered sugar, sifted**

Cream together butter and cream cheese; beat until light and fluffy. Add flour, mixing well. Roll out dough onto lightly floured surface to ⅛-inch thickness; cut into rounds with 2-inch cookie cutter. Place on lightly greased cookie sheets. Spoon ¼ teaspoon jam on each cookie and fold in opposite sides, slightly overlapping edges. Bake at 375° for 15 minutes. Remove from cookie sheets and sprinkle with powdered sugar.

Sausage may be substituted for jam; omit powdered sugar.

Raisin Coffee Cake

Yield: 12 servings

Coffee Cake:
1 **stick butter or margarine**
1 **cup sugar**
2 **eggs, beaten**
1 **teaspoon vanilla extract**
1 **cup sour cream**
2 **cups flour**
1½ **teaspoons baking powder**
1 **teaspoon baking soda**
½ **cup raisins**
Topping:
½ **cup sugar**
½ **teaspoon cinnamon**

Coffee Cake:
In large mixing bowl, beat butter and sugar together. Mix eggs, vanilla, and sour cream; add to butter mixture. Sift next 3 ingredients; add to mixture. Stir in raisins; set aside.
Topping:
Mix sugar and cinnamon. Grease 9x12-inch cake pan. Pour half the batter in pan and sprinkle with half the topping. Add remaining batter and topping to cake. Bake at 350° for 35 to 40 minutes.

Beneath the Palms

The Biggest and Best
Sour Cream Coffee Cake

Yield: 8 servings

Coffee Cake:
- 2 sticks butter, softened
- 2 cups sugar
- 3 eggs
- 3 cups sifted flour
- 1 teaspoon baking soda
- 2½ teaspoons baking powder
- 1 (16 ounce) carton sour cream
- 1 teaspoon vanilla extract

Swirl:
- ½ cup sugar
- 4 teaspoons cinnamon
- ½ cup pecan pieces

Coffee Cake:
Cream together butter and sugar until fluffy. Add eggs, one at a time, blending well after each one. Add next 5 ingredients. Continue to beat only until well blended. Pour into buttered and floured 9x12-inch baking pan.

Swirl:
Mix ingredients together and spread over top of batter. With spatula, swirl small amount into batter. Gently pat the ingredients into batter, so swirl will stick to cake when cooked. Bake at 350° for 45 to 50 minutes or until tester inserted in center comes out clean.

Crustless
Quiche Lorraine

Yield: 6 servings

- ½ pound bacon, cooked and crumbled
- 1 cup grated Swiss cheese
- ¼ cup minced onions
- 4 eggs
- 1 cup evaporated milk
- ¾ teaspoon salt
- ⅛ teaspoon cayenne pepper
- 1 (4 ¼ ounce) can chopped black olives
- Chopped parsley
- Sliced mushrooms

Sprinkle bacon, cheese, and onions in 9-inch glass pie plate. Beat eggs, milk, and seasonings together, pour over bacon mixture. Top with black olives, parsley, and mushrooms. Microwave on high for 9 to 11 minutes. Let stand 5 minutes before slicing.

Spinach Quiche

Yield: 6 servings

- 1 **(10 ounce) package frozen chopped spinach**
- 1 **(9-inch) pastry shell, unbaked**
- ¼ **cup Parmesan cheese**
- 3 **eggs, beaten**
- 1 **cup cottage cheese**
- 1 **cup heavy cream**
- 2 **tablespoons dried minced onion**
- 1½ **teaspoons salt**
- ½ **teaspoon pepper**
- 1 **teaspoon caraway seeds**
- ¼ **teaspoon nutmeg**
- ½ **teaspoon Worcestershire sauce**
- 2 **drops Tabasco Sauce**
- 2 **tablespoons butter**

Cook spinach and drain well. Bake pastry shell at 400° for 8 minutes. Cool, reduce oven temperature to 350°. Sprinkle Parmesan in bottom of pastry shell. Combine remaining ingredients, except butter; pour into pastry shell. Brown butter and pour over top of quiche. Bake at 350° for 40 minutes or until tester inserted in center comes out clean.

Zucchini-Tomato Pie

Yield: 6 servings

- 2 **cups chopped zucchini**
- 1 **cup chopped tomatoes**
- ½ **cup chopped onion**
- ⅓ **cup Parmesan cheese**
- 1½ **cups milk**
- ¾ **cup biscuit baking mix**
- 3 **eggs**
- ½ **teaspoon salt**
- ¼ **teaspoon black pepper**

Sprinkle first 4 ingredients into greased 9-inch pie plate. Beat remaining ingredients together until smooth, about 15 seconds. Pour into pie plate. Bake at 400° for 30 minutes.

Beneath the Palms

Chicken Quiche

Yield: 4 to 6 servings

Crust:
- 1 **stick butter or margarine**
- 1 **(3 ounce) package cream cheese**
- 1 **teaspoon salt**
- 1 **cup flour**

Filling:
- 2 **cooked chicken breasts, cubed**
- ½ **cup chopped ham**
- ½ **cup grated Swiss cheese**
- 2 **cups light cream**
- 3 **eggs**
  Pinch of nutmeg
  Salt and pepper to taste

Crust:
Cut margarine, cheese, and salt into flour; pat together and chill. Roll out to fit 9-inch deep dish pie plate or 10-inch quiche pan. Bake at 450° for 10 minutes (if pastry shell is to be frozen before use, bake at 500° for 10 minutes).

Filling:
Place chicken and ham in baked shell; sprinkle with cheese. Beat remaining ingredients together, pour over meats. Bake at 375° for 30 to 35 minutes, or at 325° for 45 minutes if pastry shell was frozen.

To avoid crust shrinking and bubbling, fill unbaked crust with dry beans or raw rice before cooking.

Saturday Brunch Soufflé

Yield: 10 to 12 servings

- 1 **package English muffins, cut in half**
- 1 **dozen eggs**
- 1 **(8 ounce) carton sour cream**
- 1 **pound hot bulk sausage**
- 1 **(8 ounce) jar processed cheese spread**

Add a teaspoon of chili powder to a favorite pastry shell recipe for this quiche.

Spray glass baking dish with nonstick cooking spray. Cover bottom of dish with muffins. In large bowl, mix together eggs and sour cream. Cook sausage thoroughly; drain. Combine with egg mixture; pour over muffins. Refrigerate overnight. Bake at 350° for 25 minutes. Remove from oven, spoon cheese spread over top. Return to oven, bake an additional 10 to 15 minutes.

Ham and Cheese Strata

Yield: 12 servings

12 slices white bread,
     cubed
8   ounces shredded
     cheddar cheese
2   cups cooked ham,
     cubed
¼   cup chopped onion
1   (10 ounce) package
     frozen chopped
     broccoli, thawed and
     drained
1   (2 ounce) jar pimentos,
     drained
6   eggs
3   cups milk
½   teaspoon salt
¼   teaspoon dry mustard

Grease a 13x9-inch (3-quart) baking dish. Layer bread, cheese, ham, onion, broccoli, and pimentos in dish. In medium bowl, combine remaining ingredients, mix well. Pour over ham mixture. Cover and refrigerate at least 6 hours or overnight. Bake, uncovered, at 325° for 55 to 70 minutes or until tester inserted in center comes out clean. Let stand 10 minutes before serving.

Jalapeño Corn Quiche

Yield: 6 servings

1   (9-inch) pastry shell,
     unbaked
3   slices bacon
½   cup chopped onion
1   (17 ounce) can cream-
     style corn
2   jalapeño peppers,
     seeded and chopped
2   eggs, beaten
¼   cup half and half
½   cup grated sharp
     cheddar cheese
1   tablespoon flour
¼   teaspoon salt
⅛   teaspoon black pepper
     Jalapeño slices
       (optional)

Bake pastry shell at 400° for 3 minutes. Remove from oven, prick with fork and bake 5 more minutes. Cook bacon in skillet, remove and crumble. Sauté onion in bacon grease. Combine all ingredients and pour into pastry shell. Bake at 375° for 45 minutes. Garnish with jalapeño slices.

Beneath the Palms

Egg Casserole

Yield: 8 servings

  9 eggs, beaten
1½ pounds bulk sausage, fried and drained
  3 cups milk
1½ teaspoons dry mustard
  1 teaspoon salt
1½ cups grated cheddar cheese
  3 slices bread

Combine first 6 ingredients and mix well. Tear bread into pieces and place in bottom of well-greased 13x9-inch casserole dish. Pour mixture over bread and refrigerate overnight. Bake, uncovered, at 350° for 1 hour.

South of the Border Grits

Yield: 6 servings

4 ½ cups water
  1 teaspoon salt
  1 cup regular grits
  1 (14 ounce) can tomatoes, drained and chopped
  1 teaspoon ground cumin
  ¼ cup sliced scallions
  ¼ cup shredded reduced fat cheddar cheese

Place all ingredients, except scallions and cheese, into a 2-quart microwave safe bowl; stirring well. Cover with lid and microwave on high 15 to 18 minutes, stirring once. Stir in scallions and cheese. Cover and let stand 5 minutes before serving.

Grits Soufflé

Yield: 4 servings

1 stick butter or margarine
1 cup grated sharp
 cheddar cheese
2 cups grits
1 teaspoon salt
8 cups water
4 egg yolks, beaten
4 egg whites, beaten
 Cracker or dry bread
 crumbs

Cook butter, cheese, and grits in salted water until done. Remove from heat, add egg yolks; mix well. Fold in egg whites. Pour into greased 1½-quart casserole dish; top with crumbs. Bake at 350° for 45 minutes.

Breakfast Pizza

Yield: 6 to 8 servings

1 pound bulk pork
 sausage
1 (8 ounce) package
 refrigerated crescent
 rolls
1 cup frozen, loose pack,
 hash brown potatoes,
 thawed
1 cup shredded sharp
 cheddar cheese
5 eggs
¼ cup milk
½ teaspoon salt
¼ teaspoon black pepper
2 tablespoons Parmesan
 cheese

In a skillet, cook sausage until browned; drain off fat. Separate crescent dough into 8 triangles; place in ungreased 12-inch pizza pan, with points towards center. Press over bottom and up sides to form crust; seal perforations. Spoon sausage over crust. Sprinkle with potatoes, top with cheese. In a bowl, beat together eggs, milk, salt, and pepper. Pour over potatoes. Sprinkle Parmesan over mixture. Bake at 375° for 25 to 30 minutes.

Beneath the Palms

Ms. Tish's Original Quiche

Yield: 6 servings

1 (9-inch) deep-dish
   pastry crust, unbaked
⅓ cup finely minced onion
½ clove garlic, minced
2 eggs
2 cups cream
   Parsley flakes to taste
½ pound bacon, crisply
   fried and crumbled
2 cups shredded Swiss
   cheese

Bake pastry crust. Mix onions, garlic, eggs, cream, and parsley well. Line baked crust with bacon and cheese, pour in egg mixture. Bake at 425° for 15 minutes. Reduce oven to 300° and bake until lightly browned. Let stand 20 minutes before serving.

Vegetable Brunch Pie

Yield: 6 servings

1 (10 ounce) package
   frozen spinach,
   chopped broccoli, or
   asparagus,
      cooked and drained
1 cup sour cream
1 cup cottage cheese
4 tablespoons butter or
   margarine
2 eggs
½ cup biscuit baking mix
1 medium tomato, sliced
   thin
¼ cup Parmesan cheese

Spread selected vegetable in greased 9-inch pie plate. Beat sour cream and cottage cheese together. Mix butter and eggs for 15 seconds; add to sour cream mixture, mix well. Stir in biscuit baking mix. Pour into pie plate. Top with tomato slices and cheese. Bake at 350° for 30 minutes.

🌴 Buttermilk and Banana Waffles

Yield: 6 waffles

1	**cup all-purpose flour**
1	**tablespoon sugar**
1	**teaspoon baking powder**
½	**teaspoon baking soda**
½	**teaspoon ground cinnamon**
¼	**teaspoon salt**
1¼	**cups buttermilk**
1	**egg**
2	**tablespoons unsalted butter, melted**
2	**ripe bananas, peeled and sliced**
	Maple syrup, warmed

In a large bowl, stir together flour, sugar, baking powder, baking soda, cinnamon, and salt; mixing well. In a large measuring cup combine buttermilk, egg, and melted butter; whisk until blended. Place half the banana slices in a small bowl and mash coarsely. Add mashed bananas to buttermilk mixture and stir into flour mixture. With a fork, mix until batter is smooth. Preheat waffle iron. Lightly grease with vegetable oil. Ladle batter into waffle iron and cook, per manufacturer's directions, or until waffle removes easily. Serve waffles with remaining banana slices and drizzle with warmed maple syrup.

Buttermilk Pancakes

Yield: 12 to 15 small pancakes

1¼	**cups buttermilk**
1	**egg**
2	**tablespoons oil**
1¼	**cups sifted flour**
1	**teaspoon sugar**
1	**teaspoon baking powder**
½	**teaspoon salt**
½	**teaspoon baking soda**

Blend buttermilk, egg, and oil. Sift dry ingredients together, add to buttermilk mixture. Using a tablespoon spoon mixture into preheated frying pan or onto griddle. Cook pancakes until golden brown in color.

Sour Cream Whole Wheat Pancakes

Yield: 1 dozen pancakes

1	**cup whole wheat flour**
½	**cup all-purpose flour**
1	**teaspoon baking powder**
½	**teaspoon salt**
1½	**cups milk**
½	**cup sour cream**
2	**tablespoons unsalted butter, melted**
2	**tablespoons honey**
1	**egg, lightly beaten**

In a mixing bowl, stir together dry ingredients. Make a well in the center and add remaining ingredients. Stir starting at center and gradually mix in dry ingredients until smooth. Cover bowl and let sit at room temperature for 1 hour or overnight in refrigerator. Using a ladle, pour mix onto lightly greased hot griddle. Cook 1 minute on each side or until lightly browned.

Banana Bran Nut Muffins

Yield: 12 large muffins

2¼	**cups oat bran cereal**
1	**tablespoon baking powder**
¼	**cup brown sugar**
½	**teaspoon cinnamon**
¼	**cup chopped pecans or walnuts**
1¼	**cups milk**
2	**ripe bananas, mashed**
2	**eggs**
2	**tablespoons oil**
1	**cup raisins**

Mix all dry ingredients together, set aside. Combine milk and next 6 ingredients; mix well. Add to dry ingredients. Line muffin pans with paper cups and fill ¾ full with batter. Bake at 425° for 17 minutes.

🌴 Banana Muffins

Yield: 12 jumbo or 18 regular muffins

3 **medium overripe bananas**
½ **cup light brown sugar**
½ **cup skim milk**
½ **cup fat free plain yogurt**
½ **cup natural applesauce**
3 **teaspoons vanilla extract**
2 **cups unbleached flour**
2 **teaspoons baking soda**
2 **teaspoons baking powder**
2 **teaspoons cinnamon, rounded**
⅛ **teaspoon nutmeg**
⅛ **teaspoon salt**
12 **naturally dehydrated oil free banana chips or a sprinkling of brown sugar**

Mash bananas and mix with next 5 ingredients. Mix dry ingredients in a separate bowl; add in wet ingredients, stir until moistened. Coat muffin tin with cooking spray and divide batter among cups. Place a banana chip or sprinkling of brown sugar on top of each muffin. Bake at 400° for 15 to 20 minutes or until tester inserted in center of muffin comes out clean. Cool on wire rack.

Bran Muffins

Yield: 3 dozen

2 **cups 100% bran cereal**
2 **cups boiling water**
4 **eggs**
3 **cups sugar**
1 **cup shortening**
5 **cups flour**
5 **teaspoons baking soda**
1 **teaspoon salt**
1 **quart buttermilk**
4 **cups bran flakes**

Combine first 2 ingredients; set aside to cool. Mix remaining ingredients, except bran flakes, together, add cereal mixture. Stir in bran flakes. Spoon into greased muffin tins. Bake at 375° for 20 minutes.

This makes a large amount of batter. Batter stores well in refrigerator for up to 6 weeks.

🌴 Carrot Pineapple Muffins

Yield: 12 jumbo or 18 regular muffins

2 cups unbleached all-purpose flour
1 teaspoon baking soda
2 teaspoons cinnamon
⅛ teaspoon ginger
¼ teaspoon salt
4 egg whites (at room temperature)
1 cup frozen apple juice concentrate, thawed
⅔ cup nonfat dry milk
¼ cup oat bran
1½ cups shredded carrots
1 (8 ounce) can unsweetened crushed pineapple, drained
1 (8 ounce) can unsweetened pineapple tidbits, drained

In a large bowl, mix together flour and next 4 ingredients. In a separate bowl, beat egg whites with an electric mixer at medium speed to form soft peaks, gradually beat in apple juice increasing mixer speed to high. Fold dry milk into egg whites, then fold in oat bran and flour mixture, stirring until moistened. Stir in carrots and crushed pineapple. Coat muffin tins with cooking spray and divide batter among cups. Place a pineapple tidbit on top of each muffin. Bake at 375° for 15 to 20 minutes or until tester inserted in center of muffin comes out clean. Cool on wire rack.

St. Joseph's Catholic College for boys was constructed between Sixth and Seventh on Elizabeth Street in Brownsville during the Civil War era. The school later moved to its present location in the Rio Viejo area off Palm Boulevard. It has since become a Catholic co-educational Junior and Senior High School.

Strawberry Bread

Yield: 1 loaf

Bread:
- 1½ **cups flour**
- 1 **cup sugar**
- ½ **teaspoon baking soda**
- ½ **teaspoon cinnamon**
- ¼ **teaspoon salt**
- 1 **(10 ounce) package frozen strawberries, thawed**
- 2 **eggs, well beaten**
- ½ **cup oil**
- ½ **cup chopped pecans (optional)**

Spread:
- 8 **ounces cream cheese**
- ¼ **cup strawberry juice, reserved from above**

Bread:
Mix dry ingredients. Make a well in dry ingredients and pour in liquid ingredients. Stir by hand; add nuts. Pour into greased, floured 8x4-inch pan. Bake at 350° for 1 hour or until done.

Spread:
Mix reserved cream cheese and juice.

Pumpkin Nut Bread

Yield: 1 loaf

- 2 **cups all-purpose flour**
- 2 **teaspoons baking powder**
- ½ **teaspoon salt**
- ½ **teaspoon ground ginger**
- ¼ **teaspoon baking soda**
- ¼ **teaspoon ground cloves**
- 1 **cup packed brown sugar**
- ⅓ **cup shortening**
- 2 **eggs**
- 1 **cup pumpkin**
- ¼ **cup milk**
- ½ **cup coarsely chopped walnuts**
- ½ **cup raisins**

In a mixing bowl, stir together first six ingredients; set aside. In a large mixing bowl, cream together brown sugar and shortening; beat in eggs. Add pumpkin and milk; mix well. Add flour mixture to sugar mixture; mixing well. Stir in nuts and raisins. Turn batter into greased 9x5x3-inch loaf pan. Bake at 350° for 55 to 60 minutes or until tester inserted near center comes out clean. Cool in pan 10 minutes. Remove from pan, cool thoroughly on a wire rack. Wrap and store overnight in refrigerator before slicing.

Zesty Zucchini Nut Loaf

Yield: 1 loaf

- 1 **cup all-purpose flour**
- 1 **teaspoon ground cinnamon**
- ½ **teaspoon baking soda**
- ½ **teaspoon salt**
- ½ **teaspoon ground nutmeg**
- ¼ **teaspoon baking powder**
- 1 **cup sugar**
- 1 **cup finely shredded, unpeeled zucchini**
- 1 **egg**
- ¼ **cup oil**
- ¼ **teaspoon lemon zest**
- ½ **cup chopped walnuts**

In a mixing bowl, stir together first six ingredients; set aside. In another bowl, beat together sugar, zucchini, and egg. Add oil and lemon zest; mix well. Stir flour mixture into zucchini mixture. Gently fold in nuts. Turn batter into greased 8x4x2-inch loaf pan. Bake at 350° for 55 to 60 minutes or until a tester, inserted near center, comes out clean. Cool in pan for 10 minutes. Remove from pan, cool thoroughly on a rack. Wrap and store loaf overnight before slicing.

Orange Rolls

Yield: 2 dozen rolls

Rolls:
- 2 **packages dry yeast**
- 1 **cup lukewarm water**
- 1 **teaspoon salt**
- ⅓ **cup sugar**
- ⅓ **cup salad oil**
- 2 **eggs, well beaten**
- 4 **cups flour, divided into 2 parts**

Orange Butter:
- ¼ **cup frozen orange juice concentrate, undiluted**
- 1⅓ **sticks butter**
- 3½ **cups powdered sugar**

Rolls:
Dissolve yeast in lukewarm water. Add salt, sugar, oil, and eggs. Add flour in 2 parts; beat until elastic. Let rise until more than doubled in bulk. Punch dough down, form into balls or rolls. Place on cookie sheet or muffin tins. Let rise again. Bake at 375° until brown.

Orange Butter:
Cream orange juice, butter, and sugar together. Place in a covered container. Spread on warm rolls.

Country Biscuits

Yield: 2 dozen

6 cups all-purpose flour
½ cup nonfat dry milk
¼ cup double-acting
   baking powder
¼ cup sugar
2 teaspoons salt
2 teaspoons cream of
   tartar
2 cups shortening
1½ cups water

In a large bowl, use a fork to combine first 6 ingredients. Using a pastry blender, cut shortening into flour mixture until crumbly. Stir in water until moistened. Add ¼ to ½ cup more water if too dry. Turn dough onto floured surface. With floured hands, knead 8 to 10 times until smooth. With floured rolling pin, roll dough ¾-inch thick. Cut biscuits with a floured 2½-inch round cutter; place on cookie sheet 1-inch apart. Press trimmings together, re-roll and cut. Repeat until all dough used. Bake at 400° for 15 to 20 minutes.

To freeze, prepare as above but do not bake. Place biscuits on cookie sheet and freeze. When biscuits are frozen, remove from sheet and place in freezer bags. To bake, place on cookie sheet and bake at 400° for 30 to 35 minutes.

Beneath the Palms

Beer Biscuits

Yield: 2 dozen

3 **cups biscuit baking mix**
2 **tablespoons sugar**
1 **(12 ounce) can warm beer (never refrigerated)**

In a large mixing bowl, mix together all ingredients. Spoon batter into greased muffin tins. Bake at 425° for 23 to 30 minutes.

60 Minute Rolls

Yield: 2 dozen rolls

2 **packages dry yeast**
1½ **cups warm water**
2 **tablespoons sugar**
6 **tablespoons shortening, melted**
3 **cups self-rising flour**
2 **tablespoons nonfat dry milk**

Dissolve yeast in warm water, add sugar and shortening. Mix in flour and dry milk; let stand 30 minutes. Dip with spoon into a greased muffin tin. Let rise 30 minutes. Bake at 400° until lightly browned, about 12 minutes.

Border Beer Bread

Yield: 1 loaf

4 **tablespoons butter**
3 **cups self-rising flour**
2 **tablespoons sugar**
1 **(12 ounce) can warm beer (never refrigerated)**

Butter a 9x5-inch loaf pan using 1 tablespoon of butter. In a large bowl, mix together flour, sugar, and beer. Spoon dough into pan. Melt remaining butter and pour over top. Bake at 350° for 50 to 60 minutes or until bread is a light golden color. Let stand 10 minutes before cutting.

Hearty Honey Bread

Yield: 2 loaves

1½	**cups water**
1	**cup cottage cheese**
½	**cup honey**
¼	**cup butter or margarine**
6	**cups bread flour**
1	**cup whole wheat flour**
2	**tablespoons sugar**
3	**teaspoons salt**
2	**packages dry yeast**
1	**egg**

Combine water, cottage cheese, honey, and butter in a saucepan and heat to very warm (120° to 140°). In a large mixing bowl, combine 4 cups of bread flour with 1 cup of whole wheat flour. Set aside. In a blender, mix the additional 2 cups of bread flour, sugar, salt, yeast, and egg. Blend well and add to the flour in the mixing bowl. Pour in the cottage cheese mixture. Mix well; and knead for 2 minutes. Place in a greased or oiled bowl; cover, let rise for 40 to 50 minutes. Punch dough down. Divide into two; place in 2 greased loaf pans. Cover; let rise for 45 to 60 minutes. Bake at 350° for 30 to 40 minutes.

The town of Shannondale began adjacent to the International Bridge in the area now known as Amigoland in Brownsville. The town never grew and was abandoned. The remains dissolved into the ever-shifting Rio Grande river.

Refrigerator Yeast Rolls

Yield: 4 dozen rolls

1	package active dry yeast
1	cup hot water
9	cups all-purpose flour
1	cup shortening
½	cup sugar
1	egg
1½	teaspoons salt
1¾	cups cold water
1	cup nonfat dry milk
	Melted butter

Proof yeast in hot water (110° to 115°). Sift flour. Mix shortening, sugar, egg, and salt in mixing bowl. Add yeast and cold water to shortening mixture. Stir in 1 cup flour and some milk. Mix just until blended. Continue adding flour, 1 cup at a time, up to 8 cups, and milk, until a soft dough is formed. Place dough in an airtight container and refrigerate overnight. Remove from refrigerator and knead dough with 1 cup of remaining flour. Shape into rolls and brush with melted butter. Allow to rise in a warm place without a draft until double in size (about 2½ hours). Bake at 400° for 15 to 20 minutes.

These may be partially baked and frozen or refrigerated until ready to use.

Gingerbread

Yield: 35 to 40 servings

2½	cups flour
1½	teaspoons baking soda
1	teaspoon cinnamon
1	teaspoon ginger
½	teaspoon cloves
½	teaspoon salt
½	cup sugar
½	cup shortening
1	egg
1	cup molasses
1	cup hot water

Sift together flour and next 5 ingredients. Mix together remaining ingredients except hot water; stir in flour mixture. Add hot water and use a pastry blender to mix well. Bake in a shallow pan at 350° for 35 minutes.

Sour Dough Ranch Biscuits

Yield: 2 dozen biscuits

2 **packages active dry yeast**
⅓ **cup warm water**
2 **cups buttermilk**
4 ½ **cups flour**
2 **teaspoons baking powder**
½ **teaspoon baking soda**
1 **teaspoon salt**
2 **tablespoons sugar**
½ **cup oil**

Dissolve yeast in warm water; add buttermilk. In a large bowl, mix together remaining ingredients; add yeast mixture. Knead dough until smooth, form into ball. Place in bowl, cover and refrigerate. The following day, pinch dough off into round balls. Form into biscuits, place in greased 9-inch round cake pan. Bake at 450° for 8 minutes or until lightly browned.

Jalapeño Cornbread

Yield: 24 squares

3 **cups cornmeal mix**
2½ **cups milk**
½ **cup bacon drippings or vegetable oil**
1 **(8 ounce) can creamed corn**
3 **eggs, beaten**
½ **(9 ounce) can chopped jalapeños**
1½ **cups grated sharp cheddar cheese**
1 **(2 ounce) jar chopped pimentos**
1 **onion, diced**

Combine all ingredients in order listed. Pour into well oiled 9x 13-inch baking dish. Bake at 375° for 35 minutes. More baking time may be needed, but do not cook too long or bread will be dry. Allow to cool slightly before cutting into squares.

Beneath the Palms

Sweet Potato Corn Sticks

Yield: 14 cornsticks

2 medium sweet potatoes
  Vegetable oil
½ cup buttermilk
6 tablespoons unsalted
  butter, melted
2 eggs
1 cup yellow cornmeal
1 cup unbleached all-
  purpose flour
½ cup sugar
2½ teaspoons baking
  powder
½ teaspoon salt

Position rack in center of oven. Place potatoes in pan and bake at 400° until knife pierces potatoes easily, about 1 hour. Maintain oven temperature. Peel potatoes. Purée. Transfer 1½ cups purée to a large bowl. Generously brush corn stick pans with vegetable oil. Heat pans in oven until oil smokes slightly, about 10 minutes. Meanwhile, mix buttermilk, butter, and eggs into potato purée. Combine cornmeal, flour, sugar, baking powder, and salt. Add to purée and stir just until combined. Spoon batter into pans, filling each ¾ full. Bake until crisp and golden brown, 15 to 20 minutes. Unmold. Serve warm.

Onion Cheese Bread

Yield: 1 loaf

½ cup chopped onion
1 tablespoon oil
1 egg, beaten
½ cup milk
1½ cups biscuit baking mix
1 cup grated sharp
  cheddar cheese
1 tablespoon poppy seeds
2 tablespoons butter,
  melted

Sauté onion in oil until translucent. Combine egg and milk, add to biscuit mix and stir only until dry ingredients are moistened. Add onion and half the cheese. Spread dough in greased 8-inch pan. Sprinkle top with remaining cheese and poppy seeds. Drizzle butter over all. Bake at 400° for 25 minutes.

All Corn Muffins

Yield: 10 large muffins

1 cup cornmeal
1 teaspoon salt
1 cup boiling water
½ cup milk
1 egg
2 teaspoons baking
   powder
1 tablespoon bacon
   grease, melted

Mix cornmeal and salt. Add boiling water, stir well (water must be boiling, not just hot). Add milk and stir. Add egg and mix well. Stir in baking powder and bacon grease just before pouring into greased and heated muffin tins. Bake at 475° for 12 to 15 minutes, or until browned.

🌴 Fort Brown Cornbread

Yield: 12 servings

1 cup yellow cornmeal
1 cup all-purpose flour or
   whole wheat flour
3 tablespoons sugar
1 tablespoon baking
   powder
⅓ cup nonfat dry milk
¼ teaspoon salt
1 cup water
3 tablespoons safflower
   oil
2 egg whites, lightly
   beaten or 1 egg
   substitute

Combine first 6 ingredients in a medium bowl. Mix the water, oil, and egg whites. Add to dry ingredients and mix just until blended. Bake in a greased 9-inch square pan until tester inserted in center comes out clean, about 20 to 25 minutes. Serve hot.

Beneath the Palms

Bacon Cheese Loaf

Yield: 1 loaf

- ½ **cup butter or margarine, melted**
- 3 **tablespoons minced onion**
- 1 **tablespoon mustard**
- 1 **tablespoon poppy seeds**
- 1 **loaf French bread**
- 8 **slices Swiss cheese, cut in half**
- 2 **slices bacon**

Mix butter with onions, mustard, and poppy seeds. Trim crust off sides of bread; cut crosswise into 1-inch slices, being careful not to cut through bread. Insert cheese into slices, pour butter mixture over bread. Top with bacon. Bake at 400° for 20 minutes.

Hurricane Herb Bread

Yield: 1 loaf

- 1 **package active dry yeast**
- ¼ **cup warm water (105° to 115°)**
- 1 **teaspoon sugar**
- 1 **cup creamed cottage cheese, warmed**
- 1 **egg, slightly beaten**
- 2 **tablespoons sugar**
- 1 **tablespoon minced onions**
- 1 **tablespoon butter, melted**
- 2 **teaspoons dill seed**
- ½ **teaspoon dill weed**
- 1 **teaspoon salt**
- ¼ **teaspoon baking soda**
- 2½ **cups all-purpose flour**

Dissolve yeast in warm water with sugar. Let stand for 10 minutes. Combine cottage cheese with next 8 ingredients and yeast mixture, stirring until well blended. Stir in flour, working dough until all flour is moistened. Beat well. Cover with damp towel and let rise in warm place until doubled in bulk (about 1 hour). Punch down and turn dough into well-greased 2-quart casserole dish. Let rise until doubled in bulk (about 30 minutes). Bake at 375° for 15 minutes; lower temperature to 300° and bake for another 25 minutes or until golden brown.

The first Episcopal Church in Brownsville was built on the corner of Tenth and Washington streets in 1854. It was twice destroyed. First, by the October 1867 hurricane and again, by fire in 1928.

🌴 Herb Loaves

Yield: 2 loaves

2	**cups rolled oats**
1½	**cups boiling water**
2	**tablespoons active dry yeast**
½	**cup warm water**
1	**cup skim milk**
¼	**cup honey**
¼	**cup olive oil**
1	**teaspoon salt (optional)**
½	**cup minced onions**
⅓	**cup minced celery leaves**
¼	**cup minced fresh parsley**
1	**tablespoon minced fresh sage, or 1 teaspoon dried**
1	**tablespoon minced fresh marjoram, or 1 teaspoon dried**
1	**tablespoon minced fresh thyme, or 1 teaspoon dried**
2	**cups whole wheat flour**
4	**cups unbleached flour**
1	**egg white**
1	**tablespoon water**
2	**tablespoons lightly ground rolled oats**

In a medium bowl, combine 2 cups rolled oats and boiling water. Let cool until lukewarm. In a large bowl, dissolve the yeast in warm water. Let stand in a warm place until foamy, about five minutes. In a one-quart saucepan, combine milk, honey, oil, and salt. Heat until lukewarm. Stir in onions, celery, parsley, sage, marjoram, and thyme. Add to yeast mixture. Stir in whole wheat flour, add cooled rolled oats. Stir in enough unbleached flour to make a kneadable dough. Let stand for 15 minutes. Turn dough onto lightly floured surface; knead, adding more flour if necessary for approximately 10 minutes or until smooth and elastic. Coat a large bowl with cooking spray. Add dough and turn to coat all sides. Cover and set in a warm place until doubled in size, about 1 hour and 15 minutes. Divide dough in half; let rest for 10 minutes. Roll each half into a 14x7-inch rectangle. Starting at short end roll into a log. Coat two 9x5-inch loaf pans with cooking spray. Add dough seam-side down. Cover and set in a warm place until doubled, about 30 to 45 minutes. In a cup lightly beat together egg white and water; brush over loaves. Sprinkle with ground oats. Bake at 375° for 45 to 50 minutes or until lightly browned.

Beneath the Palms

Pepper Cheese Bread

Yield: 2 loaves

¼ cup warm water (105° to 115°)
1 package active dry yeast
½ teaspoon sugar
⅛ teaspoon ground ginger
6 cups all-purpose flour
⅓ cup nonfat dry milk
2 tablespoons sugar
1½ teaspoons black pepper
1 teaspoon salt
2 cups shredded cheddar cheese
1½ cups very warm water (120° to 130°)
2 tablespoons cooking oil
1 egg, lightly beaten
1 egg yolk, lightly beaten
1 tablespoon water

In a small bowl, combine warm water, yeast, sugar, and ginger; let stand 5 minutes or until bubbles form. In a large bowl stir together 1½ cups of flour, milk, sugar, pepper, and salt. Stir yeast mixture, cheese, 1½ cups very warm water, oil, and whole egg into flour mixture. Beat with an electric mixer on low speed 30 seconds. Beat on high speed 3 minutes. Using a spoon, stir in as much of remaining flour as possible. Turn dough onto a lightly floured surface; knead in enough of remaining flour to make a moderately stiff dough that is smooth and elastic (6 to 8 minutes). Shape dough into a ball; place in a greased bowl, turning once to grease surface. Cover; let rise in a warm place until double in size (about 1 hour). Punch dough down; turn onto a floured surface. Cover; let rest 10 minutes. Meanwhile, grease 2 baking sheets. Divide dough in half; then divide each half into three equal portions. To shape loaves, roll each portion into a 16-inch rope. Braid by lining up three ropes, 1-inch apart on baking sheet. Starting in middle, loosely braid by bringing left rope underneath center rope; bring right rope under new center rope. Repeat to end. Press ends together to seal. Repeat on other end and with remaining dough. Cover; let rise in a warm place until nearly double (about 30 minutes). Brush loaves with a mixture of egg yolk and water. Bake at 350° for 20 minutes, or until golden and bread sounds hollow when tapped.

Main Courses

Beef Tenderloin with Peppercorn Crust and Whiskey Sauce

Yield: 4 servings

Sauce:

- 1½ pounds beef neck bones
- 4 large shallots, coarsely chopped
- 6 cloves garlic, coarsely chopped
- 2 large carrots, coarsely chopped
- 1 cup whiskey
- 1 tablespoon tomato paste
- 4 fresh thyme sprigs or 1 teaspoon dried
- 2 teaspoons whole black peppercorns or 4 peppercorn mix
- 2 cups chicken broth or canned low-salt broth
- 2 cups beef broth or canned unsalted broth

Beef:

- ¼ cup whole black peppercorns, lightly crushed
- 1 tablespoon cornstarch
- 2 teaspoons chopped fresh thyme or ½ teaspoon dried
- 1 teaspoon chopped fresh oregano or ¼ teaspoon dried
- 2 tablespoons vegetable oil
- 1 (2 pound) beef tenderloin roast

Sauce:

Brown beef bones, shallots, garlic, and carrots in heavy saucepan over medium heat, stirring occasionally, about 20 minutes. Add whiskey, increase heat and boil until liquid is reduced by half, about 5 minutes. Mix in tomato paste, thyme, and peppercorns. Add broths and boil until liquid is reduced to 1 cup, about 20 minutes. Strain through fine sieve into heavy small saucepan. Season to taste with salt. (Can prepare 1 day ahead. Cover and refrigerate.)

Beef:

Mix first 4 ingredients on large plate. Brush 1 tablespoon oil over beef. Roll beef in peppercorn mixture, coating completely. Season with salt. Heat remaining oil in heavy large ovenproof skillet over medium-high heat. Add beef and sear on all sides, about 5 minutes. Transfer skillet to oven and roast until meat thermometer inserted into center of beef registers 130° for rare, about 30 minutes. Let beef stand 10 minutes before slicing. Slice beef and arrange on plates. Bring sauce to simmer, spoon over beef.

Beef Tenderloin with Blue Cheese and Tomato Chutney

Yield: 6 to 8 servings

Chutney:
- 10 cloves garlic
- 1 (4-inch) piece fresh ginger, peeled
- ½ cup balsamic vinegar
- ¼ cup red wine vinegar
- 6 tablespoons sugar
- 1¼ teaspoons salt
- ¾ teaspoon cayenne pepper
- 1 large Roma tomato, seeded and chopped

Beef:
- 1 (3 to 4 pound) beef tenderloin roast
- 2 cups blue cheese or mild Roquefort cheese, crumbled
  Italian parsley
  Cherry tomatoes

Chutney:
In a food processor with metal blade, mince garlic and ginger. Add vinegars, sugar, salt, and cayenne. Add tomato, pulse into small pieces. Remove to an 8-cup microwave safe bowl and microwave on high for about 45 to 55 minutes, stirring every 10 minutes, until mixture is very thick and liquid on the top is absorbed when stirred. Cool thoroughly.

Beef:
Up to one hour before roasting, remove meat from refrigerator, trim off fat. Sprinkle with salt. Place on a rack in a shallow pan. Sprinkle 1 cup cheese over top, pressing into meat. Spoon enough chutney over top to press into a ¼-inch thickness (not all will be used). Roast meat at 450° for 15 minutes (don't be concerned if some of the chutney falls off). Sprinkle top with remaining cheese. For rare to medium meat, continue baking for 35 to 40 additional minutes. Temperature will go up 10 degrees as it sits. Let rest 10 to 20 minutes before carving into ½-inch slices. Serve with remaining chutney. Garnish with Italian parsley and cherry tomatoes.

Beef Roulades

Yield: 4 servings

1½	**pounds boneless round steak**
4	**slices bacon**
2	**tablespoons butter or margarine**
1	**medium onion, sliced**
1	**(10 ounce) can beef consommé, undiluted**
1	**bay leaf**
1	**teaspoon black pepper**
1½	**tablespoons all-purpose flour**
1½	**tablespoons water Hot cooked noodles**

Pound steak to ¼-inch thickness; cut into 12 (4x1½-inch) pieces. Cut each bacon slice into 3 equal pieces. Lay a piece of bacon in the center of each steak. Roll tightly and secure with a wooden pick. Set aside. Melt butter in a Dutch oven; add steak, brown on all sides. Remove steak and set aside. Add onions to pan drippings and sauté until tender. Add steak, consommé and next 2 ingredients. Cover and simmer 45 minutes or until tender. Combine flour and water, stirring until smooth. Gradually stir flour mixture into steak mixture; cook until thickened. Serve over hot cooked noodles. Remove wooden picks before serving.

Meat Marinade

Yield: 1 cup marinade

¾	**cup soy sauce**
¼	**cup brown sugar**
2	**tablespoons lemon juice**
¼	**teaspoon garlic powder**
½	**teaspoon salt**
¼	**cup Worcestershire sauce**

Mix all ingredients together. Pour over meat and let stand for at least 2 hours.

Great for roast, steaks, beef-kabobs.

The first paving of City streets in Brownsville was accomplished by the use of wooden blocks. On one occasion, a street caught fire when gasoline leaking from an automobile was accidentally ignited. The Fire Department was called to extinguish the blaze.

Steamboat Brisket

Yield: 6 to 8 servings

1 **whole brisket, trimmed
  of fat
  Liquid Smoke flavoring
  Meat tenderizer**
2 **tablespoons dry onion
  flakes
  Garlic powder to taste
  Black pepper to taste**
1 **(32 ounce) can
  sauerkraut with juice**
½ **cup white wine
  (optional)**
½ **cup water (optional)**

Generously moisten both sides of brisket with Liquid Smoke flavoring. Punch holes through remaining fat and sprinkle with meat tenderizer, onion flakes, garlic powder, and pepper. Allow to stand 20 minutes then bake at 450° for 1½ hours or until fat begins to become crisp and brown. There should be juices in bottom of pan browning, if not, cook a while longer. Remove pan and cover brisket with sauerkraut. If not enough juice, add wine and water. Cover tightly with foil and return to oven. Lower temperate to 325° and bake until very tender. Juice may be thickened with flour.

Brochette Dijon Flambe

Yield: 6 servings

4 **cloves garlic**
1 **teaspoon dried thyme**
2 **tablespoons lemon juice**
⅔ **cup Drambuie**
1 **cup Dijon mustard**
2 **tablespoons honey**
2 **pounds lamb or chicken,
  cut into 1½-inch cubes
  Salt and pepper**
4 **tablespoons Drambuie**

In a saucepan, combine first four ingredients. Cook over medium heat for about 10 minutes until reduced slightly. Stir in mustard and honey, simmer a few minutes. Sprinkle meat with salt and pepper; toss with mustard mixture. Thread meat on skewers and grill or broil 8 to 10 minutes on each side. Flambe by heating remaining Drambuie until warm. Light and pour (carefully) over brochettes.

Beneath the Palms

Rolled Flank Steak

Yield: 6 servings

- 1 **cup sliced mushrooms**
- ½ **cup chopped onion**
- 1 **tablespoon olive oil**
- 2 **cups bread crumbs**
- 2 **tablespoons chopped parsley**
- ½ **teaspoon celery seed**
  Salt and pepper to taste
- 1 **flank steak**
- ½ **cup beef bouillon**

Sauté mushrooms and onions in oil until tender. Add bread crumbs and next 3 ingredients, mix lightly. Place mixture lengthwise down center of flank steak. Roll meat around filling and fasten edges with toothpicks or twine. Be sure it is rolled lengthwise. In a heavy skillet, brown on all sides. Add bouillon, cover tightly and simmer for 1 hour and 30 minutes. Add more liquid as needed. Remove meat from skillet. If desired, make gravy from drippings by adding sour cream, wine, and flour to thicken. For perfect slices, let roast cool before slicing.

Steak Marinade

Yield: 1 cup marinade

- ¼ **cup soy sauce**
- ½ **cup Sauterne wine**
- 1 **clove garlic, minced**
- 1 **tablespoon chopped parsley**
- 2 **tablespoons olive oil**
- 1 **teaspoon oregano leaves, crushed**
- 1 **teaspoon coarse ground black pepper**

Mix all ingredients together. Pour marinade over steak and refrigerate for 8 hours or overnight.

Buddy's Fajitas

Yield: 6 to 8 servings

2 tablespoons soy sauce
6 tablespoons teriyaki
  sauce
  Juice of 5 limes
1 tablespoon wine vinegar
1 teaspoon garlic powder
2 tablespoons chopped
  onion
1 tablespoon honey
  Pinch of chili powder
1 teaspoon picante sauce
1 tablespoon Woody's
  Smoke sauce
½ stick butter
  Salt and pepper to taste
2 pounds cleaned fijitas

Mix all ingredients together. Pour over cleaned fajitas and let stand for 30 minutes. Grill fajitas over hot coals.

Serve with warm tortillas, pico de gallo, chopped cilantro, and sliced avocados.

West Texas Casserole

Yield: 4 to 6 servings

1 pound ground round
  steak
2 (15 ounce) cans black-
  eyed peas with
  jalapeños
2 cups cooked rice
1 (14 ½ ounce) can stewed
  tomatoes, drained
1 cup grated cheddar
  cheese
½ cup minced onion
1 tablespoon butter
  Salt and pepper to taste

Brown meat in large skillet; add other ingredients in order listed. Salt and pepper to taste. Bake in a 13x 9x2-inch baking dish at 350° for 20 minutes.

Beneath the Palms

Cajun Sauce Piquante

Yield: 6 servings

1   tablespoon vegetable oil
2   pounds stew meat
1   pound chopped smoked
       sausage
2   large onions, chopped
¾   cup chopped celery
¾   cup chopped bell pepper
1   (10 ounce) can chopped
       tomatoes with green
       chilies
2   (15 ounce) cans tomato
       sauce
2   cloves garlic, minced
¼   teaspoon cayenne
       pepper
     Salt and pepper to taste
3   tablespoons chopped
       parsley
1   bunch green onions with
       tops, chopped

Cover bottom of a Dutch oven with oil. On medium heat, brown meat and sausage well. Add onions, celery, and bell pepper; cook until translucent. Add tomatoes and next 3 ingredients. Bring to a rapid boil. Add parsley, onion, and enough water to cover meat. Pot should be ¾ full of water at all times. Bring to a rapid boil for 2 minutes. Reduce heat, cover with tight fitting lid, simmer until tender, about 2 to 3 hours. Add water as needed. Serve over white rice.

Lazy Beef Casserole

Yield: 4 to 6 servings

1   pound lean beef chuck,
       cut in 1½-inch cubes
½   cup red wine
1   (10 ounce) can
       consommé
¼   teaspoon rosemary
     Fresh ground black
       pepper
1   medium onion, chopped
¼   cup fine dry bread
       crumbs
¼   cup all-purpose flour

Put meat in a casserole with wine, consommé, rosemary, pepper, and onion. Mix bread crumbs and flour, stir into mixture. Cover and bake at 300° for approximately 3 hours. Serve over rice or noodles.

Sombrero Casserole

1 **pound lean ground beef**
2 **tablespoons olive oil**
⅓ **cup chopped onion**
⅓ **cup chopped bell pepper**
1 **(15 ounce) can whole kernel corn**
1 **(15 ounce) can kidney beans**
4 **(8 ounce) cans tomato sauce**
1 **Tabasco pepper (optional)**
Salt and pepper to taste
1 **(12 ounce) package egg noodles**
Parmesan cheese

Brown meat in oil, add onion and pepper; sauté. Add corn, beans, and tomato sauce; stir. Add Tabasco pepper, salt, and pepper to taste. While sauce is simmering, prepare noodles according to package directions. Drain and add to sauce. To capture flavors and thicken slightly, simmer 25 to 30 minutes. Sprinkle Parmesan cheese on top before serving.

This dish is similar to a goulash. For a casserole, place sliced cheese on top and microwave until cheese is bubbly.

Rolled Stuffed Meat Loaf

2 **cups seasoned stuffing mix**
2 **tablespoons chopped parsley**
¼ **cup water**
½ **cup peeled, sliced carrots**
2 **pounds ground chuck**
2 **(10 ¾ ounce) cans cream of mushroom soup**
1 **egg, beaten**
⅓ **cup diced onion**
1 **teaspoon salt**
½ **cup milk**

Mix 1½ cups stuffing mix with parsley, water, and carrots. Set aside. Combine ground chuck, ½ cup soup, egg, onion, salt, and ½ cup stuffing mix. Shape into 9x13-inch rectangle on waxed paper. Spread stuffing mixture over meat, leaving ½-inch border on each side. Begin rolling from one end, lifting wax paper as you go. Press edges together to seal. Place in lightly greased baking dish. Bake at 350° for 45 minutes. Make gravy by stirring 3 tablespoons of grease from pan with remaining soup and milk. Heat over low heat, stirring occasionally.

Cheese Mushroom Meatloaf

Yield: 6 servings

- 1 **medium yellow onion, chopped**
- 2 **tablespoons of water**
- 2 **cloves garlic, minced**
- 8 **ounces fresh mushrooms, sliced**
- 1½ **pounds ground meat**
- ⅔ **cup fresh bread crumbs**
- ½ **cup chopped fresh parsley**
- ¼ **cup ketchup**
- 1 **egg, beaten**
- 1 **teaspoon salt**
- ½ **teaspoon black pepper**
- ½ **teaspoon dried thyme, crumbled**
- ½ **teaspoon dried ground or rubbed sage**
- 1½ **cups grated cheese, (Swiss, Monterey Jack, or cheddar)**

In a skillet, sauté onion in 2 tablespoons of water, until translucent. Add garlic and mushrooms, stirring frequently. Cook until mushrooms are golden brown. Cool. Mix meat with bread crumbs and next 7 ingredients. Put half the mixture into loaf pan, layer with onion mixture and cheese. Top with remaining meat mixture. Bake at 350° for one hour or until loaf shrinks from sides of pan and browns. Pour off any drippings.

Construction of the Immaculate Conception Cathedral located on Twelfth and Jefferson streets began in 1854. Designed by Father Pierre Keralum, the first Mass was celebrated there in 1859.

✦ Port Pork Medallions

Yield: 4 to 6 servings

2 **pounds pork tenderloin, trimmed and sliced**
Salt and pepper to taste
Flour as needed
2 **tablespoons unsalted butter**
2 **tablespoons olive oil**
1 **cup chicken broth**
1 **cup port wine**

Slice tenderloin into ½-inch thick medallions. Season slices with salt and pepper; dredge in flour to coat. Heat butter and oil in a heavy skillet on medium high heat. Sauté medallions in small batches until browned, one minute per side.

Place cooked slices in a serving dish and keep warm in a 225° oven. To prepare the sauce, add chicken broth and wine to skillet with meat drippings. Bring to a boil, scraping and stirring until it evaporates slightly. Cook for 6 to 8 minutes until sauce thickens. Spoon sauce over meat to serve.

Pork Chops with Apple Stuffing

Yield: 6 servings

6 **thick pork chops**
¼ **cup chopped onions**
¼ **cup chopped celery**
2 **tablespoons margarine**
4 **cups dry bread crumbs**
½ **teaspoon poultry seasoning**
½ **teaspoon dried sage**
1 **cup peeled, diced apples**
½ **cup chicken broth**
Freshly ground black pepper to taste

Cut a pocket into each pork chop; set aside. Sauté onions and celery in margarine for 5 minutes or until tender; combine with all other dry ingredients. Add broth and toss. Fill the pocket in the pork chop with stuffing. Place on a broiler pan and bake at 350° for 1 hour.

Beneath the Palms

🌴 Stuffed Pork Tenderloin

Yield: 4 to 6 servings

1 (2 pound) pork
tenderloin
1 tablespoon olive oil
2 tablespoons Dijon
mustard
2 tablespoons teriyaki
sauce
1 cup fresh spinach,
washed
½ cup sliced fresh
mushrooms
½ cup chopped onion
Salt and pepper to taste
Fresh sage to taste

Slice tenderloin length-wise, without cutting all the way through tenderloin. Place on work surface, pound to about ½-inch thickness. Mix together olive oil, Dijon, and teriyaki to form a medium thick paste. Spray a saucepan with nonstick cooking spray, sauté spinach, mushrooms, and onions until just tender. Add salt, pepper, and sage to taste. Spread mixture over top of tenderloin. Roll tenderloin gently and secure with string or toothpicks. Grill for about 45 minutes or until done.

🌴 Dijon Rosemary Pork with Apple Tomato Sauce

Yield: 4 servings

1 pound lean pork
tenderloin
2 cloves garlic, minced
2 teaspoons Dijon
mustard
1 teaspoon dried
rosemary leaves
¼ teaspoon ground cloves
2 tablespoons apple juice
1½ cups fresh or canned
crushed tomatoes
2 large apples, peeled,
cored, and cut into ½-
inch slices

Place pork tenderloin in baking dish sprayed with nonstick cooking spray. Combine garlic, mustard, rosemary, and cloves. Spread over pork. Bake at 450° for 10 minutes. Reduce heat to 400°, sprinkle apple juice over pork, bake for 10 minutes. Spoon tomatoes and apples over and around the pork. Bake 20 minutes.

🌴 *Rio Grande Pork Loin*

Yield: 12 to 16 servings

Roast:
1 (6-8 pound) pork loin
   roast
½ teaspoon salt
½ teaspoon garlic salt
½ teaspoon chili powder

Sauce:
½ cup apple jelly
½ cup ketchup
1 tablespoon vinegar
½ teaspoon chili powder

Roast:
Have butcher cut loin away from bone and tie back together. Mix seasonings together and rub on roast. Smoke over a mesquite charcoal fire for 3 hours. Let meat stand for 10 minutes to set juices prior to slicing.

Sauce:
Mix all ingredients and boil for 2 minutes, stirring well. Baste meat with sauce during cooking. Serve remaining sauce over loin slices.

This dish can also be baked at 325° until 170° internally on a meat thermometer. Baste with sauce and cook 10 minutes longer.

Pork Chops and Rice Casserole

Yield: 6 servings

6 (½-inch) thick pork
   chops
1 cup uncooked white rice
1 bell pepper, sliced
½ teaspoon curry powder
1 medium onion, sliced
   Salt and pepper to taste
2 cups boiling water

Brown pork chops. Place rice in greased 1½-quart casserole or 9x13-inch baking pan. Layer pork chops on top of rice. Top each chop with a slice of onion and bell pepper. Season with salt, pepper, and curry powder. Rinse skillet with boiling water, scraping up bits. Pour into casserole over pork chops. Cover with lid or foil. Bake at 375° for approximately 1 hour.

Beneath the Palms

Party Pizza

Yield: 2 pizzas

Crust:
- ⅓ cup cornmeal
- 1 teaspoon salt
- 1 tablespoon sugar
- 1½ packages active dry yeast
- 5 ½ cups flour
- 1½ cups warm water
- 4 tablespoons vegetable oil

Topping:
- 1 pound sausage
- 1 (14 ounce) jar pizza sauce
- 1 pound mozzarella cheese, shredded
- 1 (3 ounce) package pepperoni, sliced thinly
- 1 small onion, diced
- 1 medium bell pepper, diced

Crust:
Combine cornmeal, salt, sugar, yeast, 2 cups flour, water, and oil in a mixing bowl of a heavy duty mixer. Begin mixing, using regular beater and mix for 3 minutes. Change to dough hook, add 2 more cups of flour. Continue to mix 2 to 3 minutes after flour is mixed in. Mix in additional flour ½ cup at a time until dough is only slightly sticky (up to 5 ½ cups total). Don't add too much flour or dough will be too heavy. Cover bowl and let rise until it has doubled in size (about 1 hour). Punch dough down and divide in two parts. Spray two large pizza pans with nonstick cooking spray; dust lightly with cornmeal, press dough into pans. For raised crust, let dough rise in the pans for about 1 hour before adding the toppings. If raised crust is not wanted, continue without allowing time for crust to rise.

Topping:
Cook sausage, crumble, and drain fat. Spread sauce evenly on dough and cover with ½ of the cheese. Add sausage, pepperoni, onion, and bell pepper. Top with remaining cheese. Bake at 450° for 15 minutes.

🌴 Veal Chops with Apricots

Yield: 4 servings

16 **fresh apricots, peeled, pitted, and halved, or 32 canned apricot halves, drained**
 4 **tablespoons light olive oil**
 4 **veal chops, each ¾-inch thick**
 ½ **teaspoon dried thyme leaves**
 ¼ **teaspoon grated nutmeg**
 ¼ **teaspoon white pepper**
 2 **cups low sodium chicken broth**
 ½ **teaspoon dry mustard**

Purée 16 apricot halves in the work bowl of food processor or blender. Set aside. Heat olive oil in skillet over medium heat. Brown veal chops on both sides; sprinkle with thyme, nutmeg, and pepper. Add 1½ cups of chicken broth and simmer for 15 minutes or until chops are tender. Turn chops several times while simmering. Remove chops from pan, set aside. Discard any juices remaining in skillet. Combine apricot purée and dry mustard, add to skillet. Add remaining chicken broth, cook for 5 minutes. Add remaining apricot halves, stir and cook for 2 minutes. Return chops to skillet and simmer 3 minutes.

🌴 Grilled Lemon Herb Veal Chops

Yield: 4 servings

- 3 **tablespoons fresh lime juice**
- 3 **tablespoons olive oil**
- 3 **cloves garlic, quartered**
- 2 **teaspoons dried oregano**
- 1 **teaspoon freshly ground black pepper**
- 4 **veal chops, cut 1-inch thick**
- 4 **slices firm red tomato Salt (optional)**

Process lemon juice and next 4 ingredients in a food processor until it forms a paste. Reserve 1 tablespoon. Spread remaining paste on both sides of veal chops and put in shallow dish. Cover, marinate in refrigerator for two hours. Spread reserved paste on one side of each tomato slice. Grill chops over medium coals for 12 to 14 minutes uncovered and then 10 to 12 minutes covered. Place tomato slices on grill during last six minutes of grilling time. Grill until heated through, turn once.

Lamb Chops with Nut Crust

Yield: 4 servings

- ½ **cup slivered almonds**
- ½ **cup pignola nuts**
- ½ **cup pistachio nuts**
- ½ **cup walnuts Salt and pepper to taste**
- ½ **cup Italian flavored bread crumbs**
- 1 **teaspoon milk**
- 2 **eggs**
- 8 **(4 ounce) loin lamb chops**
- 1 **cup all-purpose flour**
- 2 **tablespoons olive oil**

Place almonds and next 3 ingredients in food processor and process until well chopped. Season with salt and pepper; combine with bread crumbs. Combine milk and eggs, whisk together. Coat lamb chops with flour, dip in egg mixture, and dredge in nut mixture. Brown lamb chops in olive oil. Bake at 425° about 12 minutes for medium rare.

Great for veal and pork chops as well.

Sautéed Veal Scaloppine with Lemon Sauce

Yield: 2 to 4 servings

2 **tablespoons vegetable oil**
½ **stick butter**
1 **pound veal scaloppine, sliced thin, flattened**
¾ **cup all-purpose flour, spread on wax paper**
Salt and pepper to taste
2 **tablespoons lemon juice**
2 **tablespoons finely chopped parsley**
½ **lemon, sliced thin**

Heat oil and 2 tablespoons of butter in skillet over medium heat (the oil and butter should be very hot. Thinly sliced veal must be cooked quickly or it will become leathery). Dip both sides of scaloppine in flour and shake off excess. Slip scaloppine, no more than will fit comfortably in skillet at one time, into the pan. (If oil is hot enough, meat should sizzle). Cook scaloppine until they are lightly browned on one side, then turn and brown other side. When done, transfer to a warm platter and season with salt and pepper. Off the heat, add lemon juice to skillet, scraping loose cooking residue. Add remaining 2 tablespoons of butter and parsley, stirring it into sauce. Add scaloppine, turning in sauce. Turn heat to medium very briefly, just long enough to warm up sauce and scaloppine. Transfer to warm serving platter, pour sauce over scaloppine and garnish with lemon slices. Serve immediately.

Lamb Patties

Yield: 4 servings

1½ pounds ground lamb
1 tablespoon butter
⅓ cup chopped green onion tops
½ cup fresh bread crumbs
3 tablespoons chopped parsley
1 egg, lightly beaten
Salt to taste
Freshly ground pepper to taste
3 tablespoons butter
¼ pound mushrooms, sliced
1 tablespoon chopped shallots
¼ cup dry white wine
½ cup heavy cream
2 teaspoons chopped parsley

Put ground lamb in bowl. Heat 1 tablespoon butter, add onions and cook until wilted. Add to lamb along with bread crumbs, 3 tablespoons parsley, egg, salt, and pepper. Divide into 8 patties. Heat 2 tablespoons butter and sauté patties quickly on both sides. Remove patties to heated platter. Wipe out skillet. Add remaining butter and sauté mushrooms briefly; add shallots and wine. Cook down. Add cream; cook 5 minutes. Add chopped parsley, stir. Pour sauce over patties and serve.

The Presbyterian Church of Brownsville held their first service aboard the riverboat "Whiteville" with Reverend Hiram Chamberlain presiding. A permanent structure was built on Ninth and Elizabeth streets in 1864.

Moussaka

Yield: 6 servings

1	tablespoon olive oil
¾	pound ground lamb (or beef)
1	large onion, sliced
1	large tomato, peeled and sliced
	1 clove garlic, minced
2	teaspoons parsley
½	teaspoon salt
½	cup tomato juice
	Pinch of sugar
⅛	teaspoon cinnamon
2	eggs, separated
1	small eggplant, unpeeled and cut into ¼-inch cubes
	Flour
½	teaspoon salt
2	medium potatoes, boiled and thinly sliced
1	cup béchamel sauce

Place about 1 tablespoon olive oil in skillet; crumble meat and sauté until fat is drawn. Spoon off fat and add onion, tomato, garlic, herbs, and salt. Cook 2 minutes. Add tomato juice, sugar, and cinnamon. Simmer 5 minutes. Cool. Stir egg whites into cooled meat mixture. In another skillet, add generous amount of olive oil. Dip eggplant into flour seasoned with ½ teaspoon salt, cook until lightly browned; drain on paper towels. Layer meat mixture, potatoes and eggplant slices. Top with Béchamel sauce.

Béchamel Sauce

Yield: 1½ cups sauce

2	tablespoons butter
2	tablespoons flour
½	teaspoon salt
1½	cups milk
2	egg yolks
	Dash of nutmeg

Melt butter in saucepan; stir in flour; cook until mixture bubbles. Add salt; slowly add milk stirring with wire whisk until mixture thickens. Turn off heat. Add some sauce to egg yolks in bowl, mix. Add yolks to remaining sauce, mix well. Add nutmeg; cool slightly and pour over moussaka.

🌴 *Zucchini Lasagna Casserole*

Yield: 4 servings

1 onion, chopped
1 bell pepper, chopped
4 ounces mushrooms, sliced
½ teaspoon vegetable oil
4 small zucchini, peeled and sliced thin
1 pound lean ground beef, browned and drained
8 ounces no-salt added tomato sauce
¼ teaspoon garlic powder
¼ teaspoon fennel
¼ teaspoon black pepper
1 teaspoon basil
1 teaspoon oregano
2 ounces mozzarella cheese, shredded
⅔ cup low fat cottage cheese
⅓ cup Parmesan cheese

Sauté onion, pepper, and mushrooms in oil in Dutch oven. Meanwhile, steam sliced zucchini 6 minutes on stove top with 1 tablespoon water. Stir meat, tomato sauce, and seasonings into sautéed vegetables. Combine mozzarella and cottage cheeses in separate bowl. Spray an 8-inch square baking dish with nonstick cooking spray. Layer zucchini, cheese, and meat sauce twice. Sprinkle Parmesan over last meat layer. Bake at 375° for 45 minutes. This can be assembled and frozen for later use.

Chicken in Orange Sauce with Mushrooms

Yield: 4 to 6 servings

2 (2 pound) broiler chickens, skinned and quartered
2 teaspoons salt
⅛ teaspoon black pepper
1 stick butter
½ pound mushrooms
¼ cup finely chopped onion
2 cups orange juice
1 tablespoon sugar
1 (10¾ ounce) can beef consommé

Wash chicken and pat dry, sprinkle with salt and pepper. Brown in butter; drain. Wash, trim, and quarter mushrooms; add to skillet, cook until golden brown. Remove and set aside. Stir onion in remaining drippings in skillet and cook a few minutes. Add orange juice and sugar; cook over high heat until mixture is reduced by half. Lower heat, stir in consommé. Add chicken to skillet, cover, cook for 1 hour. Add mushrooms during last 10 minutes.

Herbed Chicken

Yield: 8 servings

2 chickens, quartered (about 3½ pounds each)
1 large onion, minced
1 cup dry sherry
½ cup olive oil
1 tablespoon Worcestershire sauce
1 teaspoon soy sauce
1 teaspoon lemon juice
1 clove garlic, minced
1 teaspoon thyme
1 teaspoon rosemary
1 teaspoon dill weed

Trim fat from chicken, rinse and pat dry. Arrange chicken in shallow pan. Combine remaining ingredients in small bowl, mix well. Pour over chicken, turning chicken to coat all sides. Cover and refrigerate, at least 4 hours, turning occasionally. Preheat grill and grease lightly. Drain chicken, saving marinade. Arrange chicken on grill, close lid. Grill for 40 to 50 minutes or until chicken is tender. Baste frequently with marinade.

Beneath the Palms

Chicken Saltimbocca

Yield: 4 servings

- 4 **medium boneless chicken breasts**
- 4 **thin slices prosciutto**
- 4 **slices Swiss cheese**
- 1 **fresh tomato, chopped**
  Fresh basil leaves
- 1 **tablespoon olive oil**
- ⅓ **cup dry white wine**

Rinse chicken and pat dry. Place each breast between two pieces of plastic wrap and pound to about ⅛-inch thickness. Place 1 slice of prosciutto and cheese on each breast. Top with 2 to 3 basil leaves and tomato. Roll breast jelly roll style and secure with toothpicks. Cook in skillet with olive oil until done, about 30 minutes. Be sure to turn gently and brown on all sides. Remove from pan, cover and keep warm. Add white wine to pan, cook 2 to 3 minutes until wine is slightly reduced. Pour over chicken and serve with white rice or orzo.

To make this low fat, substitute low fat ham and fat free Swiss cheese.

Pan Fried Chicken Strips

Yield: 2 servings

- 2 **tablespoons olive oil**
- 2 **chicken breasts**
- 2 **cloves garlic, crushed**
- 6 **green onions, chopped**
- 5 **tablespoons Marsala wine**
- 2 **tablespoons lemon juice**
  Salt and pepper to taste

Skin, bone, and cut chicken breasts into ½-inch strips. Add oil, chicken strips, garlic, and green onions to large skillet. Sauté over high heat until chicken is lightly browned and tender. Remove chicken from skillet, add wine and lemon juice, reduce liquid slightly. Return chicken to skillet, add salt and pepper. Do not overcook this dish. Serve immediately.

Chicken with Lemon and Capers

Yield: 4 servings

2 boneless, skinless chicken breasts, halved
2 tablespoons unsalted butter
3 tablespoons olive oil
¼ cup flour
   Salt and freshly ground black pepper to taste
3 large garlic cloves, minced
2 tablespoons capers, chopped
4 tablespoons freshly squeezed lemon juice
1¼ tablespoons minced parsley leaves

Pound chicken to a thickness of about ⅓-inch between sheets of waxed paper. Heat butter and oil in large skillet. Meanwhile, lightly coat both sides of each chicken with flour. Sauté chicken on moderately high heat for about 1½ minutes on each side, or until just cooked through; season with salt and pepper and remove from pan. Stir in garlic, capers, and lemon juice; cook 15 seconds. Return chicken to skillet, baste for few seconds, transfer to warmed plates. Spoon pan juices over chicken; sprinkle with parsley and serve.

Strips of roasted red or yellow peppers may be added to skillet once chicken has cooked through. May substitute 2 tablespoons olive oil for butter and olive oil.

Serve with saffron tinged baked rice and buttered carrots.

Beneath the Palms

Pan Roasted Chicken with Rosemary, Garlic, and Wine

Yield: 4 to 6 servings

- 2 tablespoons butter
- 2 tablespoons vegetable oil
- 3 large garlic cloves, peeled
- 1 frying chicken, quartered
- 1 small branch of rosemary, cut in half
- ½ teaspoon dried rosemary
- ½ cup dry white wine
  Salt and pepper to taste

Heat butter and oil in deep skillet over medium high heat. Add garlic and chicken. When chicken is well browned on one side, turn and add rosemary. If garlic starts to blacken, remove it. When chicken is well browned on all sides, add wine, salt, and pepper. Bring to boil, cover, simmer until chicken is tender (35 to 40 minutes), turning chicken two or three times. If cooking liquid evaporates, add 1 to 2 tablespoons water. Remove chicken from pan, transfer to serving platter and garnish with fresh rosemary or parsley.

Brown and Wild Rice Chicken Superb

Yield: 4 to 6 servings

- 5 tablespoons butter or margarine
- 1 cup diced boneless, skinless chicken breast
- ½ cup sliced green onions
- ½ cup cubed bell pepper
- 2 ribs celery, chopped
- 2 ounces mushrooms, sliced
  Salt and pepper to taste
- 1¾ cups water
- 6 ounces long grain brown and wild rice

Melt butter in heavy 10-inch skillet, sauté chicken in butter until cooked. Remove with slotted spoon, set aside. Add next 5 ingredients, sauté 3 minutes. Return chicken to skillet, add water, and rice; cover and cook for 20 minutes.

🌴 Grilled Chicken with Creamy Mustard Sauce

Yield: 6 to 8 servings

Sauce:
- ½ cup plain no fat yogurt
- ½ cup no fat sour cream
- 1 tablespoon Parmesan cheese
- 1-2 tablespoons red wine vinegar
- 1 tablespoon soy sauce
- ¼ teaspoon dried marjoram
- ⅛ teaspoon black pepper
- 1 clove garlic, minced

Chicken:
- 8 boneless, skinless chicken breast halves

Sauce:
Combine all ingredients, and stir well. Cover and chill.

Chicken:
Grill chicken over hot coals for 45 minutes, or until done, turning every 10 minutes. Place chicken on a serving platter, spoon mustard sauce over top. Garnish with fresh basil leaves.

Chicken Artichoke Delight

Yield: 4 servings

- 1 (12 ounce) jar marinated artichoke hearts, cut up
- 2 tablespoons olive oil
- 1 large chicken, cut into pieces
  Flour
- 1 (14 ½ ounce) can tomatoes, diced
- 2 cloves garlic, minced
- 1¼ teaspoons salt
- ½ teaspoon oregano
- ½ teaspoon basil
- ½ teaspoon black pepper
- ½ pound mushrooms, sliced
- ½ cup sherry

Drain artichoke hearts, reserving liquid. Combine liquid and olive oil in large frying pan. Dredge chicken in flour, brown until golden in color. Place chicken in large casserole dish. Add tomatoes to pan; stir. Add garlic, spices, and mushrooms; stir. Pour over chicken, add artichoke hearts and cover. Bake at 350° for 1 hour or until chicken is tender. Add sherry during last few minutes of cooking.

Beneath the Palms

Apricot Chicken Breasts

Yield: 4 servings

- **4 boneless, skinless chicken breasts**
- **4 ounces Swiss or mozzarella cheese, grated**
- **¼ cup toasted almonds, chopped**

Sauce:
- **1 cup apricot preserves**
- **3 tablespoons Worcestershire sauce**
- **1 teaspoon dry mustard**

Cut pocket in each chicken breast. Combine cheese with almonds; stuff into pockets.
Sauce:
Combine ingredients until well blended. Top chicken with sauce; bake, uncovered, at 325° for 50 to 60 minutes, basting frequently with sauce. Garnish with sliced almonds, if desired.

Saté Ayam (Grilled Chicken on Skewers)

Yield: 4 servings

- **2 red chilies**
- **2 medium onions, chopped**
- **2 tablespoons light soy sauce**
- **2 tablespoons dark soy sauce**
- **1 tablespoon sesame seed oil**
- **2 tablespoons lemon juice**
- **3 tablespoons chopped fresh ginger**
- **2 tablespoons brown sugar**
- **1½ pounds boneless, skinless chicken breasts**

Put all ingredients except chicken in blender, purée. Cut chicken into cubes, marinate in sauce at least one hour or overnight. Soak bamboo skewers in water for one hour. Thread chicken cubes onto skewers. Grill over coals for 5 to 8 minutes, turning occasionally. Serve with white rice.

For a dipping sauce, make two recipes of the marinade, heat one for sauce.

Castillian Chicken

Yield: 4 servings

1 medium onion, chopped
2 cloves garlic, minced
1 tablespoon butter or
   olive oil
   Minced fresh parsley to
   taste
   Salt and pepper to taste
1 pinch saffron
½ cup dry white wine
½ cup chicken broth
   Salt and pepper to taste
1 whole chicken cut into
   pieces
1 bay leaf
¼ teaspoon thyme

Sauté onion and garlic in butter or oil until wilted. Purée, in blender or food processor, with parsley, salt, pepper, and saffron. Gradually add wine and broth. Season chicken pieces and brown in skillet. Strain liquid from blender into skillet, add remaining ingredients; simmer, covered, for 30 minutes.

Grilled Chicken with Barbecue Sauce

Yield: 6 servings

Sauce:
1 stick butter
1 medium onion, chopped
2 tablespoons brown
   sugar
½ teaspoon dry mustard
1 (28 ounce) bottle of
   ketchup
¼ cup vinegar
½ teaspoon chili powder
Chicken:
6 chicken breasts

Sauce:
Mix all ingredients in large saucepan, bring to boil. Simmer for 30 minutes. This makes 3 cups of sauce.
Chicken:
Grill chicken over hot coals, bone side down for 10 minutes, turn skin side down and cook 3 minutes. Continue cooking and turning for a total of 45 to 50 minutes, or until chicken is done. Serve chicken with sauce spooned over top. Pass additional sauce.

Great with pork

Chili-Rubbed Chicken with Barbecue Mop

Yield: 4 servings

Chili Rub:
- ¾ **cup chili powder (about 3½ ounces)**
- 3 **tablespoons brown sugar**
- 2 **teaspoons cayenne pepper**

Barbecue Mop:
- 1 **cup hickory barbecue sauce**
- ¾ **cup ketchup**
- ⅓ **cup orange juice**
- 1 **teaspoon Tabasco Sauce**
- 3 **cups mesquite wood chips, soaked in cold water (optional)**
- 1 **whole chicken, quartered**
  Salt and pepper to taste

Chili Rub:
Mix ingredients in bowl, set aside.

Barbecue Mop:
Mix first 4 ingredients in bowl. Prepare barbecue grill. When coals are white, drain chips, if using, and scatter over coals. Arrange chicken in single layer on large baking sheet, season with salt and pepper. Sprinkle chili rub generously on both sides of chicken, press to adhere. Place chicken, skin side down, on grill rack away from direct heat. Cover grill and cook chicken until cooked through, turning every 5 minutes, about 35 to 40 minutes (chili rub may look slightly burned). Serve hot or warm, passing barbecue mop separately.

Day Ahead Chicken

3 whole chicken breasts, halved
½ cup honey
½ cup Dijon mustard
1 tablespoon curry powder
2 tablespoons soy sauce

Place chicken in shallow glass baking dish, skin side down. Mix remaining ingredients and spread over chicken. Cover and refrigerate six hours or overnight. Turn chicken skin side up, cover and bake at 350° for 1 hour. Baste well with sauce and continue baking for 15 minutes, uncovered. Spoon sauce over chicken and serve.

Serve as you would a traditional curry, offering condiments such as currants, coconut, chutney, and peanuts.

🌴 Healthy Chicken Stroganoff

2 whole skinless, boneless chicken breasts
¼ teaspoon garlic powder
¼ teaspoon white pepper
½ cup cream of mushroom soup
1 cup plain yogurt
1 (6 ounce) can sliced mushrooms, drained
2 tablespoons sherry
¼ cup Parmesan cheese

Spray 8x11-inch casserole dish with cooking spray. Place chicken breasts in casserole, do not overlap. Sprinkle with garlic and pepper. Combine soup, yogurt, mushrooms, and sherry; pour over chicken. Sprinkle cheese on top. Bake at 350° for 50 minutes. Serve over noodles.

Beneath the Palms

Almond Chicken

Yield: 4 servings

Chicken:
- ¼ **teaspoon salt**
- ⅛ **teaspoon black pepper**
- 1 **teaspoon cornstarch**
- 1 **tablespoon soy sauce**
- 1 **egg white**
- 1 **pound boneless, skinless chicken breasts, cut into 1-inch cubes**
- 1 **cup vegetable oil**
- 5 **slices fresh ginger root**
- 3 **green onions, chopped**
- 1 **medium-size bell pepper, chopped**
- ½ **cup bamboo shoots, diced**

Sauce:
- 1 **tablespoon rice wine vinegar or white vinegar**
- 2 **tablespoons soy sauce**
- 1 **tablespoon rice wine or dry sherry**
- ½ **teaspoon salt**
- 1 **teaspoon sugar**
- ½ **teaspoon cornstarch**
- ⅓ **cup crisp almonds**

Chicken:
Combine first 5 ingredients in medium bowl; add chicken. Let stand 30 minutes. Heat oil in wok over high heat 30 seconds; add chicken, stir-fry 30 seconds or until very lightly browned. Remove chicken from wok with slotted spoon; drain and set aside.

Remove all but 2 tablespoons oil from wok, reheat over medium heat 30 seconds. Stir-fry ginger root 30 seconds; remove and discard. Add green onions, bell pepper, and bamboo shoots; stir-fry 1 to 2 minutes until crisp-tender.

Sauce:
Combine vinegar and next 5 ingredients in small bowl; mix well and add to wok. Bring to boil, add chicken; stir-fry until chicken is coated with sauce. Add almonds; mix well.

Crisp Almonds: Heat 4 cups oil in wok over medium heat. Add 1 cup blanched almond halves, stir 2 to 3 minutes or until golden brown. Remove, drain well on paper towels. Let stand 5 minutes before using.

Chicken Ghivetch

Yield: 4 servings

1 chicken, cut into pieces
1½ (28 ounce) cans stewed
   tomatoes
2 cloves garlic, minced
1½ cups chicken broth
3 tablespoons fresh dill or
   1 tablespoon dried
2 potatoes, peeled and
   diced
1 eggplant, peeled and
   diced
2 onions, quartered
1 bell pepper, sliced
2 stalks celery, cut into
   1-inch diagonal pieces
   Salt and pepper to taste
   Dill weed to taste
½ head cauliflower, cut
   into florets

Place first 5 ingredients in 4-quart baking dish. Bake, covered, for 1 hour at 350°. Add remaining ingredients; cover and bake 30 minutes or until vegetables are tender.

May delete tomatoes and broth and substitute other vegetables.

The first Methodist Church in Brownsville was built in 1856 on the corner of Tenth and Elizabeth streets and served until 1892. The property was sold to the Federal government and a new church was constructed on the opposite corner of Tenth Street.

Gomez's Turkey

Turkey:
- 1 (20 pound) turkey, thawed
- 1 stick butter
- ½ cup pineapple juice
  Salt

Giblets:
- 2 cups white wine
  Turkey giblets
- 2 pounds chicken giblets
- ½ tops of celery bundle, chopped
- 1 bunch green onions, chopped
  Salt and pepper to taste

Stuffing:
- 2 (8 ounce) packages seasoned stuffing
- 2 rolls round buttery crackers, crumbled
- 1 bundle celery, finely chopped
- 2 (6 ounce) packages dried mixed fruit
- 4 ounces dried dates
- 2 bell peppers, finely chopped
- ½ cup mixed nuts (pecans, walnuts), chopped
- 1 (10 ounce) jar pimento stuffed olives
- 1 medium onion, finely chopped
- 2 bunches green onions, finely chopped
- 1 large apple, peeled and chopped

- 4 cloves garlic, minced
  Salt and pepper to taste
- ⅔ cup chopped giblets
- 1 (8 ¼ ounce) can sliced pineapple, chopped
- 3 tablespoons powdered sage
- 1½ cups white wine
- ½ cup pineapple juice
- 1 cup warm giblet broth

Roasting:
- ½ cup wine
- ½ cup pineapple juice

Gravy:
- Remaining giblets
  Remaining broth
- 1 cup wine
- 3 stalks celery, diced
- 1 onion, chopped
- 1½ cups diced fresh mushrooms
  Salt and pepper to taste
  Garlic powder to taste
- 2 (.7 ounce) packages brown mushroom gravy mix

Yield: 10 to 12 servings

Turkey:
The night before serving, remove giblets from cavity, rinse turkey. Melt butter, add pineapple juice, mix well. Brush all of this mixture over turkey and in cavities. Rub salt over turkey, place in refrigerator.

Giblets:
In a large saucepan, add all ingredients. Bring to a boil; cook 30 minutes. Remove giblets from broth; cut into small pieces. Reserve broth. Place chopped giblets and broth in refrigerator.

Stuffing:
The day of serving, combine seasoned stuffing and next 15 ingredients. Mix well. Add wine, juice, and broth; form into a ball. It should not be sticky or mushy. Add additional crackers if needed. Stuff both cavities and close.

Roasting:
Place stuffed turkey in large aluminum cooking pan, pour wine and juice in pan. Cover and seal turkey with foil. Make sure foil is sealed tightly to prevent steam from escaping during cooking. Cook according to package directions. Do not overcook.

Gravy:
While turkey is cooking, blend ingredients together. Cook until the turkey is done, stirring every 30 minutes. The longer you cook gravy the better, just be careful it doesn't burn. Serve the turkey as soon as it is done.

Left over stuffing can be cooked separately or frozen.

Summer Chicken

Yield: 6 servings

½ **cup dry white wine**
1 **cup water**
½ **cup lemon juice, plus 2**
   tablespoons
3 **whole chicken breasts,**
   halved, boned and
   skinned
½ **cup mayonnaise**
4 **teaspoons peeled,**
   seeded, and diced
   cucumber
2 **teaspoons grated lemon**
   zest
¼ **teaspoon salt**
¼ **teaspoon black pepper**
6 **lemon slices**

Bring wine, water and 2 tablespoons lemon juice to boil. Add chicken. Cover and simmer 20 minutes. Set aside and cool. Combine next 5 ingredients and remaining lemon juice. Spread thinly over drained chicken. Place lemon slice on top of each chicken piece. Cover tightly and refrigerate. Serve on lettuce leaves.

Chicken Pot Pie

Yield: 4 to 6 servings

1 **whole chicken, cut into**
   pieces
1 **stick butter**
½ **cup flour**
   Salt and pepper to taste
1 **(4 ounce) can flaky**
   biscuits
1 **(5 ounce) can**
   evaporated milk

In a large saucepan, cover chicken with water and cook 45 minutes. Remove chicken, reserve broth. Skin and bone chicken, placing meat in a greased 9x13-inch baking dish. Mix reserved broth, butter and flour in saucepan, heat. Salt and pepper chicken to taste. Pour broth over chicken. Separate biscuits into 3 parts, place on top of chicken. Pour evaporated milk over biscuits. Bake at 350° until browned.

To create a hearty winter time dish, add sliced carrots, diced potatoes, and other vegetables.

Stuffed Chicken Breasts

Yield: 8 servings

- 8 **chicken breast halves, boned and skinned**
- 4 **slices cooked ham, cut in half**
- 4 **slices Swiss cheese, cut in half**
- 1 **egg, beaten**
- 2 **teaspoons water**
- 1 **cup seasoned bread crumbs**
- 1 **stick butter or margarine**
- 1 **teaspoon Italian seasoning**
- ½ **pound fresh mushrooms, sliced**
- ¼ **cup chopped onion**
- 3 **tablespoons butter or margarine, melted**
- 3 **tablespoons white wine**
- ½ **cup milk**
- 1 **(10 ¾ ounce) can cream of mushroom soup, undiluted**

Place each chicken breast half on a sheet of waxed paper; flatten to ¼-inch thickness using a meat mallet or rolling pin. Place 1 piece of ham and cheese in center of each chicken piece. Roll up lengthwise, and secure with wooden picks. Combine egg and water; dip each chicken breast in egg, and then bread crumbs. Melt butter in large skillet; stir in Italian seasoning. Add chicken, cook over low heat 30 to 40 minutes, browning on all sides. In a medium saucepan, sauté mushrooms and onion in melted butter until tender. Stir in wine, milk, and soup. Serve sauce with chicken.

Easy Crock Pot Chicken

Yield: 4 servings

- 1 **whole chicken, cut up**
  Oil
- 1 **(8 ounce) bottle creamy French dressing**
- 1 **(8 ounce) can jellied cranberry sauce**
- 1 **(1 ounce) package dried onion soup mix**

Brown chicken pieces in oil. Place in crock pot. Mix remaining ingredients, pour over chicken. Cook on low temperature for 8 to 10 hours.

Beneath the Palms

🌴 Grilled Redfish with Mango Salsa

Yield: 4 servings

Salsa:
- ½ teaspoon cumin seeds
- 1 small mango, peeled, pitted, and diced
- ½ cup diced red bell pepper
- ¼ cup minced red onion
- 1 tablespoon fresh lime juice
- ¼ teaspoon hot red pepper sauce

Fish:
- 2 pounds redfish fillets
- Salt and pepper to taste

Salsa:
In a small nonstick skillet, toast cumin seeds over low heat until fragrant. Transfer to a small bowl. Add remaining ingredients. Refrigerate until chilled.

Fish:
Wash fillets and pat dry; sprinkle with salt and pepper. Grill over hot coals; cooking until fish flakes, about 5 minutes per ½-inch thickness. Place on serving platter and spoon salsa over each fillet.

Mango salsa is also great on grilled chicken.

🌴 Broiled Salmon with Dill Sauce

Yield: 4 servings

- 3 tablespoons butter
- 2 teaspoons fresh lemon juice
- Salt and pepper to taste
- 2 fresh salmon fillets
- 2 tablespoons dry white wine
- 4 tablespoons fat free sour cream
- ½ teaspoon dill weed

Melt butter in a small saucepan on low heat, add lemon juice, salt, and pepper to taste. Spray a broiler pan with nonstick cooking spray. Brush salmon fillets on both sides with lemon butter. Place on broiler pan and broil 10 minutes per 1-inch thickness of fillet. While fish is broiling, add wine to remaining lemon butter and whisk until frothy; add sour cream and dill weed. Serve over fillets.

Grilled Sea Bass with Mushroom Stuffing

Yield: 6 servings

1	(3½ pound) whole striped bass or sea bass
8	tablespoons butter or margarine
¾	pound mushrooms, sliced
¼	cup minced green onions
2½	cups soft bread crumbs
¼	cup water
1¼	teaspoons savory leaves
¾	teaspoon salt
⅜	teaspoon black pepper
1	tablespoon lemon juice

Scale and fillet bass to make 2 large fillets, with skin left on. In a 10-inch skillet over medium heat, melt 6 tablespoons of butter; add mushrooms and green onions. Cook until tender, stirring constantly. Remove skillet from heat; stir in bread crumbs, water, 1 teaspoon savory, ½ teaspoon salt, and ¼ teaspoon pepper. On double thick heavy duty foil, place a fillet, skin side down. Spoon mushroom mixture on fillet; top with remaining fillet (skin side up). Sprinkle fish with lemon juice and remaining spices; dot with 2 tablespoons butter. Wrap in foil, being careful seam is folded several times to seal in juices. Place packet on grill, cook 30 minutes, turning once.

In November 1892, the first Post Office and Customs House in Brownsville was built on the corner of Tenth and Elizabeth streets. The structure was demolished in 1931 and replaced by the current Federal Building in 1932.

Beneath the Palms

🌴 Baked Salmon Citron

Yield: 4 servings

- 4 **tablespoons butter**
- 1½ **pounds salmon fillets,
  cut into 4 equal pieces**
  Salt and pepper to taste
- 4 **carrots, julienned**
- 1 **zucchini, julienned**
- 4 **green onions, julienned**
- 2 **tablespoons olive oil**
- 2 **tablespoons lemon juice**
- 8 **teaspoons chopped
  shallots**
- 4 **tablespoons lemon
  flavored vodka**

Tear aluminum foil into 4 equal squares, large enough to wrap fillets. Grease each piece well with butter. Place a fillet on each square, sprinkle lightly with salt and pepper. In a large skillet, sauté vegetables in olive oil. Add lemon juice and shallots, cook until tender. Place equal amounts of vegetable mix on top of each fillet. Sprinkle each with 1 tablespoon of vodka. Fold foil and seal packets as tightly as possible so juices won't escape. Bake at 475° for 10 to 15 minutes.

This may also be cooked on the grill.

🌴 Grilled Shrimp and Scallops

Yield: 6 servings

- ½ **cup Dijon mustard**
- ½ **cup brown sugar**
- ½ **cup bourbon**
- ½ **cup sliced green onions**
- ½ **cup soy sauce**
- 2 **tablespoons
  Worcestershire sauce**
- 1 **pound sea scallops**
- 1½ **pounds large shrimp,
  peeled and deveined**

Mix all ingredients together. Marinate shrimp and scallops for several hours. Skewer and grill.

Bacon may be wrapped around each piece for a different flavor.

Serve with saffron rice and a tossed salad.

Flounder Duxelles

Yield: 4 servings

1 tablespoon oil
1 tablespoon flour
¼ pound mushrooms, sliced
⅓ cup chopped shallots
¾ teaspoon tarragon, crushed
½ cup chopped fresh parsley
½ cup white wine
¼ cup heavy cream
2 flounder fillets
Salt and pepper to taste
Paprika to taste
2 tablespoons butter
3 slices bread made into crumbs
1 cup grated Swiss cheese

Place oil in a 9x13-inch glass baking dish; sprinkle flour evenly over bottom of dish. Mix mushrooms, shallots, tarragon, with ¼ cup of parsley in a small bowl and sprinkle over flour in dish. Mix wine and cream together; drizzle evenly over mushroom mixture. Wipe fish with a damp cloth; sprinkle with salt, pepper and paprika. Arrange evenly over mushroom mixture. Melt butter in a pan and stir in bread crumbs; cook, stirring over medium heat until browned; set aside. Mix remaining parsley with crumbs and sprinkle over fish. Bake at 350° uncovered for 15 to 20 minutes or until fish flakes easily with a fork. Sprinkle cheese over fish and return to oven until cheese melts.

Salmon Steaks with Spinach

Yield: 4 servings

2 **pounds fresh spinach**
4 **(1-inch) salmon steaks**
   Salt and pepper to taste
1 **teaspoon dill weed**
½ **stick butter**
1 **large onion, chopped**
1 **clove garlic, minced**
   Lemon wedges

Wash spinach and shake off water. Cut into 1-inch wide strips and set aside. Turn on broiler and preheat a broiler pan. Wipe fish with a damp cloth. Remove broiler pan, grease lightly; arrange fish in single layer on pan. Broil about 4 inches from flame for 5 minutes. Remove and turn fish; season with salt, pepper, and dill weed. Place a pat of butter on each steak. Broil fish for 5 more minutes or until it flakes readily.

In a large frying pan, melt 3 tablespoons of butter; sauté onion and garlic until limp. Stir in spinach, cover and cook, stirring occasionally over high heat until wilted, about 3 minutes. Spoon spinach onto plate, and place salmon steak on top. Garnish with lemon wedges.

Trout in Lemon Cream Sauce

Yield: 6 servings

6	tablespoons butter, divided
2½	pounds trout fillets
¼	teaspoon garlic powder
¼	pound mushrooms, sliced
1	teaspoon minced onions
2	teaspoons flour
1	cup sour cream
2	tablespoons lemon juice
1	teaspoon soy sauce
¼	teaspoon dry basil
	Salt and pepper to taste
	Chopped parsley

In a small pan, melt 3 tablespoons of butter and spread one half over large baking pan. Arrange fish evenly in single layer and pour remaining melted butter over fillets. Sprinkle with garlic powder. Bake, uncovered, at 450° until fish flakes easily, about 10 minutes. In a small saucepan, melt remaining butter, add mushrooms and onion; cook until limp. Stir in flour and cook until bubbly. Remove from flame and blend in sour cream, and next 5 ingredients. When fish is done, remove from oven. Reduce heat to 350°. Drain pan of all liquid. Pour sour cream mixture over fish and bake 5 to 7 minutes or until sauce is heated through. Sprinkle with parsley.

Baked Trout Parmesan

Yield: 6 servings

10	**trout fillets, boned**
1½	**lemons**
	Worcestershire sauce
	Salt to taste
	Red pepper to taste
	Garlic powder to taste
	Parmesan cheese
	Bread crumbs
	Butter

Line a 9x13x2-inch baking sheet with foil; place trout fillets in a row. Squeeze lemon juice over both sides of fillets. Sprinkle 3 or 4 drops of Worcestershire sauce on each fillet. Roll fillets in this mixture again to coat evenly then lay flat. Lightly sprinkle top of each fillet (in this order) with salt, red pepper, garlic powder, Parmesan cheese, and bread crumbs. Put a pat of butter on each fillet. Cook on middle rack of oven at 350° for 20 minutes. After 20 minutes, baste tops of fillets, being careful not to brush off bread crumbs. Turn oven up to broil and broil fillets until tops are toasty brown (5 to 8 minutes). Watch carefully. Allow to cool for a few minutes before serving.

Telephone service in Brownsville began with a small number of subscribers in 1904. International service was initiated when Francisco Yturria connected his store in Matamoros with his bank in Brownsville.

Laguna Madre
Fish in Curry

Yield: 4 servings

1	**stick butter**
1	**cup chopped onion**
1	**cup chopped bell pepper**
2	**tablespoons curry powder**
½	**teaspoon ground ginger**
2	**tablespoons packed brown sugar**
3	**tablespoons lemon juice**
2	**tablespoons water**
¼	**teaspoon Tabasco Sauce**
2	**pounds fish fillets or steaks**
1	**cup plain yogurt**
6	**lemon slices**
3	**eggs, hard-boiled and chopped**
⅓	**cup raisins**
⅓	**cup cashews**
⅓	**cup chutney**
1	**cucumber, peeled and sliced**

In a large frying pan, melt butter, sauté onion, bell pepper, curry powder, and ginger until onion and pepper are soft. Stir in brown sugar, lemon juice, water, and Tabasco; remove from heat. Preheat broiler and broiler pan. Wipe fish with a damp cloth. Push vegetables aside in large frying pan and dip fish pieces in "curry butter". Remove preheated broiler pan and arrange fish without crowding. Return to broiler and broil until fish flakes easily. Transfer cooked fish to serving platter. Stir yogurt into heated curry butter, do not boil, pour over fish and garnish with lemon slices. Serve eggs, raisins, cashews, chutney, and cucumber as condiments.

Beneath the Palms

Bacalao

Fish:
- 1 (16 ounce) box salted codfish

Sauce:
- ⅓ cup olive oil
- 1 small onion, sliced
- 5 cloves garlic, chopped
- 1 (14 ½ ounce) can whole tomatoes, puréed
- 1 (8 ounce) can tomato sauce

Casserole:
- 1 (14 ½ ounce) can whole new potatoes, sliced very thin
- 1 (16 ounce) can garbanzo beans
  Spanish olives, pitted

Fish:
In a saucepan, place codfish in cold water; bring to a boil. Drain and repeat this step twice more. Flake fish.

Sauce:
In a large skillet, heat olive oil; sauté onion about 3 minutes. Add garlic and simmer 1 to 2 minutes (don't let garlic brown). Add tomatoes and sauce. Simmer for 10 minutes. Cover the bottom of a 9x13-inch glass dish with sauce.

Casserole:
Layer potatoes, garbanzo beans, fish, and sauce (2 layers). Decorate top with olives. Cover loosely and bake at 350° for 30 to 45 minutes or until bubbly.

Flounder au Gratin

Yield: 6 servings

2 **pounds flounder fillets**
½ **cup dry sherry**
2 **tablespoons lemon juice**
   Salt and pepper to taste
2 **tablespoons butter**
2 **tablespoons flour**
½ **teaspoon chicken broth granules**
½ **teaspoon Dijon mustard**
⅓ **cup heavy cream**
¾ **cup shredded Swiss cheese**
2 **(10 ounce) packages chopped frozen spinach, thawed**

Wipe fish with damp cloth. Fold fillets in half and arrange side by side in a large shallow pan. Mix sherry and lemon juice; pour over fish. Sprinkle with salt and pepper. Cover tightly and bake at 400° until fish flakes easily, 1-inch thick fish equals 10 minutes. Remove from oven; drain all liquid into a measuring cup, add enough water to make 1 cup of liquid; set aside. Cover fish. Melt butter in pan, stir in flour, chicken broth granules, and mustard; cook until bubbly. Gradually add poaching liquid and cream. Cook, stirring until thickened. Stir in ½ cup Swiss cheese. Set aside. Squeeze all liquid from spinach. Spread spinach over bottom of 1½-quart casserole; place cooked fish (still folded) over spinach. Spoon cheese sauce evenly over fish. Sprinkle with remaining cheese. Bake at 450° for 7 to 8 minutes.

Shrimp and Asparagus Cakes with Chive Vinaigrette

Yield: 8 servings

Vinaigrette:
- 1 **cup olive oil**
- ⅔ **cup chopped fresh chives**
- ¼ **cup fresh lemon juice**
- 3 **tablespoons finely chopped shallots**

Shrimp Cakes:
- 36 **spears asparagus, trimmed to 6-inch length**
- 4 **tablespoons unsalted butter**
- ⅔ **cup plus 3 tablespoons chopped shallots**
- ½ **pound sea scallops, finely chopped**
- 1½ **pounds uncooked medium shrimp, peeled, deveined, finely chopped**
- 1½ **cups fresh white bread crumbs**
- 1 **cup diced red bell pepper**
- 2 **eggs, beaten well**
- ¼ **cup chopped fresh chives or green onions**
  Salt and pepper to taste

Vinaigrette:

Whisk ingredients together in a bowl to blend. (Can be prepared 4 hours ahead. Let stand at room temperature.)

Shrimp Cakes:

Cook asparagus in large pot of boiling salted water until crisp tender, about 3 minutes. Drain. Refresh under cold water and drain well. Finely dice 4 asparagus spears. Transfer to large bowl. Reserve remaining asparagus for garnish. Melt 2 tablespoons butter in heavy skillet over medium heat. Add ⅔ cup shallots and sauté 2 minutes. Add shallots to chopped asparagus. Mix in scallops and next 5 ingredients. Season generously with salt and pepper. Form shrimp mixture into eight 3½ to 4 inch rounds. Place on baking sheet. (Can be prepared 2 hours ahead. Cover and refrigerate). Melt 2 tablespoons butter in a large nonstick skillet over medium heat. Add shrimp cakes and cook in batches until golden brown and cooked through, about 5 minutes per side. Place 1 shrimp cake in center of each plate. Arrange 4 asparagus spears around each shrimp cake, overlapping at corners to form box. Spoon vinaigrette over each. Serve, pass remaining vinaigrette.

Southern Crab Cakes with Caper Sauce

Yield: 4 servings

Crab Cakes:
- 2 cups crabmeat, flaked
- ¼ teaspoon salt
- Dash black pepper
- 1 egg
- 1 cup flour
- Oil for frying

Caper Sauce:
- 1½ cups chicken broth
- 1 tablespoon butter
- 1 tablespoon flour
- 1 teaspoon white vinegar
- 1 tablespoon capers
- 1 teaspoon caper liquid
- ½ teaspoon salt
- Dash of ground black pepper
- 1 tablespoon sour cream

Crab Cakes:
Mix crabmeat, salt, pepper, and egg; shape into small cakes and dredge lightly with flour. Deep fry in hot oil for 2 to 3 minutes or until golden brown.

Caper Sauce:
Pour broth into a saucepan and let boil until reduced by one half. In a separate pan, melt butter, add flour and mix to a paste. Add chicken broth gradually, stirring until smooth and slightly thickened. Add all remaining ingredients, except sour cream. Remove from heat, add sour cream. Serve crab cakes hot with caper sauce.

Beer Batter

Yield: 1½ cups

- 1 cup unsifted flour
- ½ teaspoon paprika
- ¼ teaspoon salt
- ⅛ teaspoon black pepper
- ¾ cup beer

In a bowl combine flour, paprika, salt, and pepper. Gradually stir in beer, beat until smooth. Dip fish in batter, let excess drip off before deep frying.

Stuffed Gulf Shrimp

Yield: 6 servings

24 jumbo shrimp, peeled,
    deveined and cooked
1   medium onion, minced
1   bell pepper, minced
4   tablespoons butter,
    divided
1   (7.5 ounce) can flaked
    crabmeat
1   teaspoon dry sherry
1   teaspoon dry mustard
1   teaspoon
    Worcestershire sauce
½   teaspoon salt
2   tablespoons
    mayonnaise
1   cup white sauce
    Parmesan cheese
    Paprika to taste

Split shrimp and open flat. Sauté onion and bell pepper in 2 tablespoons of butter until soft. Add next 7 ingredients, mix well. Stuff shrimp with crab mixture. Dot with remaining butter. Sprinkle with Parmesan cheese and paprika. Bake at 350° for 10 minutes.

White sauce is made by melting 2 tablespoons butter in a saucepan, stir in 2 tablespoons flour. Add 1 cup milk and stir until thickened. Salt and pepper to taste.

Barbecued Shrimp

Yield: 6 servings

½   cup olive oil
3   cloves garlic, chopped
½   teaspoon salt
1   teaspoon black pepper
1   teaspoon oregano
¼   cup white wine vinegar
¼   cup ketchup
3   pounds shrimp, peeled
    and deveined

Mix together all ingredients, except shrimp. Marinate shrimp for 1 hour in mixture. Place shrimp on skewers, or in a basket, and grill.

Isabella Fried Shrimp

Yield: 4 servings

2	**eggs**
1	**cup milk**
1	**pound shrimp, uncooked**
1	**cup flour**
1½	**teaspoons garlic salt**
36	**saltine crackers, crushed**
	Oil for frying

Beat eggs, add milk. Clean and butterfly shrimp. Mix flour and garlic salt together. Dip shrimp in seasoned flour, then egg mixture, then crackers. Deep fry in oil until golden brown.

Serve with a spicy cocktail sauce.

Deep Fried Oysters

Yield: 6 servings

2	**dozen oysters, shucked**
	Salt and pepper to taste
1	**egg**
4	**tablespoons water**
2	**tablespoons self-rising flour**
2	**tablespoons cornmeal**
3	**small green onions, chopped**
	Vegetable oil for frying
½	**lemon, juiced**

Season oysters with salt and pepper. Beat egg for 10 seconds. Add water and beat for another 5 seconds. Mix flour and cornmeal gradually into egg mixture. Add one chopped onion and blend well. Dip oysters into batter and deep fry (3 to 4 at a time) in hot oil until golden. Drain on absorbent paper. When oysters have been fried and drained, place on a well-heated dish. Sprinkle with remaining green onions and lemon juice.

The first railroad connecting Brownsville with Point Isabel began operation in 1872. The total distance was twenty-two and one-half miles.

Coquilles St. Jacques

Yield: 4 servings

½ **cup fresh bread crumbs**
5 **tablespoons margarine, divided**
1½ **cups shredded processed Gruyere cheese**
1 **cup mayonnaise**
¼ **cup white wine**
1 **tablespoon chopped parsley**
1 **pound scallops**
½ **pound mushrooms**
½ **cup chopped onion**

Toss bread crumbs in 1 tablespoon melted margarine. Set aside. Mix cheese, mayonnaise, wine, and parsley. Cook scallops in 2 tablespoons margarine until opaque. Remove from skillet, drain well and set aside. Sauté mushrooms and onions in remaining margarine. Return scallops to broiler-proof dish, add sauce and mix well. Sprinkle with bread crumbs. Broil six inches from heat until browned.

Can be made up to 12 hours ahead and refrigerated. Bake at 350° for 20 to 30 minutes, then place under broiler.

Crawfish Jubilee

Yield: 4 servings

½ **cup chopped bell pepper**
4 **cloves garlic, minced**
1 **cup chopped onion**
½ **cup chopped celery**
1 **stick butter**
2 **tablespoons crawfish fat "Paul Prudhommes Seafood Magic"**
1 **pound peeled crawfish tails**
1 **cup chopped green onions**
4 **cups cooked rice**
2 **tablespoons chopped parsley**

Sauté bell pepper, garlic, onion, and celery in an iron skillet with butter. Add crawfish fat and season highly with "Paul Prudhommes Seafood Magic". Cook uncovered for 40 minutes on low heat; stir several times. Add crawfish tails and cook for 10 minutes. Add green onions and rice. Mix well and steam for 5 minutes. Add butter if too dry. Sprinkle with parsley and serve.

Coral and Jade Stir-Fry

Yield: 4 servings

2 tablespoons cornstarch, divided
3 tablespoons soy sauce, divided
½ teaspoon sugar
1 clove garlic, minced
½ pound shrimp, peeled and deveined
1 (16 ounce) can cling peaches in juice
1 teaspoon white vinegar
4 ounces fresh snow peas
2 tablespoons oil, divided
1 medium onion, chopped
1 tablespoon slivered fresh ginger root

Combine 1 teaspoon cornstarch with 1 teaspoon soy sauce. Mix with sugar and garlic; stir in shrimp. Let stand 15 minutes. Meanwhile, drain peaches, reserving ¼ cup juice. Add enough water to juice to measure 1 cup; stir in remaining cornstarch, soy sauce, and vinegar; set aside. Cut peaches crosswise in half. Remove tips and strings from snow peas. Heat 1 tablespoon oil in wok or large skillet over high heat. Add shrimp to snow peas and stir-fry 1 minute, remove from pan. Heat remaining oil in same wok. Add onion, snow peas, and ginger; stir-fry 4 minutes. Stir in shrimp and soy sauce mixture; cook and stir until sauce starts to boil and thicken. Stir in peaches and heat through. Serve immediately.

Serve with cooked white rice.

Tartar Sauce

Yield: 2 cups

1 cup mayonnaise
⅓ cup chopped dill pickles
¼ cup chopped onion
1 teaspoon chopped capers
½ teaspoon mustard
½ teaspoon lime juice

Mix all ingredients and refrigerate at least 1 hour before serving.

Beneath the Palms

Scallops with Linguini

Yield: 2 servings

¾	**pound sea scallops**
2	**tablespoons dry white vermouth**
	Salt and pepper to taste
⅓	**pound linguini**
1	**small onion, chopped**
1	**small hot dried red pepper, minced**
¼	**cup olive oil**
2	**cloves garlic, minced**
¾	**cup sliced fresh mushrooms**
¼	**cup dry bread crumbs**

Place scallops in vermouth; let stand 15 minutes, turning occasionally. Bring a large pot of water to boil. Add salt and pepper to taste, cook pasta until tender but not overcooked. Meanwhile, sauté onion and hot pepper in olive oil briefly. Add garlic, mushrooms, and scallops; cook over medium heat until scallops are firm. Add vermouth and cook another minute or two. To serve, drain pasta thoroughly and return to cooking pot. Over low heat, add scallop mixture and toss. Toss in bread crumbs and serve.

Seafood Scampi

Yield: 4 servings

1	**pound seafood of choice**
1	**small onion, chopped**
½	**teaspoon garlic powder**
1	**tablespoon margarine**
1	**(8 ounce) can low sodium chicken broth**
1	**tablespoon flour**
1	**red bell pepper, chopped**
1	**tablespoon lemon juice**
¼	**teaspoon salt (optional)**
1½	**cups instant rice**
¼	**cup minced fresh parsley**

Using a large skillet, sauté seafood, onion, and garlic powder in margarine in large skillet until seafood turns white. Combine broth and flour in a shaker container. Shake well, until all flour is dissolved. Pour into seafood mixture, stir well. Add pepper, lemon juice, and optional salt. Bring to a boil. Stir in rice and parsley. Cover. Remove from heat and let stand for 5 minutes before serving.

Shrimp Creole
Texas Style

Yield: 6 servings

1 medium onion, chopped
2 cloves garlic, minced
½ pound hot Italian
sausage with casing
removed, sliced
1 medium bell pepper,
chopped
2 ribs celery, chopped
2 tablespoons bacon
drippings
2 (14 ounce) cans stewed
tomatoes
3 tablespoons picante
sauce
3 tablespoons tomato
paste
3 tablespoons bold flavor
steak sauce
1 pound shrimp, cleaned

Sauté onion, garlic, sausage, bell pepper, and celery in bacon drippings for about 10 minutes. Add tomatoes, picante sauce, tomato paste, and steak sauce; simmer for 10 minutes. Add shrimp and cook for 15 minutes. Serve over cooked white rice.

Seafood Gumbo

Yield: 8 servings

Shrimp:
- 7 quarts water
- 5 dried hot red chilies
- 6 lemon slices
- 2 large bay leaves
- 1 teaspoon dried thyme, crumbled
- 1 tablespoon salt
- 1 pound medium shrimp, shelled, deveined, uncooked

Roux:
- 4 tablespoons flour
- 4 tablespoons bacon drippings

Gumbo:
- ½ cup chopped onion
- 1 pound small okra pods
- ½ cup celery leaves
- 2 cloves garlic, minced
- 1 large bell pepper, chopped
- 1 (28 ounce) can tomatoes
- 1 bay leaf
- ½ teaspoon dried thyme, crumbled
- 1 tablespoon honey
- Salt and pepper to taste
- Cayenne pepper to taste
- 2 pounds andouille sausage
- 1 pound crabmeat
- ½ pint oysters
- 2 tablespoons gumbo filé powder
- ½ cup chopped parsley
- 1 bunch green onion tops, chopped
- Cooked white rice
- Lemon slices

Shrimp:
In a 10 or 12 quart pot, bring water, chilies, lemon slices, 2 of the bay leaves, 1 teaspoon thyme, to a boil. Add shrimp; cook uncovered for 3 to 5 minutes. Remove shrimp and boil stock down to 4 quarts; set aside.

Roux:
Make a roux by slowly adding flour to bacon drippings, stirring to a smooth paste. Place skillet over lowest possible heat and simmer roux for 45 minutes to an hour. Stir often until roux is very dark brown but not burned.

Gumbo:
In a heavy 10-quart pan, warm the roux over low heat; add onion, okra, celery, garlic, and bell pepper. Stir for 5 minutes until vegetables are soft. Pour in warm shrimp stock and next 6 ingredients. Simmer for 1½ hours. Brown sausage and drain well; cut into bite size pieces. At end of 1½ hours, add sausage, crabmeat and oysters, simmer for 5 minutes. Add shrimp just to heat. Turn off heat and add gumbo filé powder, parsley, and green onions; mix well. Serve over white rice with a slice of lemon on top.

Game/Fowl

Apricot Glazed Cornish Hens

Yield: 2 servings

Hens:
- ¾ **cup apricot preserves**
- 2 **tablespoons orange juice**
- **Zest from ½ orange cut into strips**
- 2 **rock Cornish game hens, thawed**
- **Salt**
- **Paprika**

Rice:
- ¼ **cup sliced green onions and tops**
- 2 **tablespoons butter or margarine**
- ½ **cup raw wild rice**
- ½ **cup raw white rice**
- **Chicken broth**
- 1 **tablespoon minced parsley**
- ½ **cup cashews**
- 4 **tablespoons butter or margarine**

Mix preserves, orange juice, and zest in small bowl. Remove giblets from hens. Place hens on rack, in roasting pan; sprinkle lightly with salt and paprika. Roast hens at 350° for 1 hour and 15 minutes to 1 hour and 30 minutes, or until thickest parts are fork tender and drumstick meat feels soft when pressed. Baste frequently with apricot mixture during last 30 minutes of cooking time. In a medium saucepan, sauté green onions in 2 tablespoons butter until tender, about 2 minutes. Stir in rice; cook according to package directions, substituting chicken broth for water and omitting salt. Stir parsley into rice. In a medium skillet, sauté cashews in remaining butter until golden, about 2 minutes; stir into rice. Spoon rice onto serving platter; arrange hens on rice.

Good with steamed asparagus.

Roast Wild Turkey

Yield: 6 servings

- 1 **wild turkey, cleaned and plucked**
- 2 **sticks butter**
- **Salt**
- **Freshly ground black pepper**
- 1 **cup white wine**

Rub turkey inside and out with 1 stick butter, salt, and pepper. Melt second stick, add wine; set aside. Roast turkey, uncovered, at 375° for 12 minutes per pound. Baste frequently with butter and wine mixture.

Roast Stuffed Cornish Hens

Yield: 6 servings

Stuffing:
- ⅓ cup uncooked long grain and wild rice
- 1 medium onion, chopped
- 2 tablespoons margarine
- 1 teaspoon sage, thyme, savory or tarragon

Hens:
- 6 Cornish hens (about 14 ounces each)
- 1 stick margarine, melted
- ½ cup water
- ¼ cup brandy
- 1 cup orange sections

Stuffing:
Cook rice until slightly firm; set aside. In large skillet, sauté onion in 2 tablespoons margarine over medium-high heat until browned. Add rice and selected herb; toss gently. Remove from heat, set aside.

Hens:
Clean, rinse, and dry hens; stuff lightly with rice mixture. Skewer or sew cavities closed. Brush hens with melted margarine, place breast side up in shallow pan. Roast, uncovered, at 350° for about 1 hour, basting occasionally with melted margarine. Remove hens from pan. Remove rice stuffing and place in serving bowl. Cut hens in half and place on warm serving platter. Place roasting pan, with juices, on top of stove over medium-high heat. Add water to drippings, stirring to dislodge browned particles from pan; add brandy and orange sections. Cook 2 minutes, stirring constantly. Spoon over hens.

Dove Breast "Moquetito"

Yield: 4 servings

10-15 White Wing or Morning
dove breasts
8 ounces Monterey Jack
cheese
1 (8 ounce) can sliced
jalapeños
15 slices bacon
Honey

Place a sliver of cheese and a jalapeño slice in the center of each dove breast. Wrap each with a slice of bacon; secure with a toothpick. Cook dove breast over a medium grill for 10 minutes. Coat breast with honey and cook 2 additional minutes.

Roast Capon

Yield: 4 servings

¼ cup kosher salt
¾ teaspoon thyme leaves
½ teaspoon rubbed sage
⅛ teaspoon cracked
pepper
1 (6-7 pound) capon
Salad oil
Parsley or watercress

One day ahead: In small bowl, mix salt and next 3 ingredients well. Remove giblets and neck from inside capon. Rinse capon with cold water; drain well. Rub salt mixture over outside and inside; place in large bowl. Cover with plastic wrap and refrigerate at least 12 hours. Next day: Place capon in open roasting pan. Brush skin with salad oil. Roast at 325° for 2 hours and 30 minutes. When bird turns golden, cover with a tent of foil. Remove foil the last minutes of roasting time and baste with pan drippings.

Roast Duckling Gourmet with Cointreau Sauce

Yield: 4 to 6 servings

1	**(5 pound) duckling**
	Lemon juice
	Celery leaves
1	**medium onion, sliced**
1½	**cups dry white wine**
1	**tablespoon honey (optional)**
2	**tablespoons butter**
	Orange zest
½	**cup sliced mushrooms**
1	**clove garlic, crushed**
3	**tablespoons flour**
¼	**cup dry sherry**
¼	**cup cognac**
½	**cup orange juice**
½	**cup Cointreau (or orange flavored liqueur)**
1	**tablespoon currant jelly**
	Salt and pepper to taste
	Sautéed mushroom caps
	Orange slices

Trim wings and cut off neck of duckling. Wash thoroughly inside and out with cold water; dry carefully. Rub cavity with lemon juice; put celery leaves and onion inside. Place duckling, breast side up, on a rack in a shallow pan. Cook at 325° for 30 minutes. Drain fat from pan and add wine. Baste duckling and continue cooking for 1 hour and 30 minutes; baste with pan juices every 20 minutes. If a very crisp skin is desired, brush duckling with honey about 15 minutes before taking it from the oven. Do not baste again. Remove duckling from pan and keep warm. Skim off all fat in roasting pan and add butter, orange zest, mushrooms, and garlic to remaining juices. Bring mixture to a boil and simmer about 2 minutes. Remove pan from heat and blend in flour, sherry, cognac, orange juice, and liqueur. Return pan to stove, and stir until mixture is smooth and thick. Add currant jelly. Discard garlic and season sauce to taste with salt and pepper. Cut duckling into quarters and add to sauce. Heat until pieces are warmed through. Arrange on a platter and cover with sauce. Garnish with sautéed mushroom caps and orange slices.

Beneath the Palms

Tipsy Wild Duck

Yield: 4 to 6 servings

- 1 wild duck, cleaned and dressed
- 1 teaspoon salt
- ½ teaspoon pepper
- ½ cup brandy
- ⅔ cup claret wine
- ¾ cup sliced onion
- 1 teaspoon chopped parsley
- ½ teaspoon thyme
- 1 bay leaf
- ¼ teaspoon allspice
- ¼ pound salt pork, diced
- 1 tablespoon vegetable oil
- 2 cups sliced mushrooms
- 1 clove garlic, minced

Cut duck into serving pieces; wipe with damp cloth, dust with salt and pepper. Place in large bowl with brandy, wine, and next 4 ingredients. Let stand overnight. Remove duck and strain marinade through fine sieve. Cook salt pork in skillet until crisp. Add oil to skillet and brown duck, turning on all sides. Add marinade, mushrooms, and garlic. Cover and cook until tender.

Venison Stew

Yield: 8 servings

- 2 pounds venison cut into 1-inch cubes
- 2 tablespoons bacon fat
- 3 cups water
- 1 teaspoon Worcestershire sauce
- 1 teaspoon garlic powder
- ½ cup chopped onion
- 2 teaspoons salt
- ¼ teaspoon black pepper
- 4 potatoes cut into 1-inch cubes
- 6 carrots, sliced
- 2 cups diced celery
- 5 onions, halved
- 2 tablespoons flour
- ¼ cup cold water

In Dutch oven, brown venison in bacon fat; add 3 cups water, Worcestershire sauce, garlic powder, chopped onion, salt, and pepper. Cover and simmer 2 hours. Add more water if needed. After 2 hours, add potatoes and next 3 ingredients. Cook 15 minutes, adding flour and water to thicken mixture.

Herb Marinated Venison Steaks

Yield: 6 servings

Marinade:
- 2 tablespoons white wine
- 5 tablespoons olive oil
- 1 teaspoon thyme
- 1 teaspoon tarragon
- 1 teaspoon chopped parsley

Venison:
- 6 steaks from leg or loin (deer, antelope)
- Salt and pepper to taste

Marinade:
Mix all ingredients together.

Steaks:
Place steaks in shallow dish; add marinade. Let stand for at least 2 hours, turning once. Remove steaks from marinade and season with salt and pepper. Fry on hot grill.

Hunter's Delight Venison Filets

Yield: 6 servings

- 3 pounds venison
- ¼ teaspoon garlic salt
- Bacon slices
- 2 (10 ounce) cans diced tomatoes with chilies
- 1 (8 ounce) can tomato sauce
- ⅓ cup brown sugar
- ½ cup Worcestershire sauce
- ½ teaspoon honey
- Dash black pepper

Have "hunter" deliver venison cleaned and ready. Trim any excess fat and bone from meat; cut into 3-inch strips. Sprinkle with garlic salt; tenderize with a mallet (meat should resemble cube steak). After preparing strips, roll with bacon slices in jelly-roll fashion and secure with a toothpick. Arrange on dish and pour a little tomato sauce on each; marinate while preparing barbecue sauce. The longer it marinates the better. Stir ingredients together and simmer over low heat for about 1 hour. Grill the rolled meat; basting frequently with the sauce.

Venison Guisado

Yield: 4 servings

2 pounds venison, antelope or beef, cut into 1-inch cubes
½ cup flour
⅛ cup vegetable oil
2 medium onions, sliced thin
1 tablespoon minced garlic
2 tablespoons Worcestershire sauce
2 cups meat based broth
1 tablespoon ground comino (cumin)
2 tablespoons chili powder
1 teaspoon cayenne pepper
1 teaspoon ground oregano
2 teaspoons black pepper
1 (16 ounce) can Mexican style diced tomatoes or 2 fresh

Dredge meat in flour to lightly coat. Discard remaining flour. Braise meat in oil, stirring frequently to prevent sticking (do not add salt to flour, it toughens the meat). Sauté onions and garlic with meat until translucent. Add Worcestershire and reduce until meat is evenly coated. Add 1 cup broth and remaining spices; return to simmering state. Remaining broth will be incorporated during the cooking time. Cook 1 hour and 20 minutes to 2 hours, depending on the type of meat. Adjust accordingly. When meat is tender, add tomatoes and simmer another 15 minutes to blend flavors. Gravy should be dark brown and slightly thickened.

Serve with chopped fresh cilantro, chopped onions, serranos, and corn tortillas.

Venison Medallions with Madeira Sauce

Yield: 4 servings

2 tablespoons olive oil
1 tablespoon butter
8 (3 ounce) medallions of deer, lamb, or veal
Salt and pepper to taste
Pinch of thyme
Flour
4 tablespoons dry white wine
4 tablespoons Madeira wine
½ cup beef or game broth
1 tablespoon cornstarch
1 tablespoon water

Heat oil and butter in large frying pan over medium high heat. Season meat with salt, pepper, and thyme. Dip into flour, shake off excess. Pan fry medallions, remove to plate to hold juices and keep warm. Add wine and Madeira to pan and boil down by half. Add broth and meat juices from platter; reduce again until desired consistency. Place 2 medallions on each warmed plate and pour sauce on top.

If beef broth is used, gradually whisk in cornstarch mixed with water.

Compliment with spinach and pasta or mashed potatoes.

Venison Shish Kabobs

Yield: 6 to 8 servings

2 pounds venison roast (up to 3 pounds), cut into 1-inch cubes
Italian salad dressing
3 dozen shrimp, peeled
2 large bell peppers, cut in large squares
1 large onion, cut in large squares
Melted butter

Marinate venison overnight in dressing. Remove vein and tail from shrimp. Thread venison, pepper, shrimp, and onion alternately on skewers. Brush shrimp with melted butter before and during cooking over the grill at medium to low heat. Turn skewers to avoid burning. Cook for 6 to 8 minutes or until desired doneness is reached.

Beneath the Palms

Texas Venison in Wine Sauce

Yield: 6 servings

1½ **pounds venison, thinly sliced**
¾ **cup flour**
½ **teaspoon salt**
  Black pepper to taste
½ **stick butter**
¼ **cup oil**
½ **cup chicken broth**
1 **cup dry white wine**
  Salt and pepper to taste
1 **lemon, thinly sliced**

Dredge venison slices in flour seasoned with salt and pepper. Mix butter and oil in a skillet over medium heat. Sauté venison quickly. Remove venison and keep warm. Add broth to skillet, stirring to remove browned bits. Add wine and salt and cook one minute. Return venison to skillet and cook 2 to 3 minutes until bubbly. Sprinkle with pepper. Arrange slices on a serving platter, pour wine sauce over and top with lemon slices.

Vension Tampico

Yield: 4 servings

1 **pound venison loin**
½ **cup pickled jalapeños**
½ **cup jalapeño juice**
¼ **cup flour**
  Salt and pepper to taste
⅓ **cup vegetable oil**

Cut venison into ½-inch thick medallions, remove any excess fat or membrane. Pound medallions to tenderize. Dice jalapeños, including garlic, onion, and carrots. Place meat in glass pan; cover with jalapeños and juice. Marinate at least 2 hours, stirring occasionally. Dredge medallions in flour mixed with salt and pepper. Heat oil in heavy skillet; pan fry venison until done, remove from skillet. Make gravy with 2 tablespoons skillet drippings, remaining seasoned flour, and 1 teaspoon chopped jalapeños.

Game Soufflé

Yield: *4 servings*

2 **cups milk**
½ **small onion, peeled**
1 **bay leaf**
2 **cloves garlic, minced**
10 **ounces game or game fowl roast**
1 **tablespoon butter**
2 **tablespoons bread crumbs**
2 **tablespoons butter, softened**
3 **tablespoons flour**
5 **egg yolks**
 Salt and pepper to taste
 Pinch paprika
1 **teaspoon dry mustard**
3½ **ounces grated Swiss cheese**
5 **egg whites**
½ **cup milk to thin sauce, use more or less, as needed**

In saucepan, place 2 cups milk, onion, bay leaf, and cloves. Bring to a boil and set aside. Grind meat using coarsest blade of grinder and set aside. Brush soufflé dish with 1 tablespoon butter and cover with bread crumbs. With slotted spoon, remove seasonings from milk and discard. Mix softened butter with flour. Set pan with milk over medium high heat, stir in butter mixture and boil for 1 minute, stirring constantly. Pour half the sauce over meat; set other half aside. Stir egg yolks, salt, pepper, paprika, mustard, and cheese into meat mixture. Beat egg whites until stiff peaks form; fold into meat mixture. Spoon into prepared soufflé dish, filling ¾ full. Place dish on baking sheet and bake at 375° for about 50 minutes. Meanwhile, place remaining sauce back on stove, add milk and simmer 30 minutes. Sauce should keep creamy consistency. Serve soufflé immediately, pouring sauce on top.

Good with steamed broccoli or carrots and cranberry sauce.

Lasagna with Game Meat

Yield: 6 servings

1½ **pounds ground game meat**
1 **(.7 ounce) package spaghetti sauce mix**
1 **(6 ounce) can tomato paste**
1¼ **cups water**
1 **(6 ounce) can mushrooms or 8 ounces fresh**
Pinch of basil
Pinch of oregano
1 **(16 ounce) package lasagna noodles**
1 **teaspoon olive oil**
Dash of basil
Dash oregano
½ **pound ricotta cheese**
1 **egg**
1 **pound grated mozzarella cheese**
¼ **pound grated provolone cheese**
Parmesan cheese
Romano cheese

Brown meat, add mix, tomato paste, water, and mushrooms. Sprinkle basil and oregano in sauce; simmer for about 20 minutes. Bring water to boil for noodles; add oil, basil, and oregano. When boiling, carefully add noodles; boil for about 15 minutes or until soft. Drain noodles and cool on counter or wax paper. Mix ricotta with egg, set aside. In a 13x9x2-inch pan, layer meat sauce, noodles, ricotta mixture, meat sauce, mozzarella, noodles, meat sauce, mozzarella, and provolone. Sprinkle Parmesan and Romano cheeses on top. Bake uncovered at 350° for 40 minutes.

Goulash

Yield: 6 servings

1   **pound elk, venison, or moose (from shoulder)**
3   **tablespoons oil**
    Salt and pepper to taste
1   **small onion, chopped**
1   **clove garlic, crushed**
1   **teaspoon paprika**
1½ **tablespoons tomato paste**
4   **tablespoons flour**
6   **cups beef broth**
½   **teaspoon marjoram**
1   **bay leaf**
2   **medium potatoes, peeled and cubed**

Trim and cube meat, heat in saucepan with oil over medium heat; season with salt and pepper. Set aside. Sauté onion and garlic until onion starts to brown. In a large saucepan or Dutch oven, mix paprika and tomato paste; add meat and fry for 2 to 3 minutes. Add flour and stir thoroughly. Turn heat to medium high, stir in 2 cups beef broth; bring to a boil. Add remaining broth, marjoram, and bay leaf; stir. Simmer, partially covered for 1 hour 15 minutes or until meat starts to become tender.

Cube potatoes same size as meat. Add to pot; simmer until meat and potatoes are tender. Goulash should have a creamy consistency; otherwise, boil down or add water if necessary. Adjust seasoning with salt and pepper.

Add crusty rolls for a complete meal.

Authentic Texas Border Chili

Yield: 8 servings

2 **pounds ground venison, hog, or chuck roast**
1½ **cups undrained stewed tomatoes**
1 **pound chorizo (Mexican sausage)**
1½ **cups chopped green onions**
1 **tablespoon finely chopped serrano peppers**
4½ **cups water**
8 **tablespoons chili powder**
2 **tablespoons cumin**
Kidney beans (optional)
Pinto beans (optional)

Brown meat in large saucepan or chili pot; add tomatoes. In separate skillet, cook chorizo, onions, and serranos. Drain fat; add chorizo to meat and tomatoes. Add water and chili powder; simmer for 2 hours. Add cumin; simmer 2 additional hours. If beans are desired, add with cumin.

Serve with jalapeño cornbread.

Game Sausage

Yield: 8 pounds

1 **quart water**
5 **pounds venison, cut into 1-inch cubes**
3 **pounds wild hog, cut into 1-inch cubes**
5 **tablespoons salt**
3 **tablespoons black pepper**
2 **large cloves garlic, minced**
1 **tablespoon red pepper**
1 **tablespoon sage**

Chill meat. Mix dry ingredients with water and mix thoroughly with meat. Grind through ³⁄₁₆-inch or ¼-inch grinder plate. Stuff casings.

Wild Duck, Sausage and Oyster Gumbo

Yield: 6 servings

2 large wild ducks (or 1 small goose)
2 stalks celery with leaves, chopped
1 medium onion, sliced
1 tablespoon seafood seasoning
Chicken broth
1 pound hot smoked sausage, chopped
½ cup vegetable oil
½ cup all-purpose flour
¾ cup finely chopped celery
1 bell pepper, chopped
Salt and pepper to taste
1 tablespoon Worcestershire sauce
2 drops Tabasco Sauce
1 tablespoon honey
6 green onions, finely chopped
2 tablespoons finely chopped parsley
1 pint oysters, undrained
Cooked white rice
Gumbo filé powder

Combine ducks (or goose), celery, onions, and seafood seasoning in large heavy pot; cover and simmer 1 hour or until meat is tender. Remove ducks from broth, cut off meat; return bones and skin to pot and simmer another hour. Cut meat into bite-size pieces, set aside. Strain stock; add enough chicken broth to make 2½ quarts liquid (can be refrigerated at this point and cooked following day). Cook smoked sausage over medium heat about 5 minutes, stirring occasionally. Drain on paper towels, set aside. Heat oil in 5-quart pot, stir in flour. Cook over medium heat until a dark roux is formed, stirring constantly. Be very careful not to burn the roux. Add chopped celery, bell pepper, cook until vegetables are wilted, about 1 minute. Remove from heat, gradually add hot broth. Bring to boil, reduce heat and simmer 20 minutes. Add meat, sausage, salt and pepper, and next 3 ingredients. Simmer 20 minutes. Stir in green onions and parsley; simmer 20 minutes. Add undrained oysters and simmer 10 minutes. Remove from heat and serve over hot rice with lemon slice on top. Allow diners to thicken each bowl to their taste with filé powder.

Traditional Texas Mincemeat Pie

Yield: 6 to 8 servings

- 4 **pounds lean beef or venison**
- 2 **pounds beef suet Baldwin apples**
- 3 **quinces, finely chopped**
- 3 **pounds sugar**
- 2 **cups molasses**
- 2 **quarts apple cider**
- 4 **pounds raisins**
- 3 **pounds currants**
- 1 **pound citron, finely cut**
- 1 **quart cooking brandy**
- 1 **tablespoon cinnamon**
- 1 **tablespoon mace**
- 1 **tablespoon powdered cloves**
- 2 **whole nutmegs, grated Salt**

Cover meat and suet with boiling water, cook until tender. Cool in cooking water. The suet will rise to the top forming a cake of fat which must be removed. Finely chop meat; add to twice the amount of finely chopped apples (the apples should be quartered, cored, and pared, previous to chopping, or skins may be left on, which is not an objection if the apples are finely chopped). Add quinces, and next 6 ingredients, mix well. Add reserved suet and 1½ cups reduced meat stock. Heat mixture gradually, stirring occasionally. Cook two hours; add brandy and spices; blend well. Mixture may be placed in an unbaked pie shell and topped with a second crust. Bake at 350° for 45 minutes. Serve warm topped with vanilla ice cream or a slice of cheddar cheese.

Vegetables

Asparagus with Sun-Dried Tomato Vinaigrette

Yield: 4 servings

1	**pound fresh asparagus**
1	**clove garlic**
1	**shallot, peeled**
¼	**cup sun-dried tomatoes packed in oil**
3	**tablespoons balsamic vinegar**
2	**teaspoons lemon juice**
¼	**teaspoon freshly ground black pepper**
1	**tablespoon chopped fresh basil**
⅓	**cup olive oil**

Blanch asparagus, chill. Fit a food processor with the metal blade. With processor running, drop garlic and shallot through feed tube to mince. With machine off, add tomatoes and pulse to chop. Add vinegar, lemon juice, pepper, and basil; process until combined. With motor running, slowly add olive oil in thin, steady stream until mixture is emulsified and thickened. Arrange asparagus on a serving platter, spoon vinaigrette over asparagus.

Classic Baked Beans

Yield: 6 servings

2	**tablespoons butter**
1	**onion, chopped**
1	**(15 ounce) can green lima beans**
1	**(15 ounce) can kidney beans**
1	**(15 ounce) can pork and beans**
½	**cup brown sugar**
¼	**cup vinegar**
¼	**cup ketchup**
	Dash garlic salt

In a small skillet, melt butter and sauté onion. Mix together with all remaining ingredients. Bake uncovered at 325° for one hour.

Asparagus Mousse

Yield: 2 servings

8	ounces fresh asparagus
⅔	cup light cream
1	tablespoon minced green onion and tops
2	tablespoons butter or margarine
⅔	cup fresh bread crumbs
2	eggs
½	teaspoon lemon juice
⅛	teaspoon ground nutmeg
¼	teaspoon salt
2	dashes of white pepper

Cut tips from asparagus; reserve. Cut stems into ½-inch pieces. Cook stems in boiling salted water (½ teaspoon salt to 1 cup water) until very tender, about 10 minutes; drain. Process stems and cream in blender or food processor until smooth; transfer mixture to bowl. In a small skillet, sauté green onion in butter until tender, about 2 minutes. Stir onion, bread crumbs, eggs, lemon juice, nutmeg, salt, and pepper into cream mixture; blend thoroughly. Pour mixture into two greased 8-ounce timbale molds or custard cups; place in a 13x9x2-inch baking pan. Fill baking pan with hot water to come halfway up sides of molds. Bake at 350° until knife inserted halfway between center and edge of mixture comes out clean, about 20 minutes. Remove molds from baking pan; let stand 5 minutes. Loosen edges of molds with a sharp knife; invert onto serving platter. Cook reserved asparagus tips in boiling salted water until crisp-tender, 4 to 5 minutes. Drain. Lay asparagus tips around molds.

Beneath the Palms

Artichoke Fritatta

Yield: 6 to 8 servings

- 2 (6 ounce) cans marinated artichoke hearts, chopped
- 1 small onion, chopped
- 1 clove garlic, minced
- 4 eggs
- ¼ cup dry bread crumbs
- ¼ teaspoon black pepper
- ¼ teaspoon salt
- ¼ teaspoon oregano
- ¼ teaspoon Tabasco Sauce
- 2 tablespoons chopped parsley

Drain marinade from one jar of artichoke hearts into a sauté pan. Sauté onion and garlic in marinade. In a small bowl, beat eggs. Add remaining ingredients and pour into a greased 7x11-inch baking pan. Bake at 325° for 30 minutes. Cut into small squares and serve.

Broccoli with Sesame Seeds

Yield: 6 servings

- 1 pound fresh broccoli
- 1 clove garlic, minced
- 3 tablespoons vegetable oil
- 3 tablespoons white wine
- 1 (8 ounce) can water chestnuts
- 3 tablespoons soy sauce
- ½ teaspoon salt
- 2 tablespoons sesame seeds, toasted

Cut broccoli into florets and thinly slice stems. Stir-fry broccoli and garlic over high heat in oil for five minutes. Lower heat to medium. Add wine, water chestnuts, soy sauce, and salt. Cover; cook for 5 minutes. Sprinkle sesame seeds over broccoli and serve.

Red Cabbage

1 **pound purple cabbage**
2 **slices bacon, cut into strips**
½ **onion, sliced**
½ **tablespoon oil**
2 **tablespoons red wine vinegar**
½ **cup chicken broth**
 Salt and pepper to taste
4 **tablespoons cranberry jelly**

Shred cabbage. In a saucepan, fry bacon and onion in oil until onion is soft. Add cabbage and vinegar. Pour in broth, salt, and pepper to taste. Cover and simmer 1 hour. Make sure there is always some liquid in bottom. Stir in jelly before serving. May peel, core, and cook a large apple with the cabbage instead of jelly. If desired, to bind liquid to cabbage, mix 1 tablespoon cornstarch with tablespoon red wine and stir into cabbage before serving.

Excellent with goose and duck.

Sabal Sauerkraut

1½ **pounds fresh sauerkraut or a 1 pound 13 ounce can**
4 **juniper berries, crushed**
2 **tablespoons lard or bacon fat**
1 **small onion, minced**
1 **tablespoon flour**
1 **teaspoon salt**
1 **teaspoon black pepper**
 Dash of nutmeg
 Pinch of sugar

Put sauerkraut in a large pot, add water to cover. Add juniper berries and simmer, covered, for 20 minutes or until liquid is absorbed. Heat fat in a small skillet; sauté onion until dark, golden brown. Stir in flour and brown until cocoa color. Turn into sauerkraut and stir until well mixed. Add salt, pepper, nutmeg, and sugar if necessary. Simmer another 20 minutes.

Jalapeño Cabbage

Yield: 6 to 8 servings

- 1 tablespoon butter or margarine
- 1 cup chopped bell pepper
- ½ cup chopped celery
- 1 cup diced ripe or green tomatoes
- ¼ cup chopped onions
- 1 jalapeño, chopped
- ¾ teaspoon salt
- 2 cups shredded cabbage
- ½ teaspoon sugar

Melt butter or margarine in a heavy skillet, sauté bell pepper and next 5 ingredients; add cabbage, and sugar. Cover; cook over medium heat 10 to 12 minutes.

Sweet and Sour Carrots

Yield: 6 servings

- 2 slices bacon
- 1 medium bell pepper, cubed
- 1 clove garlic, minced
- 1 (10 ¾ ounce) can tomato soup
- 2 tablespoons water
- 4 teaspoons vinegar
- 1 teaspoon sugar
- 3 cups carrots, sliced diagonally, cooked
- ¼ cup chopped parsley

In a skillet, cook bacon until crisp; remove and crumble reserving drippings. Cook green pepper with garlic in drippings until tender. Stir in bacon and remaining ingredients. Heat thoroughly.

Bitter Sweet Carrots

Yield: 6 servings

- 6 large carrots, sliced
- ½ medium onion, chopped fine
- 1 tablespoon butter or margarine
- 2 large lemons

Boil carrots until slightly tender. Sauté onions in butter or margarine. Add carrots to onions. Squeeze lemon juice over carrots and onions. Toss and serve.

🌴*Honey-Ginger Carrots*

Yield: 4 servings

6 **medium carrots**
½ **cup water**
¼ **stick margarine or butter**
3 **tablespoons honey**
1 **tablespoon lemon juice**
½ **teaspoon ground ginger**
¼ **teaspoon salt**
 Parsley

Stove top:
Cut carrots lengthwise into 3x½-inch strips. Heat carrots and water to boiling in 10-inch skillet; reduce heat. Cover; simmer until tender, 15 to 20 minutes. Drain carrots and set aside. Cook margarine, honey, lemon juice, ginger and salt until bubbly; add carrots. Cook uncovered, stirring occasionally, until carrots are glazed, about 5 minutes. Parsley for garnish.

Microwave:
Place ¼ cup water and carrots in 1-quart microwave casserole. Cover tightly and microwave on high 4 minutes; stir. Cover and microwave until tender, 4 to 7 minutes longer; drain. Place margarine, honey, lemon juice, ginger, and salt in a bowl. Microwave uncovered on high 1 minute, stir. Microwave until sauce is hot, 30 to 45 seconds longer if needed. Pour over carrots, stir. Microwave on high, stirring every minute until carrots are glazed. Parsley for garnish.

The Masonic Temple, formerly the Cameron County Courthouse located in downtown Brownsville, was constructed in 1886. It is still in use today by the Masons.

Beneath the Palms

🌴 Marinated Carrots

Yield: 8 side dish servings

- 5 **cups sliced carrots**
- 1 **medium sweet onion**
- 1 **small bell pepper**
- 1 **(10 ¾ ounce) can condensed tomato soup**
- ½ **cup salad oil**
- 1 **cup sugar**
- ¾ **cup vinegar**
- 1 **teaspoon prepared mustard**
- 1 **teaspoon Worcestershire sauce**
- 1 **teaspoon salt**
- 1 **teaspoon black pepper**

In a large saucepan, cover carrots with water, cook until tender. Drain and cool. Cut onion and bell pepper in thin round slices and mix with cooled carrots. Combine remaining ingredients and pour over vegetables. Cover; marinate 12 hours or more. Serve as a side dish, appetizers, or salad.

Will keep up to two weeks in refrigerator.

🌴 Carrot Bake

Yield: 6 servings

- 6 **medium carrots**
- 1 **medium cauliflower, separated**
- ¼ **stick butter or margarine**
- 1 **teaspoon salt**
- ¼ **teaspoon ground nutmeg**
  Parmesan cheese (optional)
  Parsley

Cut carrots into 2-inch strips; arrange in an ungreased rectangular baking dish. Layer cauliflower over carrots, dot with margarine. Sprinkle with salt and nutmeg. Cover and bake at 375° for 50 to 55 minutes, or until tender. Sprinkle with cheese; garnish with parsley.

Baked Corn

Yield: 4 to 6 servings

1 (15 ounce) can creamed corn
1 (11 ounce) can whole kernel corn, drained
1 teaspoon salt
½ cup sugar
2 tablespoons flour
2 eggs, beaten
½ cup milk
2 teaspoons baking powder

In a 2-quart casserole dish, mix all ingredients. Bake at 350° for 1 hour.

Celery with Nuts

Yield: 6 servings

4 cups sliced celery, cut into 1-inch pieces
2 cups chicken broth
3 tablespoons butter or margarine, melted
3 tablespoons flour
1½ cups milk
1½ teaspoons salt
½ cup chopped pecans
½ cup Parmesan cheese

Cook celery in chicken broth until tender, about 8 to 10 minutes. Drain through a colander. In a saucepan, blend flour with butter; add milk and salt. Cook until thick. Stir in celery and pecans. Pour into a buttered 1-quart casserole dish; top with cheese. Refrigerate overnight. On serving day, bake at 350° for 15 minutes.

Spinach and Artichoke Sauté

Yield: 4 servings

1 tablespoon olive oil
1 (10 ounce) bag washed spinach
1 (14 ounce) can artichoke hearts, quartered
½ cup Parmesan cheese

Place olive oil in a skillet and heat. Add spinach and artichoke hearts, sauté until spinach is just wilted, about 2 to 3 minutes. Add cheese; cook until melted. Serve immediately.

Beneath the Palms

Ratatouille Provençal

Yield: 6 to 8 servings

¼ **cup olive oil**
¼ **cup butter**
3 **cloves garlic, crushed**
2 **onions, sliced**
1 **eggplant, peeled and cubed**
2 **zucchini, washed and sliced**
2 **bell peppers, seeded and sliced**
¼ **cup flour**
4 **large tomatoes, peeled and sliced**
 Salt and pepper to taste
½ **teaspoon sugar**
2 **teaspoons capers, drained**
 French bread, toasted and buttered

In a large skillet, heat oil and butter; add garlic and onions. Sauté until transparent. Add eggplant, zucchini and bell peppers. Sprinkle with flour and mix well. Cover and simmer about ½ hour, stirring occasionally. Add tomatoes and simmer uncovered until thick. Season with salt and pepper. Add sugar and capers last 15 minutes. Serve hot or cold with toast slices.

Texas Red Beans

Yield: 4 servings

¼ **cup canned crushed tomatoes**
2 **tablespoons honey**
2 **tablespoons Dijon mustard**
2 **tablespoons cider vinegar**
 Hot sauce to taste
1 **medium clove garlic, chopped**
1 **(15 ½ ounce) can red kidney beans, rinsed and drained**
 Salt and pepper to taste

Mix first six ingredients in a saucepan. Cook for 5 minutes, add beans. Simmer 2 minutes. Add salt and pepper to taste.

Spiced Green Beans

Yield: 4 to 6 servings

Beans:
- 2 pounds fresh green beans or 16 ounces frozen
- 1 teaspoon salt
- ½ teaspoon black pepper

Dressing:
- ¼ cup tarragon vinegar
- ¾ cup olive oil
- 1 tablespoon capers
- ½ teaspoon garlic juice
- ½ teaspoon dried rosemary, crushed

Beans:
Snap fresh green beans, cover with water and cook just to tender stage; if using frozen, cook according to directions on package. Drain and season with salt and pepper.

Dressing:
Mix all ingredients together, pour over beans while hot. Allow to stand several hours before serving. Can be served hot, cold, or room temperature.

Garlicky Green Beans with Mushrooms

Yield: 4 servings

- 1 pound fresh green beans
- 1 teaspoon butter
- Cooking spray
- 1 cup fresh mushrooms, quartered
- 2 cloves garlic, minced
- ¼ teaspoon onion powder
- ¼ teaspoon salt
- ⅛ teaspoon black pepper

Wash beans; trim ends, and remove strings. Arrange in a vegetable steamer; place over boiling water. Cover and steam 5 minutes. Drain and plunge into cold water; drain again.

Melt butter in a non stick skillet coated with cooking spray. Add mushrooms and garlic; sauté 3 minutes or until mushrooms are tender. Add beans, onion powder, salt, and pepper; stir well. Cook 3 minutes or until heated.

Sautéed Mushrooms with Sweet Peppers

Yield: 6 servings

¼	**cup unsalted butter**
2	**slices lean bacon, chopped**
1	**medium onion, chopped**
1	**pinch dried thyme, crumbled**
1	**pinch dried oregano, crumbled**
1	**small bell pepper, minced**
1	**small red bell pepper, minced**
1	**pound small mushrooms**
¾	**teaspoon salt**
¼	**cup dry red wine**
½	**teaspoon black pepper**
¼	**cup heavy cream**
¼	**cup minced fresh parsley**

In a heavy saucepan, heat butter over moderate heat until foam subsides; cook bacon, stirring, for 2 minutes, or until it is cooked partially, but not crisp. Add onion, thyme, oregano, and cook mixture, stirring occasionally, for 5 minutes. Increase heat to high, add bell peppers, and cook mixture while stirring, for 1 minute. Add mushrooms and salt; cook mixture, stirring occasionally, for 5 minutes, or until all liquid is evaporated. Add wine and black pepper; cook for 1 minute. Stir in cream and cook for 1 minute. Spoon mushroom mixture into a heated serving dish and sprinkle with parsley.

Eggplant Casserole

Yield: 8 servings

2	**large eggplants, peeled and sliced**
½	**cup chopped onion**
½	**teaspoon salt**
1½	**cups grated cheddar cheese**
1½	**cups crushed saltine crackers**
1½	**cups milk**
4	**eggs**
½	**teaspoon black pepper**
1	**stick butter or margarine**

Cook eggplant, onion, and salt in a small amount of water until tender. Drain well. Place eggplant in a 1½-quart casserole. Add remaining ingredients, reserving ½ cup of crackers, cheese, and small amount of butter. Combine the reserved cheese, crumbs, and butter; sprinkle over mixture. Bake at 350° for 30 minutes.

Mushrooms au Gratin

Yield: 4 servings

1 **pound mushrooms**
2 **tablespoons butter**
⅓ **cup sour cream**
1 **teaspoon salt**
  Dash of black pepper
1 **tablespoon flour**
½ **cup shredded cheddar cheese**

Clean mushrooms, slice lengthwise through stems into about ¼-inch thick slices. In a large frying pan, heat butter over medium high heat. Sauté mushrooms, stirring until lightly browned. Cover pan until mushrooms start releasing juices, about 2 minutes. Blend sour cream with salt, pepper, and flour until smooth. Stir into mushrooms; heat until blended and mixture begins to boil. Stir constantly. Remove from heat and pour into dish. Sprinkle cheese evenly over top. Cover and refrigerate 2 hours. Bake at 425° for 10 minutes or until cheese melts.

Marinated 1015 Onions

Yield: 4 cups

4 **1015 onions, peeled and sliced**
½ **cup sugar**
¾ **cup salad oil**
¼ **cup vinegar**
½ **teaspoon salt**
⅛ **teaspoon cracked black pepper**

Mix all ingredients together. Place into a 2-quart covered dish and chill 24 hours, or longer. Stir occasionally.

Great served on sandwiches or with steaks.

Cucumber and carrot may be added to make a salad.

Beneath the Palms

Valley Fried Okra

Yield: 4 to 6 servings

1 **crate fresh okra**
1 **egg**
2 **tablespoons water**
1 **cup flour**
  Salt and pepper to taste
  Dash of hot pepper
   sauce
  Oil for frying

Select small uniform size okra; parboil about 5 minutes in unsalted water; drain well and allow to cool, spread okra on sheet of waxed paper, slightly mash down each pod with a fork. Make wash of egg, water, and hot pepper sauce; in another shallow dish, mix flour, salt, and pepper. Dip okra first in flour, then in egg mixture, finally in flour again. Place on cookie sheet lined with wax paper and chill 1 hour or so to set coating. Deep fry in hot oil or shortening until a golden color, drain well and salt to taste. Serve piping hot.

Baked 1015 Onions

Yield: 4 to 8 servings

4 **1015 sweet onions**
  Tabasco Sauce
4 **tablespoons butter**
  Salt and pepper to taste

Slice each onion in a grid pattern, not all the way through. Sprinkle each with Tabasco Sauce, as much as you like. Place a tablespoon of butter on each, salt and pepper to taste. Wrap in foil and bake at 350° for 30 to 40 minutes, depending on size of onion.

1015 onions were developed at Texas A&M University. 1015 is the date they are to be planted. They rival the Vidalia onions from Georgia in sweetness.

Onion Pie

Yield: 6 to 8 servings

1 (9-inch) pie crust, unbaked
10 medium onions, thinly sliced
3 tablespoons butter
3 eggs
1 cup sour cream
¼ cup dry sherry
1 teaspoon salt
½ teaspoon black pepper
1 egg white, lightly beaten
4 slices bacon

Line 9-inch pie pan with pie dough and chill. Sauté thinly sliced onions in butter over low heat. Set aside to cool. Combine eggs, sour cream, dry sherry, salt, and pepper; heat slowly in a saucepan. Stir mixture into onions. Brush bottom of pie shell with 1 slightly beaten egg white and fill with onion mixture. Cut bacon into squares and place over top. Bake at 350° for 10 minutes. Reduce to 300° and bake until crust is light brown, about 1/2 hour. Serve hot.

Swiss Onion Zucchini Bake

Yield: 6 to 8 servings

3 cups sliced onion
3 cups thinly sliced zucchini or yellow squash
½ stick butter
2 eggs, beaten
¼ cup milk
1 teaspoon salt
⅛ teaspoon black pepper
½ teaspoon dry mustard
1 cup grated Swiss cheese

Peel and thinly slice onions, separate into rings. Sauté onion and squash in butter until tender. Place into a shallow 1½-quart baking dish. Combine eggs, milk, salt, pepper, mustard and half of Swiss cheese. Pour over vegetables. Sprinkle with remaining cheese. Bake at 375° for 20 minutes or until firm.

🌴 Roasted Tri-Color Peppers

Yield: 6 servings

5 **large peppers (2 green, 2 red, 1 yellow)**
1 **large clove garlic, chopped fine**
⅛ **cup olive oil**
  Salt and pepper

Wash and dry peppers. Place peppers in a baking dish, so that they are at least 2 inches apart. Place baking dish on middle oven rack. Set oven to broil. Broil peppers on all sides just until outer skin turns a golden brown and starts to puff up. When all sides are done, remove peppers; place in a clean cool dish. Let sit until completely cooled. Peel off outer skin, remove stem and seeds. Cut peppers lengthwise to your desired thickness. Place in a serving dish or bowl. Add garlic, olive oil, salt and pepper. Let sit at least 30 minutes before serving. You can make this dish up to two days ahead of time. Just cover and refrigerate.

Great side dish for summer barbecues or with garlic bread.

Baked Sliced Potatoes

Yield: 8 servings

4 **large baking potatoes**
¼ **cup butter, melted**
¼ **cup salad oil**
2 **cloves garlic, minced**
½ **teaspoon salt**
½ **teaspoon thyme leaves**

Cut unpared potatoes into ¼-inch slices. Place in a 9x13-inch baking dish overlapping potatoes. Mix butter and oil; brush slices, pouring any remaining oil on potatoes. Sprinkle spices over all. Bake 400° for 25 to 30 minutes.

New Potatoes Bagna Cauda

Yield: 6 to 8 servings

1 **pound fresh green beans, snapped**
1 **pound new potatoes**
⅔ **cup vegetable or olive oil**
⅓ **cup cider vinegar**
1 **cup scallions, thinly sliced**
1 **teaspoon salt**
   Dash of sugar
   Dash of black pepper

Steam beans until crisp-tender. Set aside. Scrub potatoes; place in a medium saucepan, cover with water and cook until tender. In a small saucepan, mix remaining ingredients, heat until warm. Pierce potatoes, add green beans, pour sauce over all. Serve warm.

Potatoes with Leeks

Yield: 4 servings

1 **pound small red potatoes, scrubbed, unpeeled**
1 **cup thinly sliced leeks, white and green parts**
½ **stick butter**
¼ **cup dry white wine**
¼ **cup heavy cream**
¼ **cup sour cream**
2 **cloves garlic**
   Salt and pepper to taste
   Chives or fresh parsley (optional)

Boil potatoes until tender. Meanwhile, in a small skillet, cook leeks in butter until tender. Add wine and cream; simmer on low for 5 minutes. Drain potatoes; mash coarse with a fork. Mix leeks, sour cream, salt, pepper, and minced garlic into potatoes. Mixture should be coarse, not creamy. Garnish with fresh parsley or chives if desired.

For a sweeter garlic flavor, boil garlic cloves in water for 2 minutes. Mince through a press, add to potato mixture with leeks.

🌴 Sweet Potato Puff

Yield: 6 servings

4 **large sweet potatoes, (3½ pounds)**
½ **cup apricot preserves**
¼ **cup light brown sugar**
½ **cup freshly squeezed orange juice**
2 **teaspoons almond extract**
3 **egg whites**
2 **tablespoons almond slivers**

Bake sweet potatoes until tender. Cool and peel. In a large bowl, mash potatoes; add preserves, sugar, orange juice, and almond extract; beat with an electric mixer until smooth. In a separate bowl, beat egg whites to stiff peaks; fold into potato mixture. Coat a 2-quart casserole dish with cooking spray. Add mixture and sprinkle with almonds. Bake at 350° for 30 to 40 minutes, or until puffy and set.

Twice Baked Potatoes

Yield: 12 servings

6 **large baking potatoes**
6 **cloves garlic**
2 **tablespoons olive oil**
1 **cup grated Romano cheese**
¼ **cup ranch salad dressing**
⅔ **(14 ounce) can chicken broth**
¼ **teaspoon white pepper**
  Salt and pepper to taste
  Butter

Cut potatoes in half, lengthwise. Loosely wrap each garlic clove in foil, pouring ½ tablespoon oil over each clove. Bake potatoes and garlic at 350° for 1 hour. Scoop out pulp from potatoes (saving potato shells) and place in large mixing bowl. Cut garlic at tip and squeeze garlic pulp into potatoes. Add ¾ cup Romano cheese and rest of ingredients. Mash and blend well. If mixture seems too dry, add additional chicken broth. Refill potato shells with mixture. Sprinkle remaining cheese on top of potatoes. Place a pat of butter on top of each. Bake at 350° for 15 minutes.

⚶ Quick Hot Potatoes

Yield: 8 servings

7 medium potatoes,
  peeled and sliced
1 large onion, sliced
1 (10 ounce) can chopped
  tomatoes with green
  chilies
  Salt and pepper to taste

Layer potatoes and onion rings in a 2.5 liter, microwave safe dish, until full. Pour tomatoes over potatoes, add salt and pepper to taste. Cover with plastic wrap; microwave on high power for 20 minutes or until tender, turning the baking dish 3 or 4 times during cooking.

Snow Peas with Celery

Yield: 6 servings

1 tablespoon cornstarch
1 teaspoon sugar
½ teaspoon salt
1 tablespoon soy sauce
½ cup water
1 pound fresh snow peas
½ cup chopped green
  onions
¾ cup diagonally cut
  celery
2 tablespoons sesame oil

Mix together cornstarch, sugar, salt, soy sauce, and water. Set aside. Wash pea pods and remove any strings. Sauté peas, green onions, and celery in sesame oil for 2 to 3 minutes. Stir in cornstarch mixture. Stirring constantly, cook until thickened, about 2 to 3 minutes.

⚶ Lemon Sesame Spinach

Yield: 4 servings

2 teaspoons sesame
  seeds
12 cups tightly packed
  washed and torn
  spinach leaves
2 teaspoons fresh lemon
  juice
½ teaspoon cracked black
  pepper

Place sesame seed in a Dutch oven over medium heat. Cook 3 minutes or until toasted, stirring frequently. Add spinach; cover and cook 1 minute or until spinach begins to wilt. Remove from heat, stir in lemon juice and pepper. Serve immediately.

Beneath the Palms

Spinach Pudding Rolls

Yield: 6 servings

- 2 **cups spinach**
- 3 **eggs, beaten**
- ¾ **cup heavy cream**
  Salt
- ⅛ **teaspoon black pepper**
- 1 **tablespoon grated onion**
  Tabasco Sauce
- 2 **tablespoons butter**
- 2 **tablespoons fine bread**
  crumbs

Cook spinach, chop, and squeeze out all water. Mix eggs and next 5 ingredients. Add spinach, mix well. Spread a 9-inch square of cheese cloth with soft butter, cover with bread crumbs, place spinach mixture on one side and roll up. Tie ends and center with string. Place roll on rack in a flat pan over water; steam 30 minutes. When done, remove cloth; glaze with melted butter. Cut roll into 12 slices.

Acorn Squash with Cranberry Chutney

Yield: 8 servings

Squash:
- 4 **medium acorn squash (1 pound each)**

Chutney:
- 1 **(6 ounce) package mixed dried fruit pieces**
- 2 **cups cranberries**
- ½ **cup packed light brown sugar**
- ¼ **cup light corn syrup**
- 2 **tablespoons orange zest**
- ½ **teaspoon ground cinnamon**
- ½ **teaspoon dry mustard**
- ¼ **teaspoon salt**
- ½ **cup water**

Squash:
Cut squash in half, crosswise, remove seeds. Cut thin slice from bottom of squash half so it will stand level. Place squash, cavity-side down, in greased roasting pan; brush (bottoms) with oil. Bake at 350° for 40 minutes or until fork tender.

Chutney:
In a 3-quart saucepan, combine remaining ingredients; bring to a boil. Reduce heat to low. Simmer, uncovered, 20 to 25 minutes, stirring frequently, until chutney thickens slightly. To serve, spoon chutney into cavity of each squash.

This can also be made using yellow squash.

Tomato Tart

Yield: 6 to 8 servings

1 (9-inch) pie shell, unbaked
2 thinly sliced tomatoes
12 finely chopped Calamata olives
½ cup Feta cheese, crumbled
Fresh basil leaves
2 tablespoons olive oil
2 cloves garlic, minced

Place pie shell in a tart pan, prick bottom with a fork. Bake at 350° until slightly brown, remove and cool. On top of pie shell, layer tomato slices, olives, and cheese. Top with basil leaves. Drizzle olive oil and garlic over tart and bake at 350° until cheese is softened, about 30 minutes.

You can layer tomatoes on top and garnish with fresh basil for a different presentation.

Spinach Topped Tomatoes

Yield: 6 servings

2 (10 ounce) packages frozen chopped spinach
2 cups herb seasoned stuffing mix
1 cup finely chopped onion
6 eggs, beaten
¾ cup butter, melted
½ cup Parmesan cheese
1 teaspoon garlic, minced
½ teaspoon thyme
½ teaspoon black pepper
¼ teaspoon red pepper
Salt to taste
2 sliced tomatoes

Cook spinach according to package directions. Drain very well. Add herb seasoned stuffing mix and remaining ingredients, mix well. Use ice cream scoop to make mounds. Place the mounds on a cookie sheet; freeze. To serve, slice tomatoes, place on a foil lined cookie sheet. Place a frozen mound on top of each tomato. Bake at 350° for 20 minutes.

Beneath the Palms

Double Baked Yams

Yield: 4 to 6 servings

4 **medium yams**
1 **tablespoon reduced calorie soft margarine**
⅓ **cup apricot preserves**
2 **teaspoons fresh orange juice**
½ **teaspoon salt**
 Skim milk
 Pinch of ground nutmeg

Using a fork, prick yams. Place them on oven rack and bake at 350° for 40 to 50 minutes or until tender. Cut a thin slice in top of each. Scoop out pulp without breaking the skin. In a medium bowl, mash pulp, stirring in margarine until melted. Add preserves, juice, and salt. Stir in enough milk to moisten. Spoon mixture into empty yams. Sprinkle with nutmeg, place on a baking sheet; bake for 15 to 20 minutes until heated thoroughly.

Stir-Fry Vegetables

Yield: 4 servings

1 **tablespoon butter**
1 **bell pepper, thinly sliced**
4 **large carrots, ½-inch pieces**
2 **medium onions, thinly sliced**
3 **cloves garlic, chopped**
4 **ribs celery, 2-inch pieces**
½ **cup chopped cabbage**
1 **pound fresh greens**
 Pinch of marjoram
 Pinch of thyme
2 **tablespoons soy sauce**
 Fresh ground pepper
2 **tablespoons grated cheese (optional)**

In a skillet, melt butter on low heat. Slice bell pepper, carrots, onion, garlic, and celery in that order, add to skillet, stirring occasionally. Increase heat to medium for 2 to 3 minutes, then add cabbage, greens, marjoram, and thyme. Cook on medium to medium high heat, stirring constantly until greens have wilted but other vegetables are still crisp. Add soy sauce and pepper to taste. Serve with brown or wild rice and 2 tablespoons of grated cheese, if desired.

Tip O'Tex Tomato and Zucchini

Yield: 6 servings

2 slices bacon
1 (14 ounce) can tomatoes
   or 2 fresh tomatoes,
   chopped
¼ cup chopped onion
2 large zucchini, sliced
   Salt and pepper to taste
½ cup grated mozzarella
   cheese (optional)

Fry bacon until crisp, drain. Leave bacon grease in pan; add onion and tomatoes, with liquid. Cook until tender. Add zucchini, salt, and pepper to taste. Cover and cook until tender. Reduce liquid by increasing temperature and removing the lid. When reduced to desired amount, crumble bacon over squash and add grated cheese, if desired. Cover with lid until cheese has melted.

Moroccan Vegetables

Yield: 12 servings

2 tablespoons olive oil
1 yellow onion, diced
2 cloves garlic, minced
1 teaspoon paprika
½ teaspoon cayenne
1 teaspoon ground ginger
   Salt and pepper to taste
1 cup chicken broth
6 carrots peeled and cut
   into 2-inch pieces
1 cauliflower cut into
   florets
1 pound potatoes peeled
   and cut into 2-inch
   cubes
4 tablespoons chopped
   mint

Place oil in a small skillet, sauté onion and garlic until translucent. Add spices and broth; bring to a boil. Place vegetables in roasting pan and pour in broth mixture. Cover and roast 30 to 45 minutes at 375°. Vegetables are done when potatoes can be pierced with a fork. Garnish with the mint.

Beneath the Palms

Zesty Zucchini

Yield: 4 to 6 servings

6	**medium zucchini, sliced**
½	**cup shredded cheddar cheese**
1	**(4 ounce) can chopped green chilies**
½	**cup toasted coarse bread crumbs**
1	**tablespoon butter**
	Salt and pepper to taste

Cook zucchini briefly and drain well. Layer squash with chilies, cheese, and seasonings. Top with bread crumbs mixed with melted butter. Bake at 350° for 10 minutes.

Easy Hollandaise Sauce

Yield: ½ cup

1	**stick butter, cut into small pieces**
3	**egg yolks**
3	**tablespoons fresh lemon juice**

Combine all ingredients in top of a double boiler. Let stand 30 minutes at room temperature. Just before serving, place over gently boiling water for 1 minute 30 seconds, stirring briskly, constantly. Serve at once.

Dash of cayenne pepper may be added.

Valley Vegetable Marinade

Yield: 1½ cups marinade

1	**(0.7 ounce) package Italian salad dressing mix**
½	**(0.7 ounce) Parmesan salad dressing mix**
⅓	**cup vinegar**
1	**teaspoon tarragon vinegar**
½	**cup olive oil**
⅛	**cup water**
¼	**cup dried parsley**

Put dry ingredients in a pint size jar. Add vinegars, olive oil, water, and parsley. Shake; put in small saucepan. Bring to a boil. Pour over vegetables, cover, and let sit until cool. Put in refrigerator and leave overnight. Stir occasionally while in refrigerator.

Pasta/Rice/Grains

Cilantro Pesto

Yield: 1 cup

4 **cloves garlic**
2 **cups fresh parsley, stemmed**
2 **cups fresh cilantro, stemmed**
4 **tablespoons safflower oil**
2 **tablespoons pine nuts, toasted**
1 **tablespoon Parmesan cheese**
1 **teaspoon lemon juice**
¼ **teaspoon salt**
1 **pinch of white pepper**

In a food processor, combine all ingredients until well blended. Store in a covered container.

Use to baste grilled fish or chicken. Also good tossed with pasta.

Sausage Pasta Salad

Yield: 6 servings

1¼ **cups medium shell macaroni**
4 **ounces Polish sausage links, cooked and sliced**
3 **slices bacon**
½ **cup sliced fresh mushrooms**
4 **teaspoons sugar**
1½ **teaspoons flour**
⅓ **cup water**
Salt and pepper to taste
2 **teaspoons vinegar**
1 **tablespoon snipped parsley**

Cook macaroni according to package directions, drain. Meanwhile, slice sausage into ½-inch slices, set aside. In a 10-inch skillet, cook bacon until crisp, drain, reserving 1 tablespoon drippings. Cook mushrooms in reserved drippings until tender.
Stir in sugar, flour, salt and pepper. Add water and vinegar; cook, stirring, until thick and bubbly (about 1 minute). Crumble bacon and stir into mixture, add sausage. Gently stir in pasta and parsley. Turn into a serving dish.

Sun-Dried Tomato Pesto

Yield: 1½ cups

- ¾ **cup sun-dried tomatoes, packed in oil**
- ¼ **cup pine nuts**
- ¼ **cup parsley leaves**
- 1 **clove garlic**
- ¾ **cup chicken broth**
- ¼ **cup olive oil**
- ⅛ **teaspoon crushed red pepper**

In a food processor, purée tomatoes, nuts, parsley, and garlic. With the motor running, add broth and oil; process until blended. Stir in pepper.

Tomato and Cream Sauce (Sugo Di Pomodoro Epanna)

Yield: 6 servings

- 1 **stick butter**
- 3 **tablespoons finely chopped yellow onion**
- 3 **tablespoons finely chopped carrots**
- 3 **tablespoons finely chopped celery**
- 2½ **cups canned Italian plum tomatoes with juice**
- 2 **teaspoons salt**
- ¼ **teaspoon sugar**
- ½ **cup heavy cream**

Put all ingredients, except for heavy cream, in a saucepan and simmer for one hour uncovered. Stir occasionally with wooden spoon. Purée contents of saucepan in a blender or food processor. (Up to this point, the sauce can be prepared ahead of time and refrigerated for a few days or frozen.) Place in a saucepan and bring to a simmer, stirring with wooden spoon. Add cream, stir for one minute or more. Taste and correct for salt. Serve immediately over tortellini, ravioli, or fettuccine.

Beneath the Palms

Tomato Sauce

Yield: 6 servings

2 **pounds beef short ribs**
Black pepper to taste
1 **tablespoon olive oil**
2 **large onions, chopped**
3 **cloves garlic, minced**
1 **(36 ounce) can stewed**
   tomatoes, chopped
2 **(8 ounce) cans tomato**
   sauce
3 **(10 ¾ ounce) cans**
   tomato purée
3 **cups water**
   Pinch of sugar
3 **tablespoons Italian**
   seasoning blend
2 **tablespoons dried**
   parsley

Sprinkle short ribs with pepper and braise in a soup pot with olive oil. When meat is almost done, add chopped onion and garlic. Let onion turn clear. Add remaining ingredients; let simmer 3 hours.

Use as pasta sauce.

Meat can be left in or removed.

Easy Spaghetti Sauce

Yield: 6 cups

1 **large onion, chopped**
12 **cloves garlic, minced**
2 **tablespoons butter**
1½ **pounds ground beef**
⅓ **cup sugar**
½ **teaspoon garlic salt**
1 **cup fresh sliced**
   mushrooms
2 **teaspoons Italian**
   seasoning
4 **(8 ounce) cans tomato**
   sauce
2 **(6 ounce) cans tomato**
   paste

In a large skillet, sauté onion and garlic in butter until transparent. Add next 5 ingredients and continue cooking over medium heat until ground beef is browned. Transfer mixture to large pot; add tomato sauce, tomato paste, and 3 to 4 cups water. Simmer approximately 4 hours, stirring occasionally.

White Clam Sauce

Yield: 4 servings

4 tablespoons butter
4 tablespoons olive oil
1 clove garlic, crushed
¼ teaspoon black pepper
2 tablespoons finely
  chopped fresh parsley
½ teaspoon dried oregano
¼ cup dry white wine
1 (7 ounce) can minced
  clams
1 teaspoon salt

Melt butter with 2 tablespoons of olive oil in a small saucepan. Add remaining ingredients. Cover and cook gently over low heat for 15 minutes. Spoon over cooked pasta.

🌴 No-Fat Alfredo Sauce

Yield: 4 to 6 servings

1 quart fat free milk
2 cloves garlic, minced
2 tablespoons natural
  butter flavor sprinkles
¼ cup cornstarch
¼ cup water
1 cup shredded fat free
  mozzarella cheese
  Salt to taste
  White pepper to taste

In a medium saucepan, combine milk, garlic, and butter sprinkles; bring to a boil. Blend together cornstarch and cold water, slowly add to the sauce, stirring constantly. Let sauce simmer for 2 minutes. Remove from heat and slowly stir in cheese.

Following the Civil War, 50,000 Federal troops were sent to the Lower Rio Grande Valley area of Brownsville as a demonstration of force against the Maximillian government in Mexico.

Beneath the Palms

🌴 Penne Pasta with Chili and Sun-Dried Tomatoes

Yield: 6 servings

- 4 tablespoons crushed New Mexican red chilies
- ½ cup sun-dried tomatoes, cut in strips
- 1 cup pitted calamata olives, cut in half
- ½ cup chopped fresh basil
- ½ cup chopped fresh Italian parsley
- 1 tablespoon lemon zest
- 3 cloves garlic, minced
- ½ cup olive oil
- 2 tablespoons oil from tomatoes
- 2 teaspoons freshly ground black pepper
- 1 pound penne pasta
- 4 quarts salted water
- ¾ pound Parmesan cheese, grated

Combine all ingredients, except cheese, pasta, and water. Let sit at room temperature for several hours to blend flavors. Cook pasta in the water until al dente, drain. Toss pasta with sauce and cheese until well coated. Serve.

Great with spinach salad and pepper cheese bread.

🌴 Lowfat Pasta Cream Sauce

Yield: 2 cups

- 2 tablespoons butter, melted
- 1½ tablespoons flour
- 12 ounces low fat evaporated milk
  Fresh ground black pepper to taste
  Nutmeg to taste
- 2 tablespoons Parmesan cheese

Blend butter and flour. Cook one minute over moderate heat. Gradually add evaporated milk, stirring constantly with a whisk. Heat until sauce bubbles, season with pepper and nutmeg to taste. Remove from heat, add cheese. Serve immediately over hot, cooked pasta.

🌴 *Linguini with Fresh Tomato Sauce*

Yield: 4 to 6 servings

6   **pounds fresh tomatoes, peeled, seeded and chopped**
16 **cloves garlic, minced**
1   **teaspoon salt**
½   **teaspoon pepper**
1   **(16 ounce) package linguini**
¾   **cup freshly grated Parmesan cheese**
1   **stick butter**
¼   **cup chopped fresh basil**

Combine tomatoes and garlic, bring to a boil. Reduce heat and cook 15 to 20 minutes, stirring occasionally. Stir in salt and pepper, keep warm. Cook linguine according to package directions, and drain. Add cheese and remaining ingredients, tossing well. To serve, top pasta with tomato mixture.

Pasta with Garlic and Oil

Yield: 4 servings

¾   **pound spaghetti**
8   **cloves garlic, coarsely chopped**
⅓   **cup extra virgin olive oil**
½   **cup minced fresh flat leaf parsley**
¼   **teaspoon dried hot red pepper flakes**
    Salt and pepper to taste

In a saucepan of boiling salted water, cook spaghetti for 7 to 9 minutes or until al dente; drain, reserving 8 tablespoons of cooking liquid. While spaghetti is cooking, cook the garlic in oil in a small heavy skillet, over moderate heat, stirring until it is golden. Add the parsley and red pepper; cook for about 30 seconds. Divide spaghetti among 4 heated bowls, pour 2 tablespoons of reserved cooking liquid over each serving; top it with garlic oil. Add salt and pepper to taste.

Beneath the Palms

Spaghetti with Spinach

Yield: 4 to 6 servings

1 medium onion, diced
2 cloves garlic, minced
1 pound fresh spinach,
   rinsed and cleaned
2 tablespoons olive oil
2 tablespoons butter
1 teaspoon basil
½ teaspoon salt
¼ teaspoon pepper
½ cup Parmesan cheese
4 ounces vermicelli or
   spaghetti, cooked al
   dente

Sauté onion, garlic, and spinach in oil and butter for 10 minutes. Add spices and cheese; cook for 5 additional minutes. Serve immediately over hot pasta.

Good with veal.

Chicken Spaghetti

Yield: 6 servings

1 whole chicken
1 (16 ounce) package of
   spaghetti
2 small onions, diced
2 bell peppers, diced
1 (6 ounce) can sliced
   mushrooms
1 stick butter
1 (28 ounce) can crushed
   tomatoes
1 cup chicken broth
1 pound grated cheddar
   cheese

In a large stew pot, boil chicken until tender. When cool, bone and dice chicken; set aside. Cook spaghetti in cooking liquid from chicken; drain; set aside. Simmer onions, peppers, and mushrooms in butter. Mix with chicken, spaghetti, and tomatoes. Place in a 13x9-inch casserole dish and pour in broth. Bake at 350° for 30 minutes. Stir in cheese just before serving and allow to melt.

Chili Rice Casserole

Yield: 4 servings

1 cup uncooked rice
½ stick butter
1 (4 ounce) can diced
   green chilies
4 ounces Monterey Jack
   cheese, grated
½ pint sour cream
   Salt and pepper to taste

Cook rice according to package directions. Add butter, chilies, and cheese, mix well. Add sour cream, salt, and pepper. Mix; pour into a 1-quart casserole dish. Bake at 325° for 30 minutes.

Thin Spaghetti with Fresh Basil and Tomato Sauce

Yield: 4 servings

1 large bunch fresh basil
2 cups canned Italian
   plum tomatoes, seeded
   and chopped
5 cloves garlic, chopped
⅓ cup olive oil
   Salt
   Freshly ground black
   pepper
1 pound thin spaghetti

Pull all the basil leaves from the stalks, rinse briefly in cold water; chop coarsely. Put basil, tomatoes, garlic, ⅓ cup olive oil, 1 teaspoon salt and pepper in an uncovered saucepan and cook over medium high heat for 15 minutes. Taste and correct for salt. Cook spaghetti in a quart of boiling salted water. Since thin spaghetti cooks very rapidly, begin testing early for doneness. Cook until truly al dente (very firm to the bite). Drain well and transfer quickly to a large hot bowl. Add the sauce, mixing it thoroughly into the spaghetti. A few drops of olive oil may be added if desired. Serve immediately.

Rigatoni, Broccoli and Mozzarella Melt

Yield: 4 servings

- 4 **tablespoons butter or margarine**
- 2 **cloves garlic, minced**
- 4 **tablespoons flour**
- 2 **cups milk**
- ½ **teaspoon salt**
- 1 **bunch fresh broccoli**
- 2 **tablespoons olive oil**
- 12 **ounces rigatoni**
- 3 **ounces shredded mozzarella cheese**

Melt butter in medium saucepan, add garlic and cook over low heat, stirring until garlic is softened. Stir in the flour and raise heat to medium high. Cook, stirring constantly, until mixture is smooth and bubbly. Stir in milk and salt. Cook; stir until mixture boils and thickens. Remove from heat. Cool slightly and place a piece of plastic wrap directly on surface of sauce to prevent a skin from forming as sauce cools. Set aside. Remove florets from broccoli and rinse with cold water, this should make about 5 cups. Cook florets in lightly salted boiling water until crisp and tender, about 2 minutes. Drain and rinse with cold water to prevent further cooking. Drain again and return to cooking pan. Toss with 1 tablespoon olive oil and set aside. Cook rigatoni in lightly salted boiling water per package directions. Drain and rinse with cold water. Toss with remaining olive oil in colander. Set aside. Lightly grease a 13x9x2-inch baking dish. Measure about ¾ cup of reserved sauce and pour it into prepared dish. Place about half of rigatoni over sauce and scatter half of broccoli over rigatoni. Drizzle about ¾ cup of sauce over all. Repeat with remaining rigatoni, broccoli, and sauce. Sprinkle evenly with shredded cheese. Bake at 350° for 25 to 30 minutes or until heated through and cheese is melted and bubbly.

Vegetable Fettuccine

Yield: 6 servings

4   **eggs**
¼   **cup heavy cream**
8   **slices bacon, cooked**
    and crumbled
½   **cup sliced mushrooms**
½   **cup sliced carrots**
½   **cup sliced cauliflower**
½   **cup frozen peas, thawed**
½   **cup sliced zucchini**
½   **red bell pepper, cut into**
    1-inch strips
¼   **cup sliced green onion**
1   **clove garlic, chopped**
1   **pound fettucine**
4   **tablespoons butter**
1   **cup Parmesan cheese**
    Salt and pepper to taste

Beat eggs with cream in small bowl, set aside. Cook bacon in large skillet, set aside. Add next 8 ingredients, sauté until crisp and tender, about 5 to 7 minutes. Meanwhile prepare fettuccine according to package directions, drain and transfer to a large pasta bowl. Add butter, egg mixture, and vegetables; toss. Top with bacon and cheese. Season with salt and pepper; serve hot.

🌴 Pasta with Garlic and Clam Sauce

Yield: 4 servings

½   **cup chopped onion**
½   **cup chopped bell pepper**
4   **cloves garlic, minced**
2   **tablespoons olive oil**
½   **pound sliced**
    mushrooms
1½ **teaspoons dried thyme**
2   **tablespoons chopped**
    parsley
    Dash cayenne pepper
2   **(6 ounce) cans minced**
    clams, reserve juice
    Salt and pepper to taste
    Cooked pasta
    Parmesan cheese

Sauté onion, pepper, and garlic in olive oil until translucent. Add mushrooms and continue heating, covered, for about 3 minutes. Add remaining ingredients, including clam liquid, and cook until hot. Serve with cooked pasta and Parmesan cheese to taste.

Best Lasagna Florentine

Yield: 6 servings

1 **pound lasagna noodles**
1 **pound ground beef**
1 **pound ground pork**
1 **tablespoon fennel seed**
1 **onion, chopped**
2 **cloves garlic, minced**
1 **(15 ounce) can tomato sauce**
32 **ounces chopped spinach**
½ **pound dry ricotta**
½ **cup fresh basil leaves**
¾ **pound provolone cheese**
3 **tablespoons virgin olive oil**
½ **cup Parmesan cheese**
Salt and pepper to taste

Cook noodles according to package directions, drain. Brown meat in oil, add fennel seed, onion, and garlic. Stir well. Pour enough tomato sauce to cover bottom of a casserole dish, spread meat on top. Place noodles to cover, top with sauce. Add spinach mixed with ricotta and basil. Lightly press down. Add noodles and then sauce. Layer provolone cheese, oil and Parmesan. Cook, covered, 1 hour in 350° oven.

Italian Style Macaroni

Yield: 4 servings

⅓ **cup chopped onion**
⅓ **cup chopped bell pepper**
2 **tablespoons olive oil**
14 **ounces Italian style stewed tomatoes**
8 **ounces tomato sauce**
1 **cup water**
2 **Tabasco peppers (optional), chopped**
Salt and pepper to taste
10 **ounces elbow macaroni**
5 **slices American cheese**

Sauté onions and bell pepper in olive oil until onions are tender. Add tomatoes, tomato sauce, and water. Add Tabasco peppers, salt and pepper to taste. While sauce is simmering, prepare macaroni according to package directions. Drain macaroni and add to sauce. Continue simmering 5 to 10 minutes. Place slices of cheese over macaroni.

This macaroni can be served a little soupy or dry.

Large Shells and Sausage

Yield: 6 servings

1 **pound bulk sausage**
½ **cup chopped bell pepper**
¼ **cup chopped onion**
1 **(14 ½ ounce) can tomatoes**
1 **(8 ounce) can tomato paste**
2 **tablespoons sugar**
1 **teaspoon salt**
2 **teaspoons chili powder**
1 **(12 ounce) package large shell macaroni**
½ **cup sour cream**
   Parmesan cheese

In a large skillet, brown sausage; drain off fat. Add peppers and onion, cook until tender. Stir in tomatoes and tomato paste; cut tomatoes with a fork. Add sugar, salt, and chili powder. Mix well, cover, and simmer for 45 minutes. Cook macaroni according to package directions, drain. Add to sauce and mix well. Stir in sour cream and heat thoroughly. Top with Parmesan cheese.

Spiced Rice

Yield: 4 to 6 servings

1 **cup uncooked white rice**
2 **tablespoons butter**
1 **teaspoon curry powder**
1 **small package almond slivers**
⅔ **cup chopped celery**
1 **bunch spring onions, chopped**
1 **(8 ½ ounce) can small green peas**
½ **cup raisins**

Cook rice, add remaining ingredients, mix well. Serve with chicken or pork.

197

Beneath the Palms

🌴 Macaroni and Cheese

Yield: 6 servings

- 1 **pound elbow macaroni**
- 1 **(16 ounce) container low fat cottage cheese**
- 2 **cups low fat milk**
- 2 **tablespoons unsalted butter**
- 2 **tablespoons unbleached flour**
- ½ **teaspoon nutmeg**
- ¼ **teaspoon salt**
- ⅛ **teaspoon ground pepper**
- ¾ **cup fat free Parmesan cheese**

In a 3-quart saucepan, boil macaroni in lightly salted water. Purée cottage cheese in blender or food processor; set aside. Heat milk until warm. While macaroni is cooking, melt butter in saucepan until bubbly, add flour. Cook over low heat, stirring constantly, until mixture is a light golden brown roux. Add milk to roux along with nutmeg, salt, and pepper. Stir constantly and cook until thickened. Add puréed cottage cheese and ½ cup of Parmesan. Thoroughly drain macaroni and return to pot adding cheese sauce. Simmer 5 minutes, stirring so cheese does not stick to sides. Pour mixture into a baking dish lightly coated with nonstick cooking spray. Sprinkle with remaining Parmesan, place under broiler until brown and bubbly.

🌴 Orzo and Rice

Yield: 4 to 6 servings

- ¼ **cup orzo**
- 1 **tablespoon olive oil or butter**
- 1 **cup rice**
- ½ **teaspoon cinnamon**
- 1 **teaspoon salt**
- 2½ **cups chicken broth**

Brown orzo in olive oil or butter. Add remaining ingredients, cover and simmer for 20 minutes.

Paella

Yield: 6 servings

- 1 **whole chicken, cut into pieces**
- 1 **large onion, chopped**
- 1 **clove garlic, minced**
- 1 **cup uncooked rice**
- 6 **slices salami, diced**
- 1 **teaspoon sugar**
 Salt and pepper to taste
- 1 **(14½ ounce) can tomatoes, diced**
- 1 **pound shrimp, cleaned and deveined**
- 1½ **cups water**
- 1 **chicken bouillon cube**

Brown chicken pieces; sauté onion and garlic. In a 3-quart baking dish mix all ingredients, except bouillon and water. Dissolve cube in water; pour over ingredients. Arrange chicken on top, cover and bake at 350° for 1 hour.

Creamy Wild Rice Casserole

Yield: 4 servings

- 1 **(6 ounce) package long grain wild rice**
- 1½ **cups sliced mushrooms**
- ¼ **cup chopped onion**
- 1 **cup sliced celery**
- 2 **teaspoons butter**
- 2¼ **cups water**
- 1 **teaspoon Worcestershire sauce**
- 1 **cup sour cream**

Place contents of rice package with seasoning packet in a 1½-quart casserole. Sauté mushrooms, onion, and celery in butter until tender. Add water and Worcestershire; bring to a boil. Pour over rice mixture, stir and cover. Bake at 350° for 30 minutes. Uncover, stir in sour cream and bake for 10 minutes.

🌴 Spicy Couscous

Yield: 6 servings

- 1 **cup chicken broth**
- ¼ **cup sliced green onion**
- 1 **(4 ounce) can diced green chilies**
- ⅔ **cup couscous**

In a saucepan, bring stock, onions, and undrained chilies to a boil; remove from heat. Stir in couscous, let stand covered for 15 minutes. Fluff with a fork before serving.

🌴 🌴 🌴 🌴 🌴

Beneath the Palms

Arroz con Jocoque (Rice and Sour Cream Casserole)

Yield: 12 servings

1 (8 ounce) can green chilies, chopped and seeded
2 tablespoons chopped onion
3 cups sour cream
3 cups cooked rice
1 teaspoon salt
¼ teaspoon black pepper
¾ pound Monterey Jack cheese, cut into strips
½ cup grated cheddar cheese

Combine green chilies and onions with sour cream. Season rice with salt and pepper. Grease a 1½-quart casserole dish. Layer rice, sour cream mixture, and cheese strips into casserole, ending with rice on top. Bake at 350° for 25 minutes. Sprinkle cheese over the top; bake another 10 minutes until cheese melts.

🌴 Black Beans and Rice

Yield: 4 servings

4 ounces dried black beans
2 cups water
1 clove garlic, minced
1 small onion, chopped
1 tablespoon butter
1 bay leaf
1 ham bone, or meaty pork rib
1 tablespoon sherry (optional)
Salt and pepper to taste
Cooked white rice
Chopped onion

Let beans soak in water overnight. The next day, put beans and soaking liquid in a large pot; cook over low heat. Sauté garlic and onion, in butter, until onion is limp. Add to beans along with bay leaf, ham bone, and sherry. Cook over low heat about 2 hours or until beans are thick and soft. Add more water if necessary. Take out bone or rib, remove meat from bone and return meat to pot. Remove bay leaf. Salt and pepper to taste. Serve over rice and top with onion.

Desserts

Luscious Orange Sponge Cake

Yield: 8 to 10 servings

Cake:
- 1 **cup flour**
- 1 **teaspoon baking powder**
- ¼ **teaspoon salt**
- ½ **cup finely chopped walnuts**
- 3 **eggs**
- ¾ **cup sugar**
- ⅓ **cup orange juice**
- ½ **teaspoon orange extract**
  Powdered sugar

Filling and Frosting:
- 1 **cup sugar**
- ⅓ **cup flour**
- 3 **egg yolks**
- ¼ **teaspoon orange zest, grated**
- ½ **cup orange juice**
- 1 **tablespoon lemon juice**
  Dash salt
- 3 **tablespoons orange flavored liqueur or orange juice**
- 2 **cups heavy cream, whipped**
- 1 **cup coarsely chopped walnuts**

Garnish:
  Orange slices
  Fresh mint leaves

Cake:
Grease a 15x10x1-inch jelly-roll pan. Line bottom with wax paper; grease paper. Sift flour, baking powder, and salt; stir in nuts. Beat eggs in a medium-size bowl with electric mixer at high speed until thick and light, about 5 minutes. Gradually beat in sugar and continue to beat 2 minutes. Blend in orange juice and extract with mixer at low speed. Fold in flour mixture gradually. Turn mixture into prepared pan, spreading evenly. Bake at 375° for 15 minutes or until center springs back when lightly pressed with fingertip. Turn cake out onto a cloth kitchen towel that has been sprinkled with powdered sugar. Place towel and cake on wire rack, cool completely.

Filling and Frosting:
Combine sugar, flour, and egg yolks in top of a double boiler, beat until well blended. Stir in zest, juices, and salt. Place pan over simmering water. Cook, stirring constantly, until thickened, about 20 minutes. Cool quickly by emptying bottom of double boiler, filling it with ice and water and replacing the top. Stir mixture occasionally as it

cools. Cut cake, crosswise, into 3 equal size rectangles, each 5x10-inches. Sprinkle pieces with orange liqueur or juice. Fold orange mixture into whipped cream. Spread ⅓ of mixture on two of the pieces. Layer pieces with plain one on top. Spread remaining mixture on top and sides of cake. Sprinkle sides with nuts. Chill cake.
Garnish with orange slices and mint.

Lady Orange Cake

Yield: 16 to 20 servings

Orange Sauce:
- 1 **cup orange juice, strained**
- 2 **cups sugar**

Cake:
- 1 **cup shortening**
- 2 **cups sugar**
- 4 **eggs**
- 1⅓ **cups buttermilk**
- 1 **teaspoon baking soda**
- ½ **teaspoon salt**
- 4 **cups flour**
- 2 **tablespoons orange zest, grated**
- 1 **cup chopped dates**
- 1 **cup pecans**

Sauce:
Mix orange juice and sugar. Stir several times while cake is baking.

Cake:
Cream together shortening, sugar, and eggs. Add buttermilk. Sift together soda, salt, and flour; add to creamed mixture. Add zest. Roll dates and pecans in small amount of flour, add to mixture. Pour batter into a 10-inch tube pan. Bake at 350° for 1 hour. Remove cake from pan and place on serving dish. Slowly pour orange juice mixture over entire cake.

This makes a large cake.

Apricot Doboschtorte

Yield: 15 to 18 servings

Cake:
- 6 eggs, separated
- ⅓ cup sugar, for egg whites
- ½ cup sugar, for egg yolks
- 1 cup flour

Apricot Filling:
- 1 (17 ounce) can apricot halves, chopped
- ¼ cup apricot preserves

Frosting:
- ¾ cup sugar
- 3 eggs
- 2 egg yolks
- 2 ounces semisweet chocolate
- 1 teaspoon instant coffee
- 1 teaspoon vanilla
- 2 sticks butter, softened
- ½ cup chopped pecans
  Apricot halves, quartered
  Chocolate curls

Cake:
Beat egg whites in large bowl until foamy. Gradually add ⅓ cup of sugar, beating until stiff peaks form. Beat egg yolks with ½ cup of sugar until thick and pale yellow, fold into egg whites. Gradually fold in flour. Grease and flour six 9-inch layer cake pans. Spread batter thinly in each one. Bake at 350° for 15 minutes or until golden. Using a sharp knife, remove layers from pan, cool on racks.

Apricot Filling:
Quarter 3 apricot halves and save for garnish. Chop remaining apricots and mix with preserves.

Frosting:
In top of a double boiler, beat together all ingredients. Cook over simmering water for 10 to 15 minutes or until thickened, stirring frequently. Cool completely. Beat butter until fluffy; gradually beat in chocolate mixture. Spread 3 cake layers with frosting and 2 with apricot filling. Stack, invert top layer. Spread remaining frosting over sides of cake, press in nuts. Spread apricot filling on top. Garnish with apricot slices and chocolate curls.

Raspberries may be substituted for the apricots in this recipe.

Orange Date Cake

Yield: 24 servings

Cake:

3½	**cups all-purpose flour**
1	**teaspoon baking soda**
1	**teaspoon baking powder**
¼	**teaspoon salt**
2	**sticks butter**
2	**cups sugar**
4	**eggs, separated**
1½	**cups buttermilk**
2	**cups chopped pecans**
1	**(12 ounce) package pitted dates, chopped**
½	**cup all-purpose flour**

Orange Glaze:

½	**cup powdered sugar**
2	**tablespoons grated orange zest**
1	**cup orange juice**
1	**tablespoon brandy**

Cake:
Sift first 4 ingredients together, set aside. Beat butter, sugar, and egg yolks, in a large bowl, at high speed until light and fluffy. Beat in flour mixture, alternating with buttermilk at low speed; begin and end with flour mixture until batter is smooth. Toss nuts and dates with remaining flour in medium bowl until coated, fold into cake batter. Beat egg whites until stiff, fold into batter until no white streaks remain. Pour batter into a greased and floured 10-inch tube pan. Bake at 300° for 1 hour 45 minutes. Cool 10 minutes.

Orange Glaze:
Mix all ingredients until smooth. Remove cake from pan, poke holes all over with skewer. Brush glaze over cake and refrigerate overnight.

The "Brownsville Herald" began publication on July 4, 1892. It is the only newspaper publishing presently that began in the 1800's.

Beneath the Palms

Carrot Cake

Yield: 20 servings

Cake:
- 1½ cups vegetable oil
- 3 cups self-rising flour
- 2 cups sugar
- 1 teaspoon cinnamon
- ⅛ teaspoon salt
- 4 eggs
- 2 cups grated carrots
- 1 cup chopped pecans

Frosting:
- 1 (1 pound) box powdered sugar
- 1 (8 ounce) package cream cheese, softened
- 1 teaspoon vanilla extract
- 1 (3½ ounce) can evaporated milk
- ½ cup chopped pecans

Cake:
Pour oil in a medium-size mixing bowl. Sift together dry ingredients. Alternate mixing dry ingredients and one egg at a time with oil. Add carrots and pecans, mix well. Pour into a greased and floured 10-inch tube pan. Bake at 325° for 60 minutes. Remove cake from pan and cool on rack.

Frosting:
Mix ingredients together with enough milk to reach a spreading consistency. All milk will not be used. Frost cake.

Mississippi Mud Cake

Yield: 24 servings

- 2 sticks margarine
- ½ cup cocoa
- 2 cups sugar
- 4 eggs, lightly beaten
- 1½ cups all-purpose flour
- 1 teaspoon baking soda
- 1 pinch salt
- 1½ cups chopped nuts
- 1 teaspoon vanilla extract
- 1 (10 ounce) bag miniature marshmallows

Melt margarine with cocoa; remove from heat. Stir in sugar and eggs, mix well. Add flour, salt, nuts, and vanilla. Mix until well blended. Spoon batter into greased and floured 13x9x2-inch pan. Bake at 325° for 35 to 40 minutes. Spread marshmallows over cake; return to oven until melted, about 10 minutes. Cool and frost with chocolate icing.

Mississippi Mud Cake Frosting

Yield: Icing for a 13x9-inch cake

1 **stick butter, melted**
⅓ **cup cocoa**
1 **(1 pound) box powdered sugar**
¼ **cup evaporated milk**
1 **teaspoon vanilla**
1 **cup chopped nuts**

Mix all ingredients, except nuts, with an electric mixer. Stir in nuts. Spread on hot cake.

Butter Pecan Cake

Yield: 16 servings

Cake:
2 **cups chopped pecans**
2½ **sticks butter**
3 **cups flour**
2 **teaspoons baking powder**
½ **teaspoon salt**
2 **cups sugar**
4 **eggs**
1 **cup milk**
2 **teaspoons vanilla**
Frosting:
8 **tablespoons butter**
2 **pounds powdered sugar**
2 **teaspoons vanilla extract**
8 **tablespoons evaporated milk**

Cake:
Toast pecans in 4 tablespoons of butter at 350° for 20 to 25 minutes. Sift flour with baking powder and salt. Using an electric mixer, cream remaining butter. Slowly add sugar. Blend in eggs, one at a time. Add dry ingredients, alternate with milk. Blend after each addition on low speed. Stir in vanilla and 1⅓ cup pecans. Turn into 3 greased and floured 8-inch round cake pans. Bake at 350° for 25 to 30 minutes. Cool before frosting.
Frosting:
Cream butter; add powdered sugar, vanilla, and evaporated milk. Stir in remaining pecans. Spread a thin layer of frosting on one layer, top with another layer and thinly frost. Place remaining cake layer on top and spread remaining frosting evenly over entire cake.

Beneath the Palms

Sour Cream Pound Cake with Orange-Raspberry Sauce

Yield: 24 servings

Cake:
- 2 sticks butter or margarine, softened
- 3 cups sugar
- 6 eggs
- 3 cups all-purpose flour
- ¼ teaspoon baking soda
- 8 ounces sour cream
- 1 teaspoon vanilla extract
- 1 teaspoon almond extract

Orange-Raspberry Sauce:
- 2 cups fresh or frozen raspberries, thawed
- ¾ cup powdered sugar
- ¼ cup orange flavored liqueur
- 1 tablespoon frozen orange juice concentrate, thawed
  Additional fruit (optional)

Cake:
Beat butter, at medium speed, with an electric mixer about 2 minutes or until soft and creamy. Gradually add sugar, beating at medium speed 5 to 7 minutes. Add eggs, one at a time, beating just until the yellow disappears. Combine flour and baking soda; add to creamed mixture alternately with sour cream, beginning and ending with flour mixture. Mix at lowest speed, just until blended, after each addition. Stir in vanilla and almond extracts. Spoon batter into one greased and floured 10-inch tube pan or three 9-inch circular cake pans. Bake at 325° for 1 hour and 20 minutes or until a tester inserted in center comes out clean. Cool, in pan, on a wire rack for 10 to 15 minutes. Remove from pan and let cool completely on a wire rack.

Sauce:
Use a blender or food processor to process raspberries until smooth. Add powdered sugar and remaining ingredients; process until blended. Pour through a wire-mesh strainer; pressing mixture with back of spoon against the sides of strainer to squeeze out liquid. Discard seeds.
Serve sauce and additional fruit on the side.

🌴 *Lemon Poppy Seed Cake*

Yield: 24 servings

1   **fat free yellow cake mix (97% fat free)**
½   **cup sugar**
⅓   **cup vegetable oil**
¼   **cup water**
1   **cup fat free plain yogurt**
1   **cup egg substitute**
3   **tablespoons lemon juice**
3   **tablespoons poppy seeds**
Lemon Glaze:
½   **cup powdered sugar**
2   **tablespoons lemon juice**
Mix ingredients well.

Combine all ingredients, except poppy seeds, beat at medium speed with an electric mixer for 6 minutes. Stir in poppy seeds. Pour batter into a 10-inch tube pan coated with nonstick cooking spray. Bake at 350° for 40 minutes, or until a tester comes out clean. Cool in pan, on wire rack, for 10 minutes. Remove from pan, drizzle with lemon glaze; cool completely on rack.

This cake freezes well.

Black Walnut Pound Cake

Yield: 24 servings

1   **pound butter**
3   **cups sugar**
1   **cup black walnuts**
4 ½   **cups unsifted flour**
½   **cup evaporated milk**
½   **cup water**
8   **eggs**
1   **tablespoon vanilla extract**
1   **tablespoon lemon extract**

Cream butter and sugar in mixer. Dredge walnuts in flour. Add walnuts and remaining ingredients to butter mixture, mix on low speed until well blended. Pour into a greased and floured 10-inch tube pan. Bake at 300° for 1 hour and 30 minutes, or until a tester placed in the center comes out clean.

Triple Chocolate Cheesecake

Yield: 16 servings

Crust:
- 2 **cups crushed chocolate cookie crumbs**
- ¼ **cup sugar**
- ½ **stick butter or margarine, melted**

Cake:
- 4 **(8 ounce) packages cream cheese**
- 1½ **cups sugar**
- 6 **eggs**
- ½ **cup unsweetened cocoa powder**
- ½ **cup hot water**
- 4 **ounces unsweetened chocolate, melted and cooled**
- ½ **stick butter or margarine, melted**
- 1 **tablespoon vanilla extract**
  Whipped cream (optional)
  Chocolate curls (optional)

Crust:
In a medium size mixing bowl, stir together cookie crumbs and sugar. Add melted butter or margarine. Press mixture into bottom and up sides of 10-inch springform pan. Set aside.

Cake:
In a large mixing bowl, beat cream cheese and remaining sugar together. Add eggs, one at a time, until well blended. In a separate bowl, stir cocoa powder and water until well mixed. Add to cream cheese mixture. Add remaining ingredients, beating until combined. Pour mixture into crust and place pan on cookie sheet. Bake at 325° for 1 hour or until center appears nearly set when pan is shaken. Cool for 15 minutes. Loosen crust from sides, cool for 30 minutes. Remove sides of pan, cool completely. Cover and chill at least 4 hours. Top with whipped cream and chocolate curls, if desired.

Cocoanut Meringue Cheesecake

Yield: 16 servings

Crust:
- 1½ cups flaked coconut
- ¼ cup chopped pecans
- 2 tablespoons butter or margarine, melted

Filling:
- 2 (8 ounce) packages cream cheese, softened
- 3 eggs, separated
- ⅓ cup sugar
- 3 tablespoons cocoa
- 2 tablespoons water
- 1 teaspoon vanilla extract

Topping:
- 3 egg whites
- Dash of salt
- 1 (7 ounce) jar marshmallow cream
- ½ cup chopped pecans

Crust:
Combine coconut, pecans, and butter or margarine; press into bottom of 9-inch springform pan. Bake at 325° for 15 minutes or until light golden. Set aside. Increase oven temperature to 350°.

Filling:
Combine cream cheese, egg yolks, sugar, cocoa, water, and vanilla; mix at medium speed until well blended. Pour over crust. Bake at 350° for 30 minutes. Loosen cake from rim of pan, cool before removing rim.

Topping:
Beat egg whites and salt until soft peaks form. Gradually add marshmallow cream, beating until stiff peaks form. Sprinkle pecans on cheesecake, spread marshmallow cream mixture over nuts, sealing cheesecake surface. Bake at 350° for 15 minutes. Cool completely prior to serving.

Pineapple Cheesecake

Yield: 16 servings

Crust:
- 1½ cups graham cracker crumbs
- 3 tablespoons sugar
- 1 stick butter, melted
- ¼ teaspoon cinnamon

Cake:
- 1 (16 ounce) carton creamed cottage cheese, small curd
- 4 eggs
- 3 (8 ounce) packages cream cheese, softened
- 2 tablespoons flour
- ¼ teaspoon salt
- 1 cup sugar
- 1½ teaspoons vanilla extract
- 2 (8 ¼ ounce) cans crushed pineapple, well drained

Topping:
- 1 pint sour cream
- 3 tablespoons sugar
- 1 teaspoon vanilla extract

Crust:
Mix crumbs and 3 tablespoons sugar together; stir in butter and cinnamon. Press mixture evenly on bottom and 1½-inches up side of 10-inch springform pan. Bake at 350° for 10 minutes.

Cake:
Mix cottage cheese and eggs in blender at high speed until smooth. Beat cream cheese, flour, salt, sugar, vanilla, and cottage cheese mixture in large bowl until smooth. Gently fold in pineapple. Pour into crust. Bake at 350° for 1 hour 30 minutes. Turn oven off, with door ajar let cake cool in oven 1 hour.

Topping:
Mix sour cream, sugar, and vanilla together. Spread on cake. Bake at 350° for 10 minutes. Cool slightly and refrigerate. To serve, loosen crust with knife, then remove side of pan.

In 1912, a new jail was constructed in Brownsville on the corner of Twelfth and Van Buren streets. This building replaced the old structure behind the first Courthouse. Today, it houses private law offices.

🌴 *Pumpkin Cheesecake*

Yield: 16 servings

Crust:
- ½ cup graham cracker crumbs

Filling:
- 2 (8 ounce) packages fat-free cream cheese, softened
- 1 (14 ounce) can fat-free sweetened condensed milk
- 1 cup brown sugar
- 1 teaspoon ground cinnamon
- ½ teaspoon ground nutmeg
- 1 (8 ounce) carton egg substitute
- 1 (16 ounce) can pumpkin
- ⅓ cup unsifted flour
  Lite whipped topping

Crust:
Spray bottom of springform pan with cooking spray. Spread cracker crumbs evenly on bottom and sides, set aside.

Cake:
Using an electric mixer, beat cream cheese, slowly add milk. Beat until smooth. Add sugar, spices, egg substitute, and pumpkin. Mix until smooth. Add flour a little at a time, slowly mixing until smooth. Pour mixture into pan. Bake at 325° for 55 to 60 minutes until set. Cook on rack, remove side of pan and refrigerate. Top with whipped topping just prior to serving.

Chocolate Hazelnut Cake

Yield: 12 servings

Filling:
- ½ cup heavy cream
- 1 tablespoon light corn syrup
- 8 ounces imported milk chocolate, chopped
- ½ cup hazelnuts, toasted and husked
- 2 teaspoons powdered sugar

Cake:
- 1 cup all-purpose flour
- ⅓ cup unsweetened cocoa powder
- ½ teaspoon salt
- ¼ teaspoon baking powder
- ¼ teaspoon baking soda
- 1½ tablespoons hot water
- 1 tablespoon instant coffee powder or instant espresso
- ½ cup buttermilk
- 1½ sticks unsalted butter, at room temperature
- 1⅓ cups sugar
- 1 teaspoon vanilla extract
- 3 large eggs

Glaze:
- 6 ounces bittersweet chocolate, chopped
- 1 stick unsalted butter, cut into pieces
- 1 tablespoon light corn syrup
- 12 whole hazelnuts (optional)

Filling:
In a heavy saucepan, bring cream and corn syrup to simmer. Place chocolate in a medium bowl; pour hot cream mixture over chocolate and let stand 1 minute. Stir until chocolate melts and mixture is smooth. Set aside. Blend hazelnuts and powdered sugar in processor until paste forms, stopping to scrape down sides. Stir paste into chocolate mixture. Chill until cool but still spreadable, about 2 hours.

Cake:
Butter a 9-inch cake pan with 2-inch sides; line bottom with parchment paper. Dust pan with flour; tap out excess. Sift flour and next 4 ingredients into medium bowl. Stir hot water and coffee powder together in small bowl until powder dissolves; mix in buttermilk. Using an electric mixer, beat butter in a large bowl until light and fluffy; gradually beat in sugar and vanilla. Add eggs 1 at a time, beating well after each addition. Beat in dry ingredients alternately with buttermilk mixture in small portions until all is incorporated into batter. Pour batter into prepared pan. Bake at 350° for 45 minutes or until tester inserted in center comes out

clean. Cool cake, in pan, on rack 5 minutes. Turn out cake onto rack. Peel off paper. Turn right side up onto another rack and cool. Using a wooden spoon, beat filling until slightly softened and lightened in color, about 30 seconds. Cut cake horizontally in half. Place one layer, cut side up on platter; spread with half of filling. Top with second layer, cut side down. Spread remaining filling over top and sides of cake. Chill 10 minutes.

Glaze:
Combine all ingredients in top of a double boiler over simmering water. Stir until smooth. Remove from heat; cool to lukewarm, stirring occasionally. Pour glaze in pool over center of cake. Using icing spatula, spread over top and sides of cake. Arrange 12 hazelnuts around top edge (optional).

Pumpkin Roll Cake

Yield: 8 to 10 servings

Cake:
- 3 eggs
- 1 cup sugar
- ⅔ cup pumpkin filling
- 1 teaspoon lemon juice
- ¾ cup flour
- 1 teaspoon baking powder
- 2 teaspoons cinnamon
- 1 teaspoon ginger
- ½ teaspoon nutmeg
- ½ teaspoon salt
- 1 cup chopped pecans or walnuts
  Powdered sugar

Filling:
- 1 cup powdered sugar
- 6 ounces cream cheese
- 4 tablespoons butter or margarine
- ½ teaspoon vanilla extract

Cake:
Beat eggs with an electric mixer about 5 minutes. Add sugar; stir in pumpkin and lemon juice. Combine dry ingredients together and fold into egg mixture. Spread in greased and floured 15x10x1-inch pan; top with nuts. Bake at 375° for 15 minutes. Turn cake out onto a kitchen towel sprinkled with powdered sugar. Roll towel and cake together. Cool, unroll.

Filling:
Blend ingredients until spreading consistency. Spread over cake. Roll again without towel, chill.

Buttermilk Chocolate Sheet Cake

Yield: 16 servings

Cake:

2	cups sugar
2	cups flour
1	teaspoon baking soda
1	teaspoon ground cinnamon
1	cup water
1	stick margarine
½	cup vegetable oil
4	tablespoons cocoa
½	cup buttermilk
2	eggs, slightly beaten
1	teaspoon vanilla extract

Icing:

1	stick margarine
4	tablespoons cocoa
6	tablespoons milk
1	(1 pound) box powdered sugar
1	teaspoon vanilla extract
1	cup chopped pecans

Cake:
Sift together sugar, flour, soda, and cinnamon, set aside. In a saucepan, add water, margarine, oil, and cocoa; bring to a boil. Pour over dry ingredients, mixing well. Set aside. Mix together buttermilk, eggs, and vanilla; add to chocolate batter. Pour batter into a greased and floured 13x9x2-inch baking pan. Bake at 400° for 20 to 30 minutes. Start chocolate icing about 5 minutes before cake is done and frost in pan.

Icing:
Place margarine, cocoa, and milk in saucepan. Bring to a boil, being careful not to let it scorch. Add powdered sugar, vanilla, and pecans, mix well. Spread on hot cake.

Meltaways

Yield: 3 dozen

2	sticks margarine
3	cups powdered sugar
1½	cups peanut butter
⅔	stick paraffin
1	bar German chocolate

Mix margarine, powdered sugar, and peanut butter. Roll into balls. Refrigerate. Melt paraffin and German chocolate in double boiler. Dip each ball in paraffin-chocolate mixture; place on wax paper. Refrigerate.

Chocolate Sheet Cake

Yield: 24 servings

Cake:
- 2 sticks butter or margarine
- ¼ cup unsweetened cocoa powder
- 1 cup water
- 2 cups flour
- 1½ cups packed brown sugar
- ½ teaspoon baking soda
- 1 teaspoon cinnamon
- ½ teaspoon salt
- 2 eggs
- 1 teaspoon vanilla
- 1 (14 ounce) can sweetened condensed milk

Icing:
- ½ stick butter or margarine
- ¼ cup unsweetened cocoa powder
- 1 cup powdered sugar
- 1 cup chopped nuts

Cake:
In a small saucepan, melt butter or margarine; stir in cocoa and water. Bring to a boil, remove from heat. In a large mixing bowl, combine flour, brown sugar, baking soda, cinnamon, and salt. Add cocoa mixture, beat well. Stir in eggs, vanilla, and ⅓ cup condensed milk. Pour into a greased 15x10-inch jelly-roll pan. Bake at 350° for 15 minutes or until cake springs back when lightly touched.
Icing:
In a small saucepan, melt butter or margarine. Stir in cocoa powder and remaining condensed milk. Add powdered sugar and nuts, stir until thoroughly mixed. Spread on warm cake.

🌴 Wonderously Lowfat Vanilla Sauce

Yield: 1½ cups

- ½ cup sugar
- 1 tablespoon cornstarch
- 1 cup boiling water
- 2 tablespoons low fat unsalted margarine
- 1 teaspoon (generous) pure vanilla extract
- Pinch of salt

Combine sugar and cornstarch, gradually stir in boiling water, stirring for 5 minutes on low heat. Remove from heat; add margarine, vanilla, and salt. Serve over angel food cake, or fresh fruit. Especially good over bananas and berries.

Beneath the Palms

Never Fail Pie Crust

Yield: Three 9-inch pie crusts

1¼ **cups shortening**
3 **cups sifted flour**
1 **tablespoon salt**
1 **egg, well beaten**
5 **tablespoons water**
1 **tablespoon vinegar**

Cut shortening into flour and add salt. Combine egg, water, and vinegar. Pour liquid into flour mixture all at once. Blend with a spoon just until flour is moistened. Divide dough into three balls. Roll pastry to ⅛-inch thickness on a lightly floured surface. Place in a 9-inch pie pan; trim excess pastry along edges. Fold under edges and flute.

This is an easy crust to handle and can be re-rolled without toughening. Can be refrigerated up to 2 weeks.

Toffee Brittle

Yield: 24 servings

1 **stick butter**
Chopped nuts
1 **(12 ounce) bag milk chocolate chips**
¾ **cup packed brown sugar**

Grease, with butter, a 9x9-inch glass baking dish. Evenly sprinkle nuts in bottom. Combine remaining butter and brown sugar in a heavy pan, heat to boiling. When it reaches a boil, stir constantly for 7 minutes. Pour immediately into greased dish. Pour chocolate chips over toffee. Cover with a cookie sheet until chips are melted. With a spatula, spread softened chocolate. Cut into small squares. Refrigerate to harden. To serve, break into squares.

Southern Crunch Apple Pie

Yield: 2 pies

Pie:
- 1½ **cups sugar**
- ¼ **cup flour**
- 3 **cups sour cream**
- 2 **eggs, beaten**
- 1 **teaspoon vanilla extract**
  Pinch of salt
- 1 **pound Granny Smith apples, finely chopped**
- 2 **(9-inch) pie shells, unbaked**

Topping:
- ½ **pound brown sugar**
- ¾ **cup flour**
- 1½ **teaspoons cinnamon**
- 1 **stick butter**

Pie:
Mix sugar and flour, add sour cream, eggs, vanilla, and salt. Stir in apples. Divide evenly between pie shells. Bake at 400° for 30 minutes. Remove from oven.

Topping:
Mix ingredients together to resemble crumbs. Sprinkle over baked pies. Return to oven and bake 10 more minutes. Cool completely before serving.

This recipe has been in the family for generations. The ingredients have been converted from pounds and ounces into cups for easier baking.

Texas Pecan Pie

Yield: 6 to 8 servings

- ½ **stick butter**
- 1 **cup sugar**
- 3 **eggs**
- ½ **cup light corn syrup**
- ½ **cup sorghum molasses**
- 1 **teaspoon vanilla extract**
- 1 **cup pecan halves**
- 1 **(9-inch) pie crust, unbaked**

Cream butter and sugar; add eggs 1 at a time, beating well after each addition. Add syrups slowly while continuing to beat. Add vanilla and pecans, mix well. Pour into pie crust. Bake at 400° for 10 minutes; reduce heat to 350° and bake until tester inserted comes out clean.

The first public schools in Brownsville were housed in vacant store buildings. A permanent school house constructed adjacent to Washington Park was completed in 1891.

Cranberry-Apple Pie

Yield: 6 to 8 servings

- 1 (9-inch) double pie-crust, unbaked
- 4 cups peeled and sliced apples (Macintosh or Cortland)
- 2 cups fresh cranberries, rinsed well
- ¼ cup apple juice
- ¼ teaspoon lemon juice
- 4 tablespoons cornstarch
- 1½ cup sugar
- ⅛ teaspoon nutmeg
- ¾ teaspoon cinnamon
- ½ teaspoon apple pie spice
- 3 tablespoons butter

Line a 9-inch pie pan with half the crust. Mix apples and cranberries, put half the fruit in bottom of pie pan. Mix water, apple juice, and lemon juice. Drizzle half over fruit. Mix cornstarch, sugar, nutmeg, cinnamon, and apple pie spice. Sprinkle half of this mixture over fruit. Repeat layers of mixed fruit, liquid, and dry ingredients. Cube butter and distribute across top. Put top crust in place, crimp edges. Use a fork or knife tip to make multiple punctures in top to allow steam to escape. Bake at 425° for 10 minutes; lower heat to 350° and bake 50 more minutes. Allow to cool before serving.

Lemon Chess Pie

Yield: 6 to 8 servings

- 2 cups sugar
- 1 tablespoon flour
- ¼ cup milk
- 4 eggs
- 1 tablespoon cornmeal
- ½ stick butter, melted and cooled
- Juice and zest of a lemon
- 1 (9-inch) pie shell, unbaked

Combine all ingredients in a blender. Pour into pie shell and bake at 325° for 45 minutes or until set.

Fresh Country Peach Pie

Yield: 6 to 8 servings

4   cups sliced fresh
    peaches
1   (9-inch) pie shell,
    unbaked
¾   cup sugar
5   tablespoons flour
¼   teaspoon salt
¼   teaspoon cinnamon
¼   teaspoon nutmeg
1   cup light cream
1   tablespoon brown sugar
¼   teaspoon cinnamon

Place peaches in pie shell. Mix sugar and next 4 ingredients together. Blend in cream; pour over peaches. Mix brown sugar and remaining cinnamon; sprinkle over top of pie. Bake at 400° for 50 to 60 minutes.

Poteet Strawberry Pie

Yield: 6 to 8 servings

3   tablespoons cream
1   (3 ounce) package
    cream cheese
1   (9-inch) pie crust, baked
    and chilled
2   pints fresh strawberries
1   cup plus 2 tablespoons
    sugar, divided
2   tablespoons cornstarch
    Frozen whipped topping
    (optional)

Mix cream and cream cheese until spreading consistency. Spread over bottom and up the sides of pie crust. Wash and stem strawberries, pat very dry with paper towels. Line bottom and sides of crust with half of the strawberries (if berries are large, slice in half and turn cut sides up). Sprinkle 2 tablespoons sugar over berries and refrigerate. Crush remaining strawberries. In sauce pan, mix strawberries, remaining sugar, and cornstarch. Cook over low heat until liquid is clear and very thick, about 5 to 7 minutes. Chill mixture. Pour mixture over prepared crust and refrigerate at least 4 hours. Before serving, top with whipped topping if desired.

Beneath the Palms

🌴 Pink Lemonade Pie

6 ounces frozen pink
  lemonade, thawed
1 (14 ounce) can fat free
  sweetened condensed
  milk
8 ounces nondairy
  whipped topping
  Red food coloring
  (optional)
1 (9-inch) fat free vanilla
  wafer pie crust

In a large bowl, combine lemonade and milk; stir well. Fold in whipped topping, stir until smooth. Add food coloring if desired. Pour into pie crust and refrigerate until set, 1 to 2 hours.

Mexican Lime Pie

4 eggs yolks
1 (14 ounce) can
  sweetened condensed
  milk
½ cup fresh Mexican lime
  juice
3 teaspoons lime zest,
  grated
  Few drops green food
  coloring (optional)
1 (9-inch) pie shell, baked
3 egg whites
½ teaspoon cream of tartar
½ cup sugar

Beat egg yolks; stir in milk, lime juice, zest, and food coloring, if desired. Beat 1 egg white until stiff, fold into milk mixture. Turn into cooled pie shell. Beat reserved egg whites with cream of tartar until foamy; gradually add sugar, beating until stiff but not dry. Spread meringue over filling, sealing edges. Bake at 350° for 15 minutes or until golden. Chill before serving.

Sweet Potato Pie

Yield: 2 pies

4   **medium sweet potatoes, peeled and quartered**
4   **tablespoons butter, softened**
¾   **cup brown sugar**
3   **eggs, lightly beaten**
⅓   **cup white corn syrup**
⅓   **cup milk**
2   **teaspoons lemon zest, finely grated**
1   **teaspoon vanilla extract**
½   **teaspoon nutmeg**
½   **teaspoon salt**
2   **(9-inch) pie shells, unbaked**

Boil potatoes, uncovered, until tender; drain, return to heat. Shake pan to dry potatoes completely. Put through sieve; set aside to cool to room temperature. In large bowl, cream butter and brown sugar together. Add cooled potatoes; beat until blended. Add eggs, one at a time, beating well after each addition. Add syrup, milk, lemon zest, vanilla extract, nutmeg, and salt. Continue beating until smooth. Divide and pour into pie shells and bake at 450° for 10 minutes; reduce heat to 325° and bake 35 minutes. Put collar of aluminum foil around crust if it begins to brown too much.

Chocolate Chess Pie

Yield: 6 to 8 servings

2   **eggs**
1½   **cups sugar**
½   **stick butter, melted and cooled**
3   **tablespoons cocoa**
1   **(6 ounce) can evaporated milk**
     Pinch of salt
¾   **teaspoon vanilla or almond extract**
1   **(9-inch) pie shell, unbaked**

Mix all ingredients in a blender and pour into pie shell. Bake at 325° for 45 minutes or until set.

Tropical Fruit Glazed Cheesecake Tart

Yield: 6 to 8 servings

Pastry for single crust pie
1 envelope unflavored gelatin, divided
5 tablespoons sugar, divided
1½ cups boiling water, divided
3 tablespoons brandy, divided
1 (8 ounce) package cream cheese, softened
1 teaspoon orange zest
Sliced fresh fruit

Crust:
Between two sheets of wax paper, roll pastry into an 11-inch circle. Turn into a 9-inch tart pan. Bake at 425° for 10 minutes or until light brown.

Glaze:
In a small bowl, mix 1 teaspoon gelatin with 1 tablespoon sugar and ¾ cup boiling water. Stir until dissolved. Set aside 1 tablespoon liquid and chill the rest.

Filling:
Mix remaining gelatin with remaining sugar. Add ¾ cup boiling water and stir until dissolved. With an electric mixer, beat in cream cheese, reserved liquid, and zest until smooth. Turn into prepared crust. Chill until partially set. Arrange fresh fruit on top of tart and brush with glaze.

Lemon Curd Tartlets

Yield: 16 servings

Dough:
- 2 sticks butter or margarine
- ½ cup powdered sugar
- 1 teaspoon vanilla extract
- 2 cups all-purpose flour
- ½ cup finely chopped blanched almonds
- Pinch of salt

Lemon Curd:
- 5 tablespoons unsalted butter
- 3 eggs
- 1 cup sugar
- Juice and finely grated zest of 2 lemons

Dough:
Cream butter and powdered sugar. Add vanilla and beat well. Mix flour, almonds, and salt until evenly distributed. Divide in half and wrap each half in foil; chill at least 1 hour. Working with half of the dough at a time, roll out to ⅛-inch thickness. Fit into 1½-inch tartlet pans or mini-muffin tins. Bake at 325° for 25 minutes or until pale gold. Cool completely.

Lemon Curd:
Melt butter in top of a double boiler, over barely simmering water. Whisk in eggs; add sugar and whisk until thoroughly combined. Add lemon juice and zest gradually while whisking constantly. Cook over simmering water until thickened while continuing to whisk. Cool to room temperature then spoon into shells. Makes 2 cups.

The first International Bridge across the Rio Grande River connecting Brownsville to Matamoros was built and placed into service in 1909. It accommodated both vehicular and rail traffic. The structure continues in service today.

Beneath the Palms

Pecan Tarts

Yield: 24 tarts

Crust:
- 1 stick butter or margarine
- 3 ounces cream cheese, softened
- 1 cup flour

Filling:
- 2 eggs, lightly beaten
- 2 tablespoons butter or margarine
- 1½ cups brown sugar
- 2 tablespoons vanilla extract
- 2 tablespoons rum or bourbon
- 1½ cups chopped pecans
- Dash of salt

Crust:
Mix butter, cream cheese, and flour together; wrap in plastic wrap and chill in refrigerator for one hour. Press dough into small fluted tart cups.

Filling:
Mix together ingredients. Fill dough-lined cups half full. Bake at 325° for 30 minutes. Remove tarts from pan and serve warm or chilled.

Island Fudge Pie

Yield: 6 to 8 servings

- ½ stick butter
- ¾ cup packed brown sugar
- 3 eggs
- 12 ounces semisweet chocolate chips, melted
- 2 teaspoons coffee
- 1 teaspoon rum extract
- 1 teaspoon vanilla extract
- 1 teaspoon water
- ¼ cup flour
- 1 cup walnut pieces
- 1 (9-inch) pie shell, unbaked
- Walnut halves

Cream together butter and sugar. Add eggs, 1 at a time, beating until well blended. Add chocolate, coffee, extracts, and water. Stir in flour and walnut pieces. Pour into pie shell, top with walnut halves. Bake at 375° for 25 minutes. Cool before serving.

Viennese Almond Torte

Pastry:

2	cups flour
⅓	cup sugar
1	teaspoon orange zest
½	teaspoon salt
¾	cup cold butter, cut into pats
1	egg yolk
1	tablespoon rum

Filling:

1¼	cups whole blanched almonds
¼	cup sugar
1	egg white
¼	cup heavy cream
1	teaspoon almond extract
½	cup raspberry jam
1	egg beaten with 1 tablespoon water

Pastry:
In a mixing bowl, combine flour, sugar, zest, and salt. Cut in butter to resemble fine meal. Add egg yolk and rum. Toss lightly to mix. Press ¾ of dough into bottom and 1¼-inch up sides of 9-inch springform pan.

Filling:
Grind almonds in food processor. Combine in mixing bowl with sugar, egg white, cream, and almond extract. Beat until thick and smooth. Spread in pastry shell. Dot jam over almond mixture, gently spread to make an even layer. Roll out remaining dough on lightly floured surface to 9x5-inch rectangle. Cut with pastry wheel into 10 strips. Arrange strips lattice fashion on top of almond mixture. Brush egg mixture on top. Sprinkle lightly with additional sugar. Bake at 350° for 25 to 30 minutes or until edges are golden.

Rocky Road Brownies

Yield: 24 brownies

Brownies:
- 4 eggs
- 2 cups sugar
- 1½ cups flour
- 2 teaspoons vanilla
- 2 cups chopped pecans
- 2 sticks butter or margarine
- 10 tablespoons cocoa, heaping
- 1 (10 ounce) package miniature marshmallows

Topping:
- 3 ounces semi-sweet chocolate
- 1 stick butter or margarine
- 1 (pound) box powdered sugar
- 1 (5 ounce) can Evaporated milk

Brownies:
In a large mixing bowl, cream eggs, sugar, flour, vanilla, and pecans. In a small saucepan, melt butter and cocoa; cool to room temperature. Blend chocolate mixture into creamed mixture. Spread batter into a greased 9x13-inch baking pan. Bake at 350° for 20 minutes. Remove from oven and sprinkle marshmallow on top.

Topping:
In top of a double boiler over simmering water, melt chocolate, add butter, stirring until smooth. Add powdered sugar and milk. Beat with hand mixer until ingredients are well mixed. Frost brownies and refrigerate for 24 hours.

Trash

Yield: 12 cups

- 1 stick butter
- 12 ounces semi-sweet chocolate chips
- 1 cup peanut butter
- 1 (12 ounce) box bite-size crispy-rice cereal squares
- 1 (1 pound) box powdered sugar

In microwave, melt butter, chips, and peanut butter together. Pour cereal squares in large bowl, fold in chocolate mixture. Pour ½ box of powdered sugar in medium trashbag. Pour in cereal mix and remaining sugar. Roll from hand to hand until coated.

Chocolate Praline
Mud Squares

Yield: 18 to 20 servings

Crust:
- ¾ cup graham cracker crumbs
- ¾ cup finely chopped pecans
- ¼ cup brown sugar, packed
- ½ stick butter, melted

Topping:
- 12 ounces caramel topping
- 3 tablespoons all-purpose flour

Filling:
- 2 sticks butter
- 4 ounces unsweetened chocolate
- 1½ cups sugar
- 1 cup all-purpose flour
- 4 eggs, beaten
- 1 teaspoon vanilla

Frosting:
- 1 tablespoon butter
- 3 tablespoons cocoa
- 3 tablespoons water
- 1 cup powdered sugar
- ¼ teaspoon vanilla
  Candied cherries
  Pecan halves

Crust:
Combine all ingredients, stirring well. Press crumb mixture into bottom of a greased 9-inch square pan. Bake at 350° for 6 to 8 minutes. Cool slightly.

Topping:
Combine caramel topping and 3 tablespoons flour, stirring well. Spread topping on crust to within one-fourth inch of edge. Set aside.

Filling:
Combine butter and chocolate in a heavy saucepan; cook over low heat until melted. Stir in sugar and next 3 ingredients. Pour mixture over reserved caramel topping in pan. Bake at 350° for 50 minutes. Cool slightly and spread with frosting.

Frosting:
Combine butter, cocoa and water in small saucepan; cook over medium heat until thickened. Remove from heat and stir in powdered sugar and vanilla. Garnish with candied cherries and pecan halves.

Beneath the Palms

Tea Time Cookies

Yield: 48 cookies

1 cup shortening
1½ cups firmly packed
    brown sugar
3 eggs
2½ cups flour
1 teaspoon baking soda
1 teaspoon cinnamon
1 cup raisins, washed in
    warm water
½ cup pecans
1 teaspoon vanilla

In a large bowl, cream shortening and sugar. Add in eggs, beat well. Sift together flour, soda, and cinnamon, gradually add to the creamed mixture. Stir in raisins, nuts, and vanilla. Drop onto greased cookie sheet by rounded tablespoons. Bake at 375° for 10 to 12 minutes.

Great with coffee or tea.

Cloud Cookies

Yield: 24 cookies

Flour for dusting
3 egg whites
⅛ teaspoon cream of tartar
1 cup sugar
3 tablespoons
    unsweetened cocoa
    powder
½ cup mint flavored
    chocolate chips
⅓ cup chopped walnuts

Line 2 cookie sheets with foil, spray evenly with nonstick spray, dust lightly with flour. In a large bowl, beat egg whites until foamy, add cream of tartar and beat until soft peaks form. Mix in sugar slowly, about 1 tablespoon at a time. Sift cocoa over mixture. With a rubber spatula, fold in chocolate chips and walnuts. Drop by teaspoonfuls onto cookie sheets and bake at 250° for 25 to 30 minutes. Remove from cookie sheet and place on wire rack to cool completely.

Chocolate Mint Snaps

Yield: 40 cookies

4 ounces unsweetened chocolate squares
1¼ cups shortening
2 cups sugar
2 eggs
⅓ cup corn syrup
1½ tablespoons water
2 teaspoons peppermint extract
1 teaspoon vanilla extract
4 cups all-purpose flour
2 teaspoons baking soda
½ teaspoon salt
½ cup sugar (plus 2 tablespoons)

In top of double boiler, melt chocolate over hot water. In a large bowl, cream shortening and sugar, beating until light and fluffy. Add melted chocolate, eggs, corn syrup, water, and extracts, mix well. Combine flour, soda, and salt, add to creamed mixture, beating just until blended. Shape dough into 1-inch balls and roll in remaining sugar. Place on ungreased cookie sheet. Bake at 350° for 10 minutes. Cool on cookie sheet 5 minutes. Remove to wire rack and cool completely.

Cavalry Cookies

Yield: 48 cookies

¾ cup shortening
1 cup sugar
1 egg
¼ cup molasses
2 cups all-purpose flour
2 teaspoons baking soda
1 teaspoon cinnamon
½ teaspoon salt
½ teaspoon ginger
½ teaspoon ground cloves
Sugar

In a large bowl, cream shortening and sugar, beat until light and fluffy; add egg and molasses. In a medium bowl, combine flour and next 5 ingredients; gradually blend into creamed mixture. Stir until smooth after each addition. Chill 1 hour. Roll dough into 1-inch balls; roll in sugar. Place 2 inches apart on ungreased cookie sheet; bake at 375° for 10 minutes. Tops will crack when done.

Beneath the Palms

Créme Brûleé

Yield: 15 servings

4 **cups heavy cream**
2 **teaspoons vanilla**
   extract
9 **egg yolks**
1 **cup plus 2 tablespoons**
   granulated sugar
⅛ **teaspoon salt**
¼ **cup plus 2 tablespoons**
   firmly packed light
   brown sugar

In a heavy saucepan, heat cream over moderate heat until it is hot, but not scalded; add vanilla. In a large bowl with an electric mixer, beat together egg yolks and granulated sugar until the mixture is thick and pale. Beat in cream mixture and salt; beat until combined. Divide custard among fifteen ¾-cup ramekins, set them in a baking pan. Add enough hot water to reach halfway up the sides of the ramekins. Bake at 325° for 40 minutes, or until a knife inserted in center comes out clean. Remove ramekins from pan and let custard cool on a rack. Force brown sugar through a sieve evenly over custards. Set custards on a baking sheet, put baking sheet under a preheated broiler, about 6-inches from the heat, for 1 to 2 minutes, or until sugar is melted and browned. Chill for 1 hour prior to serving.

The first newspaper to serve the Brownsville area was the "American Flag" published by James Barnard. The newspaper office was in Matamoros, later moving to Brownsville.

Tirami Su

3 eggs, separated
½ cup sugar
½ pound mascarpone
   cheese
2 tablespoons rum
3 ounces sweet cooking
   chocolate
3 ounces ladyfinger
   cookies
⅓ cup triple strength
   espresso

Chocolate Leaves:
12 mint or lemon leaves
   Salad oil
1 tablespoon butter or
   margarine
3 ounces sweet cooking
   chocolate
1 tablespoon light corn
   syrup
½ cup heavy whipping
   cream
¼ teaspoon vanilla extract
   Fresh or candied violets

In a large bowl, combine egg yolks and sugar with a wire whisk until lightened, about 2 minutes. Mix in mascarpone; blend in rum. In a large electric mixer bowl, beat egg whites until stiff but not dry. With a rubber spatula, gently fold egg whites into cheese mixture one third at a time. Cover bowl and refrigerate. On coarse side of metal grater or vegetable peeler shred one bar (3 ounces) of chocolate onto waxed paper. Split ladyfingers, place on cookie sheet. Brush all sides with coffee. Arrange half of ladyfingers over bottom of a 1½-quart dish. Spread half of cheese mixture over ladyfingers and sprinkle with half of shredded chocolate. Repeat, making another layer each of split ladyfingers, cheese mixture, and shredded chocolate. Cover and chill one hour or overnight.

Chocolate Leaves:
Wash leaves, dry with paper towels. Brush with salad oil. In a small saucepan, combine butter, chocolate and corn syrup, heat over medium low heat stirring until melted. Brush thick layer of chocolate mixture on back of each leaf, place on waxed paper and chill until firm. When ready to serve, peel leaves from chocolate and set aside. Fit a pastry bag with a star tip. In the small bowl of an electric mixer, beat cream with vanilla extract until thick, spoon into pastry bag and pipe around edge of dish. Garnish with chocolate leaves, violets or fresh mint leaves.

For mascarpone cheese, substitute 1 cup ricotta cheese combined with ⅓ cup heavy cream in a food processor until smooth and thickened.

🌴 Strawberry Tirami Su Torte

Yield: 12 servings

1 pint fresh strawberries
1 (8 ounce) package fat free cream cheese
1 cup fat free sour cream
1 cup lowfat vanilla yogurt
¾ cup powdered sugar, divided
1 teaspoon vanilla extract
½ cup brewed or instant espresso coffee
½ teaspoon almond extract
2 tablespoons unsweetened Dutch processed cocoa
1 10-inch angel food cake

Clean and slice strawberries; set aside. In a medium bowl, mix cream cheese, sour cream, and yogurt. Beat until light and fluffy. Stir in ½ cup powdered sugar and vanilla. In a cup, mix together espresso and almond extract; set aside. Slice angel food cake crosswise into 3 layers. Sift 1 tablespoon cocoa onto a 14-inch cake plate. Place bottom layer of cake over cocoa. Drizzle one-third of espresso mixture over cake. Cover layer with half the sliced strawberries. Top with second layer of cake; drizzle one-third espresso mixture over cake; cover with remaining strawberries and cream cheese mixture. Add top layer, drizzle remaining espresso over cake. Sift ¼ cup powdered sugar over top of cake. Sift 1 tablespoon cocoa over sugar. Cover and chill until ready to serve. Use remaining strawberries for garnish.

May be prepared up to 12 hours in advance.

🌴 *Mango Mousse*

Yield: 4 servings

2 **ripe mangoes, peeled and coarsely chopped**
½ **cup low fat yogurt**
1 **small banana**
3 **drops vanilla extract**
3 **ice cubes**
4 **sprigs fresh mint**
4 **slices kiwi fruit**

Place mangoes in a blender with yogurt, bananas, vanilla extract, and ice. Process on low, then medium speed until smooth. Remove ice that remains. Pour mixture into sherbet dishes and garnish with mint and kiwi. Serve at once.

Chocolate Mousse

Yield: 4 servings

6 **ounces semi-sweet chocolate chips**
1 **egg**
2 **egg yolks**
2 **egg whites**
1 **cup whipping cream**
1 **tablespoon rum (optional)**

Melt chocolate chips. Remove from stove and beat in whole egg and egg yolks one at a time. Beat egg whites until stiff. Whip cream until it forms a stiff peak. Fold cream and chocolate mixture into egg whites. Fold in rum, if desired. Fill 6 small stemmed glasses or leave in a decorative serving bowl. Chill 8 hours or overnight.

Mango Sorbet

Yield: 5 cups

1 **large ripe mango, peeled, pitted, cut into ¼- inch cubes**
1 **(15 ounce) can cream of coconut**
1 **cup water**
6 **tablespoons fresh·lime juice**

Combine mango and cream of coconut in blender; purée until smooth. Add water and lime juice; blend until combined. Refrigerate until cold, about 1 hour. Freeze in ice-cream maker according to manufacturer's instructions.

Bread Pudding with Hard Sauce

Yield: 12 servings

Pudding:
- 2 **tablespoons butter, melted**
- 8 **slices toasted French bread, cut thickly**
- 2 **cups milk**
- 2 **eggs**
- 1½ **cups granulated sugar**
- 5 **ounces raisins**
- 2 **tablespoons vanilla extract**
- 1 **tablespoon ground cinnamon**
- 1 **cup applesauce or crushed pineapple, undrained**
- 2 **tablespoons butter, melted**

Sauce:
- ⅔ **cup sugar**
- 2 **teaspoons cornstarch**
- ¼ **teaspoon fresh nutmeg**
  Pinch of salt
- 1 **cup boiling water**
- 2 **tablespoons orange zest**
- 3 **tablespoons brandy**

Pudding:
Grease a 13x9-inch pan with melted butter. Lay toasted bread slices in bottom of pan. Mix all other ingredients well and pour over bread slices. Let sit for 30 minutes to absorb liquid. Bake at 350° for 30 minutes, or until top is brown. Remove from oven; poke holes in top.

Sauce:
Mix sugar, cornstarch, nutmeg and salt in small saucepan. Pour boiling water into pan and stir. Add zest and gently boil over medium heat 10 to 12 minutes; do not overcook. Remove from heat, add brandy. Cover and set aside until ready to use. If needed, reheat on low temperature, careful not to boil.

🌴 Strawberry Glazed Melon Balls

Yield: 6 servings

1 **cup fresh strawberries**
½ **cup water**
3 **tablespoons sugar**
1 **tablespoon cornstarch**
1 **tablespoon lemon juice**
3 **cups cantaloupe or honeydew melon balls**
Fresh mint leaves

In a saucepan, crush strawberries, add water, and bring to a boil. Reduce heat, cover and simmer for 5 minutes. Remove from heat and press through a sieve. Return berries purée to saucepan. Combine sugar and cornstarch, stir into berries. Cook and stir until mixture thickens, and is bubbly. Cook and stir 2 minutes more. Stir in lemon juice. Remove from heat, cover surface with waxed paper and cool 45 minutes. Spoon melon balls into six serving dishes. Drizzle strawberry mixture over melon. Chill. Garnish with fresh mint leaves.

No fat and delicious.

Italian Cream Dessert

Yield: 4 to 6 servings

2 **(8 ounce) packages cream cheese, softened**
½ **cup sugar**
4 **egg yolks, beaten**
1 **cup plus 2 tablespoons heavy cream**
2 **tablespoons cognac**
4-6 **fresh strawberries**

Combine cream cheese, sugar and egg yolk in blender. Add 2 tablespoons heavy cream and cognac. Blend until smooth. Let set 15 minutes before serving. Pour into champagne glasses. Whip remaining cream. Garnish with a dollop of whipped cream and a strawberry.

Other liqueurs, such as Grand Marnier, can be substituted for cognac.

Beneath the Palms

Fresh Yogurt

Yield: 2 cups

½ **gallon milk (any type)**
1 **tablespoon plain yogurt**

Heat milk to 180°, cool to 110°. Remove ½ cup of heated milk, add yogurt and stir. Return to heated milk. Cover pan with towel, place in warm place for 6 hours. Strain through muslin cloth to remove whey.

Rice Pudding

Yield: 6 servings

1 **quart milk**
⅓ **cup uncooked rice**
½ **cup sugar**
⅓ **cup seedless raisins**
Dash of salt
1 **egg**
1 **teaspoon vanilla extract**
Cinnamon

Combine milk, rice, sugar, raisins and salt in saucepan. Bring just to a boil (be careful, milk will scorch). Stir mixture and pour into 2-quart casserole dish. Bake uncovered at 350° for 1 hour. Meanwhile, beat together egg and vanilla extract in large bowl. Remove casserole from oven; remove milk crust from top. Beat egg mixture vigorously with a fork; ladle in the milk-rice mixture, one ladle at a time (this prevents the hot mixture from cooking the egg). After incorporating about 6 ladles this way, pour in rest of the milk-rice mixture, stirring constantly. Sprinkle cinnamon on top and refrigerate until completely cold.

Frozen Fruit Mousse

Yield: 8 servings

- 1 (8 ounce) package cream cheese
- ¾ cup sugar
- 1 (14 ounce) can pineapple tidbits, drained
- 10 ounces frozen strawberries
- 2 bananas, sliced
- ½ cup chopped nuts
- 1 (17 ½ ounce) package frozen whipped topping

Beat cream cheese and sugar. In a separate bowl, combine pineapple, strawberries, bananas, nuts, and whipped topping. Fold fruit and cheese mixture together. Freeze in greased bundt pan. Unmold in hot water.

Frozen Lemon Delight

Yield: 16 servings

- 2 cups crushed vanilla wafers
- ½ stick butter, melted
- 6 egg yolks
- 1 (14 ounce) can sweetened condensed milk
- 1 (6 ounce) can frozen lemonade, thawed
- 1 pint whipping cream
- 6 egg whites
- ¾ cup sugar

Mix vanilla wafers and melted butter together. Press into a 9x13-inch pan. Refrigerate. In a large bowl, beat egg yolks, add condensed milk and lemonade concentrate. Whip cream and fold into egg mixture. Spread over crust and refrigerate. Beat egg whites until peaks form, add sugar. Spread over lemon layer. Bake at 400° just until peaks turn golden brown. Cover immediately and freeze. Serve frozen. Cut into squares to serve.

Keeps in freezer up to 1 month.

Pecos Cantaloupe Sorbet

Yield: 6 servings

- 1 **cup orange juice**
- ¼ **cup sugar**
- 2 **cups chopped cantaloupe, Texas Pecos preferred**
- ½ **cup light cream**
- 3 **tablespoons lemon juice**
- 2 **egg whites**
- ¼ **cup sugar**
  Cantaloupe halves, chilled (optional)

In a saucepan, combine orange juice and ¼ cup sugar; bring to boil, stirring occasionally to dissolve sugar. Reduce heat and simmer 5 minutes. In a blender, combine cantaloupe and cream. Cover and blend until smooth. Add lemon juice and cooled orange juice mixture. Transfer mixture to a 9x9x2-inch baking pan. Cover and freeze about 4 hours or until firm. Beat egg whites with electric mixture until soft peaks form. Gradually add ¼ cup sugar, beating until stiff peaks form. Remove frozen mixture from freezer, and break into chunks. Place in chilled mixing bowl. Beat frozen mixture with electric mixer until smooth but not melted. Fold in beaten egg whites, return to baking dish. Cover and freeze for several hours or until firm. Let sorbet stand at room temperature about 5 minutes prior to serving. Serve scoops of sorbet on chilled cantaloupe halves, if desired.

Honeydew, watermelon, and peaches may be substituted for fruit.

A Western Union line connecting Brownsville and Corpus Christi was the first telegraphic communication to the outside world on May 1, 1871.

Peach Ice Cream

Yield: 2 quarts

2 eggs
1¼ cups sugar
1 cup milk
½ teaspoon vanilla
⅛ teaspoon almond extract
5 large peaches, peeled
    and chopped
1 cup whipping cream

In large bowl, beat eggs until thick and lemon color, about 5 minutes. Beat in sugar. Stir in milk, vanilla and almond extract, set aside. Purée peaches in blender or food processor. Stir into egg mixture. Stir in whipping cream. Pour into ice cream canister; freeze according to manufacturer's directions.

Papaya Purée

Yield: 6 servings

2 cups cubed papaya
2 cups vanilla ice cream
3 ounces creme de cassis

Place papaya and ice cream into a blender. Blend until smooth. Spoon into serving bowls. Drizzle ½ ounce creme de cassis over each serving.

This is great as a palate cleanser between courses.

Buster Bar Dessert

Yield: 12 to 15 servings

1 (20 ounce) package
    chocolate sandwich
    cookies, crushed
½ cup butter, melted
½ gallon vanilla ice cream
1 (6 ounce) can chocolate
    fudge sauce
1 (8 ounce) jar dry roasted
    peanuts
1 (8 ounce) container non
    dairy whipped topping

Crush cookies and add melted butter. Press mixture (reserve 1 cup) in bottom of 9x13-inch glass pan. Press softened ice cream over cookie mixture. Spread chocolate fudge sauce over ice cream and sprinkle with peanuts. Spread whipped topping over peanuts and top with reserved crumbs. Freeze for 2 hours or overnight prior to serving. Cut into 3-inch squares to serve.

Pumpkin Loaf Cake

Yield: 12 servings

Cake:
- 1 **stick butter or margarine**
- 1 **cup sugar**
- 1 **teaspoon vanilla**
- 2 **eggs**
- 1½ **cups unsifted flour**
- 1 **teaspoon baking soda**
- ½ **teaspoon salt**
- 1 **teaspoon cinnamon**
- ½ **teaspoon nutmeg**
- ¼ **teaspoon ginger**
- ¼ **teaspoon cloves**
- ¾ **cup pumpkin**
- ¾ **cup chocolate morsels**
- ½ **cup chopped walnuts or pecans**

Topping:
- ½ **cup powdered sugar**
- ⅛ **teaspoon cinnamon**
- ⅛ **teaspoon nutmeg**
  Cream or milk

Cake:
In a bowl, cream butter until light. Gradually add sugar and vanilla. Beat in eggs, one at a time. Sift together flour and next 6 ingredients; add to creamed mixture alternately with pumpkin. When batter is well mixed, add chocolate morsels and half the nuts. Transfer to greased and floured 9x5x3-inch loaf pan and scatter remaining nuts over top. Bake at 350° for one hour or until cake springs back when touched lightly in center. Remove from oven and allow cake to cool in pan for 15 minutes. Turn out on rack to complete cooling.

Topping:
Mix powdered sugar, cinnamon, and nutmeg; add enough cream or milk to make heavy syrup-like consistency. Drizzle over cooled cake.

Ladyfingers

Yield: 24 ladyfingers

- 6 **eggs**
- ¾ **cup sugar**
- 2 **tablespoons oil**
- 1 **tablespoon vanilla extract**
- ¼ **cup cocoa powder**
- ¾ **cup all-purpose flour**

In a double boiler, combine 6 eggs, ¾ cup sugar, oil, and vanilla extract. Whip over boiling water until hot. Remove from heat and beat until cool. Fold in cocoa and flour. Using a pastry bag, pipe 24 ladyfingers onto a baking sheet. Bake at 350° for 8 to 10 minutes.

Apple Nut Cake

Yield: 16 to 20 servings

- 3 **cups sifted cake flour**
- 1 **teaspoon baking soda**
- 1 **teaspoon baking powder**
- ½ **teaspoon salt**
- 1 **teaspoon cinnamon**
- ¾ **cup vegetable oil**
- 4 **cups apples (6 Delicious), finely chopped**
- 1 **teaspoon vanilla extract**
- 2 **eggs**
- 2 **cups sugar**
- 1 **cup finely chopped nuts**

In a large mixing bowl, sift together flour, baking soda, baking powder, salt, and cinnamon. Using an electric mixer, add in oil, apples, and vanilla; beat at medium speed for 2 minutes. In a separate bowl, beat eggs until light yellow; gradually add sugar; continue to beat until light and fluffy. Fold egg mixture into apple mixture, blending very well; stir in nuts. Pour into a lightly greased and floured 10-inch tube pan. Bake at 350° for 1 hour and 10 minutes or until a tester inserted in center comes out clean.

Southern Pralines

Yield: 2 dozen

- 1½ **cups firmly packed brown sugar**
- ⅔ **cup half and half**
- ⅛ **teaspoon salt**
- 2 **tablespoons butter**
- ½ **cup pecan halves**

Combine sugar, half and half, and salt in deep 3-quart casserole, mix well. Stir in butter. Microwave at high for 7 to 9 ½ minutes (or until soft ball stage of 235° is reached) stirring once. Stir in pecans, cool one minute. Beat by hand until creamy and thickened (about 3 minutes). Drop quickly by tablespoons onto waxed paper. Let stand until firm.

🌴 Cinnamon Bread Pudding (Sugar Free)

Yield: 8 servings

6 cups cubed French or Italian bread
2 cups skim milk
4 tablespoons butter or margarine
2 eggs, or egg substitute, beaten
3½ teaspoons sugar substitute
1½ teaspoons cinnamon
¼ teaspoon salt

Place bread cubes in a 1½-quart casserole dish. Heat milk and butter to a simmer, do not boil. Combine with eggs, sugar substitute, cinnamon, and salt. Pour over bread and mix lightly. Bake at 350° for 40 to 45 minutes.

Blonde Brownies

Yield: 24 brownies

2 cups all-purpose flour
¼ teaspoon baking soda
1 teaspoon baking powder
1 teaspoon salt
2 cups firmly packed brown sugar
⅔ cup shortening, melted
2 eggs, lightly beaten
2 teaspoons vanilla
1 cup chocolate chips
⅓ cup chopped nuts (optional)

Mix flour, soda, baking powder, and salt. In a large mixing bowl, cream sugar and shortening; blend in eggs and vanilla. Add flour mixture gradually, mix well. Spread into a 9x13-inch pan. Sprinkle with chips and nuts. Bake at 350° for 30 minutes. Cool. Cut into squares.

Chocolate Hazelnut Diamonds

Yield: 35 diamonds

3 cups hazelnuts, toasted, skinned, and chopped
1 cup flour
4 eggs pinch
  Pinch of salt
2 tablespoons dark rum
½ cup sugar
1 cup dark corn syrup
6 ounces bittersweet or semisweet chocolate
6 tablespoons butter

Combine hazelnuts with flour and set aside. In a medium bowl, whisk eggs, salt, and rum. In a saucepan, combine sugar and corn syrup. Stir well. Place over low heat and bring to a boil. Remove from heat; add chocolate and butter. Allow to stand 3 to 4 minutes. Whisk smooth. Whisk chocolate mixture into egg mixture. Stir in nuts and flour. Butter a 10x15-inch jelly-roll pan, and line the bottom with a piece of parchment or wax paper. Set oven rack in middle level. Pour batter into prepared pan and bake at 350° for about 35 minutes, until set and firm. Cool in pan on rack. Unmold and cut into 2-inch diamonds.

This freezes well!

Chocolate Truffles

Yield: 30 truffles

- 2 **cups milk chocolate chips**
- ¼ **cup sour cream**
- 2 **tablespoons almond or mint liqueur**
- ⅔ **cup finely chopped almonds**
- ⅔ **cup finely chopped pecans**
- ⅔ **cup cocoa powder**
- ⅔ **cup powdered sugar**

Melt chocolate over double boiler, stir until smooth. Remove from heat; blend in sour cream and liqueur. Chill until firm. Form into marble-size balls. Roll balls in one of the remaining ingredients. Keep refrigerated.

Recipe freezes well. Other liqueurs may be used.

Glazed Blueberries, Raspberries or Strawberries

Yield: 6 servings

Vanilla Sauce:
- 1 **cup milk**
- 3 **tablespoons sugar**
- ½ **teaspoon vanilla extract**
- 2 **teaspoons cornstarch**
- 2 **egg yolks**
- 3 **pints fresh berries, or a mixture**

Glaze:
- ½ **cup heavy cream**
- 1 **tablespoon almond liqueur (optional)**

Garnish:
- 3½ **ounces almond flakes Icing sugar, to dust**

In a saucepan, bring milk (reserve 3 tablespoons for later), sugar and vanilla to a boil. Mix cornstarch and egg yolks with reserved milk; whisk gradually into boiling milk. Remove pan from heat immediately; set aside. Divide berries into 6 dessert bowls. Whip cream to soft peaks and fold with almond liqueur (if used) into vanilla extract sauce; pour over berries. Place under broiler until lightly brown. Sprinkle with almonds and dust with icing sugar.

Mexican

🌴 *Refresco de Melon (Melon Cooler)*

Yield: 6 servings

1 **medium cantaloupe or honeydew**
2 **quarts water**
1 **cup sugar**
1 **cup diced watermelon**
   Mint springs or
   Maraschino cherries

Day ahead: Halve cantaloupe; remove seeds. Soak seeds in water overnight in the refrigerator.

Next day: Strain mixture, reserving water and discarding seeds. Cut cantaloupe into small pieces to make 2 cups. In glass bowl, combine 3 cups cantaloupe water and sugar. Microwave on high 5 minutes or until sugar dissolves; cool slightly. Using blender, process sweetened cantaloupe water, with cantaloupe, and watermelon pieces until pureed. Add mixture to remaining cantaloupe water; stir well. Serve over crushed ice in goblets. Garnish with mint or cherries.

Frozen treat can be made by pouring mixture into ice-cube trays. Freeze until slushy, add wooden sticks to each cube. Freeze until firm.

🌴 *Salsa*

Yield: 4 servings

¾ **cup diced husked tomatillos (about 8 medium)**
¼ **cup diced red bell pepper**
¼ **cup diced red onion**
3 **tablespoons tarragon**
2 **tablespoons orange juice**
2 **tablespoons fresh lime juice**
1 **tablespoon sugar**
½ **teaspoon minced seeded jalapeños**

Purée ¼ cup tomatillos in food processor and pour into medium bowl. Stir in remaining ingredients. Cover and refrigerate for at least thirty minutes.

🌴 *Three Tomato Salsa*

Yield: 6 servings

½ **cup diced red onion**
¼ **cup white wine vinegar Ice water**
8 **tomatillos, husks removed, rinsed, and diced ¼-inch**
1 **pint yellow cherry tomatoes, diced ¼-inch**
4 **Roma tomatoes, diced ¼-inch**
2 **serrano chilies, stemmed, seeded, and minced**
2 **teaspoons fresh lime juice**
   Salt and pepper to taste
1 **tablespoon minced fresh cilantro**

Soak onion covered in vinegar and ice water for 30 minutes. Drain and toss with tomatillos, tomatoes, and serranos. Season to taste with lime juice, salt, pepper, and cilantro. Refrigerate at least 1 hour prior to serving.

Beneath the Palms

🌴 Pickled Carrots and Jalapeños

Yield: 5 cups

- 2 **cups cider vinegar**
- ¼ **cup fresh lime juice**
- ¼ **cup olive oil**
- 1 **cup water**
- 1 **teaspoon dried marjoram**
- 1 **large bay leaf**
- ½ **tablespoon salt**
- 1 **teaspoon cracked black pepper**
- 5 **carrots, peeled, and cut into ¼-inch pieces**
- 15 **jalapeños**
- 1 **medium onion, cut into ¼-inch wedges**
- 6 **cloves garlic, halved**

Place vinegar and next 7 ingredients in large glass dish. Bring to boil over high heat. Add carrots, jalapeños, onion, and garlic. Bring to boil, reduce heat, and simmer until vegetables start to wilt, about 2 minutes. Remove from heat; cool completely, at least 45 minutes. Transfer cooled vegetables and liquid to a glass container, cover; refrigerate overnight before serving.

Will keep refrigerated up to 2 weeks.

Shrimp Ceviche

Yield: 24 servings

- 1 **pound bay scallops**
- ¾ **cup lime juice**
- 1 **pound shrimp, shelled and deveined**
- ½ **medium onion, chopped**
- 2 **tablespoons olive oil**
- ½ **bunch fresh cilantro, chopped**
- 2 **medium avocados, peeled, pitted, and chopped**
- 3 **medium tomatoes, chopped**
  Lime slices (optional)

Place uncooked scallops in a glass baking dish; cover with lime juice. Let stand 1 hour, covered. Stir in uncooked shrimp and next 3 ingredients. Refrigerated, covered, for 8 hours or overnight. Pour off lime juice; add tomatoes and avocados. Mix well. Spoon mixture into a serving dish. Place serving dish in a large bowl of crushed ice. Garnish with lime slices.

Huevos Rancheros (Ranch-Style Eggs)

Yield: 6 servings

2 tablespoons vegetable oil
6 (6-inch) corn tortillas
2 cloves garlic, minced
½ cup chopped onion
3 large tomatoes, peeled, cored, and chopped
1 (4 ounce) can green chilies, chopped
¼ teaspoon salt
1 tablespoon cooking oil
6 eggs
Salt and pepper to taste
1 tablespoon water
1 cup shredded Monterey Jack cheese

In small skillet, heat 2 tablespoons oil. Holding tortillas with tongs, dip one at a time in hot oil for 10 seconds or until limp. Line a 10x6x2-inch baking dish with tortillas, keep warm. In same skillet, cook garlic and onion until tender. Stir in tomatoes, chilies, and salt. Simmer, uncovered, for 10 minutes. Spoon mixture over tortillas. In large skillet, heat remaining oil. Carefully break eggs into skillet; sprinkle with salt and pepper. When whites are set and edges cooked, add water. Cover skillet and cook eggs to desired doneness. Carefully arrange cooked eggs over sauce in baking dish. Sprinkle with cheese.

Arroz con Queso (Rice with Cheese)

Yield: 6 servings

1 (4 ounce) can mild green chilies, drained
5 ounces shredded Monterey Jack cheese
3 cups cooked white rice
½ cup sour cream
1 cup corn
½ cup evaporated milk
½ teaspoon salt
½ teaspoon paprika

Mix all ingredients, except 4 tablespoons of cheese, pour into a buttered 1-quart casserole dish. Top with reserved cheese. Bake at 350° for 30 minutes.

Caldo Xochitl
(Chicken Stew)

Yield: 8 servings

1 (3 pound) chicken cut into pieces
5 cloves garlic, minced
3 chicken bouillon cubes
3 bay leaves, broken into pieces
1 tablespoon dried oregano
¼ teaspoon ground cloves
1 tablespoon ground cumin
1 teaspoon black pepper
1 tablespoon salt
1 medium zucchini, sliced
1 medium onion, sliced
2 ribs celery, chopped
3 carrots, chopped
1 bell pepper, chopped
1 (17 ounce) can garbanzo beans, drained
1 bunch green onions, chopped
½ bunch cilantro, chopped
2 tomatoes, chopped
2 fresh green chilies, chopped
2 avocados, peeled, pitted, and chopped

Day before: In large kettle, bring chicken and next 8 ingredients to a boil. Lower heat; simmer, covered, for one hour. Skim foam as it accumulates. Remove chicken from broth, cut meat from bones. Chill broth and chicken separately overnight. Next day: Bring broth to boil, add zucchini and next 5 ingredients. Simmer twenty minutes. Add chicken and continue cooking until chicken is heated through. Serve soup in bowls over white rice. On a separate plate arrange green onions, cilantro, tomatoes, green chilies, and avocados; let each diner garnish soup to taste.

Fresh hot tortillas and a salad make a complete meal.

Caldo (Beef Stew)

Yield: 6 to 8 servings

6   **cups water**
¾   **pound round steak,
     sirloin tip or stew meat,
     cubed**
½   **cup picante sauce**
3   **cloves garlic, crushed**
2   **beef bouillon cubes**
1   **teaspoon salt**
6   **small new potatoes,
     halved**
5   **carrots, cut into 1-inch
     pieces**
2   **medium onions, cut in
     large chunks**
3   **ears fresh or frozen
     corn, cut in thirds**
½   **small cabbage, sliced**
1   **bell pepper, cut in ¾-
     inch chunks**
1   **rib celery, cut in ½-inch
     pieces**
2   **tomatoes, cut in large
     chunks
     Hot cooked white rice
     Lemon wedges**

Combine water and next 5 ingredients in a Dutch oven. Bring to a boil; reduce heat. Cover and simmer 1 hour. Add potatoes, carrots, and onions; cover and simmer 15 minutes. Add remaining vegetables, except tomatoes; cover and simmer 10 minutes. Add tomatoes, heat through. To serve, ladle soup into bowls, top with a scoop of rice and a lemon wedge.

Electric lights and a city water system were inaugurated in Brownsville in 1908. Both were City owned and operated.

Sopa de Pollo
(Chicken Soup)

Yield: 8 servings

4 **chicken breasts**
1 **(15 ounce) can garbanzo beans**
4 **medium potatoes**
4 **quarts water**
½ **medium bell pepper, cut into strips**
⅓ **cup long-grain rice**
¾ **cup chopped celery**
3 **chicken bouillon cubes**
   Morton's Nature's Seasons Spices to taste
   Salt to taste
1 **(14 ounce) can whole, peeled tomatoes**
1 **(8 ounce) can tomato sauce**
½ **bunch cilantro, chopped (optional)**

Cut chicken into large pieces. Peel garbanzo beans. Cut potatoes lengthwise in half, then again into sixths. Place chicken and water in soup pot, boil for 30 minutes. Add rice and next 4 ingredients; cook for 20 minutes. In separate bowl, cut tomatoes into pieces. Add this mixture, tomato sauce, and cilantro to pot. Cover; continue to simmer for 5 minutes.
Enjoy the best chicken soup ever!!!

Mexican Relish

Yield: 2½ cups

1 **(4 ounce) can green chilies, chopped**
2 **(4 ¼ ounce) cans black olives, chopped**
2 **large tomatoes, chopped**
5 **green onions, including the tops, chopped**
3 **tablespoons olive oil**
½ **teaspoon garlic salt**
   Salt and pepper to taste

Combine all ingredients. Chill and serve with corn chips.

Tortilla Soup

- 1 tablespoon butter
- 2 tablespoons oil
- 1 large onion, thinly sliced
- 2 cloves garlic, minced
- 4 Poblano chilies, roasted, peeled, cut into thin strips
  or 1 (4 ounce) can mild green chilies
- 2 jalapeños, cut in thin strips
- 1 (14 ounce) can Italian plum tomatoes
- 1 (8 ounce) can tomato sauce
- 3½ cups chicken broth
- 1 teaspoon chili powder
- ¼ teaspoon oregano
- 1 teaspoon ground cumin
- 1 teaspoon salt
- ½ cup chopped cilantro or parsley
- 6 corn tortillas
  Oil
- 12 ounces shredded Monterey Jack cheese

Heat butter and 2 tablespoons oil in large saucepan, sauté onion and garlic. Add chilies and next 7 ingredients. Bring to boil, lower heat and simmer for 15 minutes. Add cilantro; simmer 5 minutes. Cut tortillas into strips and fry in oil until crisp; drain. To serve, place several tortilla strips in each bowl, ladle soup over strips. Top each bowl with handful of cheese. Place bowls on cookie sheet under broiler until cheese melts and is lightly browned.

As a variation, two cups of diced, cooked chicken can be added to this recipe.

Beneath the Palms

🌴 Black Bean Soup, Mexican Style

Yield: 6 to 8 servings

1 **pound black beans**
1 **quart water**
2 **cups chopped onion**
1 **cup chopped bell pepper**
2 **cups chopped celery**
2 **cloves garlic, minced**
3 **slices bacon**
1 **(14 ounce) can tomato sauce**
2 **teaspoons oregano**
2 **teaspoons cumin**
3 **teaspoons sugar**
4 **teaspoons chili powder**
1 **bay leaf**
   Salt and pepper to taste

Soak beans in water overnight. Rinse and put in heavy saucepan, cover with water and cook for 1 hour; covered. Add all other ingredients and cook covered for 3 hours.

🌴 Mushroom Quesadillas

Yield: 12 servings

8 **ounces sliced fresh mushrooms**
½ **medium onion, sliced thin**
1 **teaspoon minced garlic**
3 **tablespoons chopped fresh cilantro**
3 **(8-inch) whole wheat flour tortillas**
6 **tablespoons shredded low fat Monterey Jack or cheddar cheese**
   Salsa

Spray a large skillet with nonstick cooking spray, sauté mushrooms, onion, and garlic over medium heat until onion is tender, about 5 to 7 minutes. Stir in cilantro; remove from heat. Arrange one-third of mushroom mixture on half of one tortilla and sprinkle with two tablespoons of cheese. Fold the other half of tortilla over and place on a baking sheet. Bake at 350° for 5 minutes or until filling is hot and cheese melts. Cut each quesadilla into four wedges.

Serve warm with salsa.

Chili Blanco Especial (White Chili)

Yield: 6 servings

1 **pound dried northern beans**
5 ¼ **cups chicken broth**
2 **cloves garlic, minced**
1 **large white onion, minced**
1 **tablespoon white pepper**
1 **tablespoon dried oregano**
1 **teaspoon salt**
1 **tablespoon ground cumin**
½ **teaspoon ground cloves or 3 whole**
1 **(7 ounce) can diced mild green chilies**
5 **cups diced cooked chicken**
1¾ **cups chicken broth**
1 **tablespoon diced jalapeño (optional)**
8 **flour tortillas**

Soak beans in water overnight, drain. In a large crock pot, combine beans and next 8 ingredients. Simmer, covered, at least 5 hours; stirring occasionally. Add chilies, chicken, and remaining broth. Simmer an additional 10 minutes. Serve hot!!

Guacamole

Yield: 2 cups

3 **ripe avocados**
2 **tablespoons minced onion**
1 **teaspoon minced serrano chilies**
1 **tablespoon chopped cilantro leaves**
1½ **tablespoons fresh lime juice**
½ **teaspoon salt**

Cut avocados in half; remove pits. Scoop pulp into a bowl and add all other ingredients. Mash with a fork to make a smooth mixture. Use right away, or place avocado pits in mixture and cover with plastic wrap. Place plastic wrap on surface to seal out air. Remix prior to serving.

Beneath the Palms

Sopa de Calabazas (Squash)

Yield: 6 servings

3 strips bacon, fried and crumbled, reserve drippings
1 onion, sliced
1 pound zucchini squash or yellow squash, cut in 1-inch cubes
1 clove garlic, minced
1 fresh tomato, cored and cut into strips
½ cup evaporated milk
½ teaspoon salt
¼ teaspoon black pepper
Pinch of sugar
4 ounces grated Monterey Jack cheese

Sauté onion in drippings until onion is soft. Add squash, garlic, and tomato. Cook three to four minutes, stirring constantly, until squash is tender but firm. Add milk, salt, pepper, and sugar; toss to coat vegetables. Reduce heat to low, add cheese; stir until melted. Sprinkle bacon over top. Serve immediately.

Frijoles a la Charra (Peasant Beans)

Yield: 10 servings

½ cup dry pinto beans, rinsed and drained
12 cups hot water
½ pound bacon, fried and crumbled
2 jalapeño peppers, seeded and minced
¼ cup chopped cilantro
3 fresh tomatoes, chopped
1 bunch green onions, trimmed and chopped
3 teaspoons salt
½ cup beer
3 limes, cut into wedges

Place beans and hot water in large saucepan. Bring to boil, cover partially; simmer for three hours. Add hot water, as necessary, to keep beans covered. Add next 6 ingredients, cook for thirty minutes over low heat. Add beer and heat through. Serve in bowls and garnish with lime wedges.

Best if made ahead, refrigerated and then re-heated.

Carne Guisada (Meat Stew)

Yield: 6 servings

2 **pounds boneless beef chuck**
3 **tablespoons vegetable oil**
2 **cloves garlic, minced**
1 **onion, chopped**
1 **bell pepper or 2 poblano peppers, chopped**
2 **fresh tomatoes, peeled and chopped**
2 **tablespoons tomato paste**
½ **teaspoon salt**
2 **teaspoons chili powder**
1 **teaspoon cumin**
¼ **teaspoon black pepper**

Trim fat from beef, cut into 1-inch cubes and brown in oil over high heat. Stir in remaining ingredients. Cover; simmer until meat is tender and liquid becomes a thick, rich sauce.

Mexican Lasagna

Yield: 6 to 8 servings

1 **(.7 ounce) envelope chili mix**
1½ **pounds ground beef**
1 **tablespoon vegetable oil**
1 **(14 ½ ounce) can tomatoes, chopped**
1 **(15 ounce) can ranch-style pinto beans**
½ **cup water**
½ **pound lasagna noodles**
2 **cups cottage cheese**
1½ **cups grated cheddar cheese**

Prepare chili mix according to package directions, using meat, oil, tomatoes, beans, and water. Cook lasagna noodles. Alternate noodles, meat sauce, cottage cheese, and cheese in shallow 3-quart baking pan, making 3 layers ending with sauce and cheese. Bake at 375° for 30 minutes. Let stand 15 minutes to set before serving.

Beneath the Palms

🌴 Pollo en Salsa (Chicken in Spicy Tomato Sauce)

Yield: 6 to 8 servings

6-8	**skinless chicken breasts**
1	**tablespoon vegetable oil**
1	**tablespoon salt**
1½	**teaspoons cumin**
1½	**teaspoons black peppercorns**
1	**clove garlic, minced**
¼	**cup chopped bell pepper**
1	**(8 ounce) can tomato sauce**
1	**cup warm water**
2	**tablespoons flour**
½	**cup water**

In 4½-quart Dutch oven, brown chicken pieces in oil. Add salt, cover and simmer 15 to 20 minutes. Grind cumin, peppercorns and garlic with a molcajete. Add a little water to make paste, set aside. Add spices, bell pepper, and tomato sauce to chicken. Add 1 cup warm water, cover, simmer 25 to 35 minutes, stirring occasionally. Mix flour with remaining water to make paste, add to chicken mixture. Cook and stir until thickened and bubbly.

A molcajete is a mortar made of stone, used to pound spices and small seeds.

Pico de Gallo

Yield: 2 cups

3-4	**fresh serrano chilies**
6	**sprigs fresh cilantro**
1	**small yellow onion**
4	**tomatoes**
1	**avocado, peeled and pitted**
	Dash of olive oil
1	**tablespoon fresh lime juice**
	Salt and pepper to taste

Chop first 5 ingredients into small dice and combine. Stir in remaining ingredients. Serve immediately with tortilla chips or crackers.

Arroz con Pollo Valenciana (Chicken with Rice)

Yield: 6 servings

2½	pounds chicken pieces
½	cup olive oil
2	cloves garlic, minced
1	onion, chopped
1	bell pepper, chopped
1	bay leaf
1	cup whole stewed tomatoes
1	quart chicken broth
1	tablespoon salt
½	teaspoon powdered saffron
1	cup rice

In a large skillet, brown chicken on all sides in hot olive oil. Remove chicken; add garlic, onion, and bell pepper to juices left in skillet. Sauté until onion is golden. Add bay leaf and tomatoes. Return chicken to skillet, add chicken broth. When broth boils, add salt, saffron, and rice. Pour into a 2-quart casserole, cover, and bake at 350° for 20 minutes or until rice is tender.

Chicken Chilaquiles

Yield: 8 servings

1	(3 pound) chicken
1	(10 ounce) can diced tomatoes with green chilies
½	teaspoon salt
½	cup chicken broth
1	(10 ¾ ounce) can cream of chicken soup, undiluted
1	(10 ¾ ounce) can cream of mushroom soup, undiluted
12	corn tortillas, cut into fourths
2	cups chopped onion
3	cups grated cheddar cheese

Boil chicken, bone and dice, reserving 1 cup chicken broth. Combine tomatoes and next 5 ingredients. Blend well. In greased 7x11-inch baking dish, place ⅓ of each of the following: tortillas, chicken, sauce, onions, and cheese. Repeat, in same order, two more times ending with cheese on top. Bake at 350° until cheese is melted and bubbly.

Beneath the Palms

🌴 Chicken Enchiladas

Yield: 6 servings

- 1 **cup mild green taco sauce or salsa**
- ¼ **cup chopped cilantro**
- ¼ **cup chopped parsley**
- 1 **tablespoon lime juice**
- 2 **cloves garlic**
- 2 **cups chopped cooked chicken**
- ¾ **cup shredded low-fat mozzarella cheese**
- 6 **flour tortillas**

Spray 11x7-inch baking dish with cooking spray, set aside. Place taco sauce and next 4 ingredients in a blender or food processor. Cover; blend on high speed about 30 seconds or until smooth. Reserve half of mixture. Combine remaining mixture, chicken, and ¼ cup of cheese. Spoon about ¼ cup chicken mixture onto each tortilla, roll; place seam side down in prepared dish. Cover with remaining sauce and cheese. Bake, uncovered, at 350° for 20 to 25 minutes or until heated through.

Sour Cream Enchiladas

Yield: 4 servings

- 12 **corn tortillas**
  Hot oil
- 2 **cups cooked chicken, diced**
- 1 **medium onion, chopped**
- ½ **pound grated cheddar cheese**
- ½ **pound grated Monterey Jack cheese**
- 2 **tablespoons flour**
- 1 **(14 ounce) can chicken broth**
- ½ **stick melted butter**
- 1 **cup sour cream**
- 2 **jalapeño peppers, seeded and chopped**

Soften tortillas by dipping in hot oil, drain on paper towels. Fill tortillas with chicken, onion, and cheeses, reserving one-quarter cup of each cheese. Roll tortillas, place in a large shallow baking dish, set aside. Add flour and broth to melted butter, cook over medium heat until thickened. Add sour cream; cook until hot, do not boil. Stir in jalapeños. Sprinkle reserved cheese over tortillas, add sauce. Bake at 350° for 20 minutes.

This can be made without chicken for a meatless dish.

Chicken Mole

Yield: 4 servings

- 1 **ounce blanched almonds**
- 1 **ounce hulled, unsalted pumpkin seeds**
- 2 **tablespoons sesame seeds**
- 4 **boneless skinless chicken thighs**
- 2 **5 ½-inch stale tortillas, broken into pieces**
- 2 **teaspoons vegetable oil**
- ½ **cup chopped onion**
- 3 **cloves garlic, minced**
- 1 **jalapeño pepper, seeded and minced**
- 2 **teaspoons chili powder**
- ½ **teaspoon ground cinnamon**
- ¼ **teaspoon ground cloves**
- ¼ **teaspoon ground cumin**
- 1 **(16 ounce) can whole peeled tomatoes, drained, with juices reserved**
- ½ **ounce Mexican chocolate, cut into pieces**
- ¼-½ **cup salt-free chicken broth (optional)**

In small skillet, toast almonds over medium heat, shaking pan frequently, until browned, about 5 minutes. Repeat with pumpkin seeds, then sesame seeds. Transfer to a plate to cool. Place chicken in large skillet, add water to cover. Bring to simmer; reduce heat to low and poach, uncovered, until chicken is cooked through, 12 to 15 minutes. Transfer to plate and cover loosely with foil. In food processor, process almonds, pumpkin and sesame seeds until finely ground. Add tortillas and process until ground. In large nonstick skillet, heat oil over medium heat. Add onion, garlic, and jalapeno pepper, cook stirring frequently, until onion is softened, about 5 minutes. Add spices; cook, stirring constantly, 1 minute. Add to nut mixture in food processor and puree until smooth. Add tomatoes and process until smooth. Return mixture to skillet; heat over low heat. Add chocolate, reserved tomato juice, and cook, stirring, until sauce is smooth and dark. If sauce thickens on standing, thin with chicken broth as needed. Add chicken to sauce, cook over low heat just until hot.

Serve over white rice.

Beneath the Palms

Enchiladas Tampico

Yield: 6 servings

- 1 (16 ounce) can tomatoes, drained
- 1 (4 ounce) can whole green chilies, drained and seeded
- ½ teaspoon ground coriander
- 1 teaspoon salt
- 1 cup sour cream
- 1 teaspoon margarine
- ¼ cup chopped onion
- 1 (3 ounce) package cream cheese, softened
- 2 cups chopped cooked chicken
- 12 flour tortillas
- 2 cups grated Monterey Jack cheese

Place tomatoes, chilies, coriander, and salt in a blender. Process until smooth. Add sour cream; blend and set aside. Melt margarine; sauté onion until transparent, add cream cheese and blend well. Stir in chicken. Soften flour tortillas in microwave about 30 seconds. Place equal amounts of chicken mixture in each tortilla and roll tightly, place seam side down, in a 7x11-inch baking dish. Pour sauce over enchiladas. Cover; microwave on high for 7 minutes, rotating the dish once. Sprinkle cheese over top and microwave on high for 3 minutes.

Mexican Rice

Yield: 6 servings

- ¼ cup bacon drippings
- 1 cup white rice
- 1 small onion, chopped
- 1 small bell pepper, cut in strips
- ½ cup stewed tomatoes
- 1 clove garlic, crushed
- 1 teaspoon salt
- ½ teaspoon freshly ground black pepper
- 1 (10 ¾ ounce) can chicken broth

Heat drippings, add rice and brown lightly, stirring constantly. Add onion, pepper, tomatoes, and garlic; cook until onion is translucent, continuing to stir. Add remaining ingredients, stir once. Reduce heat to a simmer, cover and cook for 20 minutes without removing the cover. Rice is done when it is dry all the way through.

Enchiladas Verdes (Green Enchiladas in the Microwave)

Yield: 4 servings

2	**cups green salsa**
12	**corn tortillas**
2	**tablespoons vegetable oil**
2½	**cups shredded cheddar cheese**
½	**cup chopped onion**
1	**cup shredded lettuce**
½	**cup chopped tomatoes**
	Salsa
	Lettuce
	Tomatoes

Pour salsa in flat-bottomed casserole dish. Cover with waxed paper. Microwave on medium-high 3 minutes, set aside. Lightly rub both sides of each tortilla with oil; place in 2 stacks of 6 tortillas each. Wrap each stack in waxed paper; microwave 50 seconds. Grease a 12x8-inch flat-bottomed casserole dish. Dip each softened tortilla in salsa. Place tortilla in casserole dish, sprinkle with cheese and onion. Top with another tortilla. Repeat alternating tortillas, cheese, and onion, building 2 stacks of 6 tortillas each. Pour remaining salsa over tortillas. Cover with waxed paper, microwave on medium-high 5 to 8 minutes or until cheese melts. Rotate dish after 3 minutes. Garnish with salsa, lettuce, and tomatoes.

Variations: After heating salsa, stir in 1 cup sour cream.

Chicken: Stir 2 cups cooked, shredded chicken and 1 can cream of chicken soup into salsa.

Tortilla Black Bean Casserole

Yield: 8 servings

2 cups chopped onion
1½ cups chopped bell pepper
1 (14 ½ ounce) can whole stewed tomatoes, cut up
¾ cup picante sauce
2 cloves garlic, minced
2 teaspoons ground cumin
2 (15 ounce) cans black beans or red kidney beans, drained
12 (6-inch) corn tortillas
2 cups shredded Monterey Jack cheese
2 medium tomatoes, sliced (optional)
2 cups shredded lettuce (optional)
Sliced green onion (optional)
Pitted ripe olives (optional)
½ cup low fat dairy sour cream (optional)

In a large skillet, combine onion and next 5 ingredients. Bring to boil, reduce heat. Simmer, uncovered, for 10 minutes. Stir in beans. In 13x9x2-inch baking dish spread one-third of the bean mixture over bottom. Top with half the tortillas, overlapping as necessary, and half the cheese. Add another third of bean mixture, then remaining tortillas and bean mixture. Cover; bake at 350° for 30 to 35 minutes or until heated through. Sprinkle with remaining cheese. Let stand for 10 minutes. If desired, top with tomato slices, lettuce, green onion, and olives. Cut into squares to serve. Can be served with sour cream or yogurt.

🌴 Calabaza con Pollo (Chicken with Squash)

6 skinless chicken breast
   Vegetable oil
1 small onion, chopped
1¼ teaspoons black
   peppercorns
1 teaspoon whole
   coriander
6 cloves garlic
   Salt and pepper to taste
3 fresh tomatoes,
   chopped
1 large calabaza, peeled,
   seeded, and cubed,
   (Mexican squash)
3 ears fresh corn, kernels
   cut from cob

Brown chicken pieces in Dutch oven or large skillet in oil. Remove and drain most of oil from pan. Sauté onion in remaining oil. Crush peppercorns, coriander, and garlic in molcajete (mortar and pestle). Add to pan along with tomatoes, sauté briefly. Add calabaza, cooking briefly. Add chicken and corn. Cover and allow to simmer about 45 minutes or until chicken is tender and well cooked.
If fresh corn is not available, substitute 1 (12 ounce) can of whole kernel corn drained. Add when chicken is almost done.

Hot, fresh corn tortillas and salsa are great with this dish.

Calabaza is a green-striped Cushaw. It is also know as a Mexican squash.

The first train into Brownsville from the north arrived in June of 1904. This connection afforded a new era in social and economic activities in the area.

Calabazitas con Puerco (Pork with Squash)

Yield: 6 to 8 servings

- 2 teaspoons cumin (comino)
- 1 tablespoon olive oil
- 1 pound ground pork
- 6 medium calabazas (Mexican squash), coarsely chopped
- 1 large onion, chopped
- 1 clove garlic, minced
- 1 (28 ounce) can stewed tomatoes, crushed
- 1 (15 ounce) can whole kernel corn
  Salt and pepper
  Hot sauce

In large skillet, brown the cumin in oil. Add pork and lightly brown. Transfer to Dutch oven. Add calabazas, onion, and garlic to pork drippings in skillet and sauté lightly; transfer to Dutch oven. Add tomatoes to meat mixture. Cover and cook slowly about 30 minutes. Add corn, salt, pepper, and desired amount of hot sauce. Add more liquid if mixture is dry. If soup is desired, serve as soon as heated through. For a thicker consistency like stew, add 2 tablespoons cornstarch to liquid from corn; cook an additional 10 to 15 minutes.

Serve with hot corn tortillas.

May substitute 6 zucchini for Mexican squash.

Baked Calabazitas (Baked Squash)

Yield: 4 servings

6   **small calabazitas (Mexican squash), cubed**
½   **small onion, chopped**
½   **cup evaporated milk**
1   **tablespoon butter or margarine, melted**
    Salt and pepper
12   **saltine crackers, crushed**
    Cheddar or American cheese, shredded

Wash squash, cut into pieces. Cover with water; cook with onion until tender. Drain and mash lightly with a fork, stir in milk, butter, salt, and pepper. Place in shallow baking dish, top with crushed crackers and grated cheese. Bake at 325° for 20 to 30 minutes.

🌴 Hot Lima Beans

Yield: 6 servings

1   **(10 ounce) package frozen baby lima beans**
¼   **cup chopped onion**
2   **tablespoons water**
1   **clove garlic, minced**
1   **large tomato, peeled and chopped**
1   **small jalapeño or serrano chili, seeded and chopped**
    Salt and pepper to taste
    Pinch of sugar
1   **egg, hard boiled and chopped**

Cook beans according to package directions, set aside. Sauté onion in water, add garlic. When onion is translucent, add next 4 ingredients. Cook 5 minutes, add beans; mix well. Transfer to serving dish, garnish with egg.

Beneath the Palms

Tortillas de Harina
(Flour Tortillas)

Yield: 2 dozen tortillas

4 **cups flour**
⅔ **cup shortening**
2 **teaspoons salt**
1 **teaspoon baking powder**
   Hot water

Mix all dry ingredients. Blend in shortening with pastry blender or fingers. Pour in hot water and mix. Knead dough, on bread board, until soft and pliable. Allow to stand 20 minutes. Preheat ungreased griddle. Make dough balls about the size of a golf-ball and then form into flat patties. Roll out on bread board until patty is round and thin. Bake on griddle, turning when top begins to show puffiness or blisters. Cook until lightly browned.

Tortillas de Manteca
(Short Corn Tortillas)

Yield: 10 tortillas

2 **cups fresh masa**
2 **teaspoons salt**
1 **cup pure lard**
½ **cup cracklings**

Combine first 3 ingredients; blend well by hand. Add cracklings; blend again. Divide dough into 8 to 10 golf-ball size balls. Pat out into small flat circles and place on a heated, ungreased griddle. Tortillas will begin to fry in their own grease. Allow each side to become golden brown. Drain.

Masa is available at specialty food stores.

Empanadas de Dulce (Sweet Pastries)

Yield: 24 servings

Filling:
- 1 medium ripe pumpkin or 1 (16 ounce) can pumpkin pie filling
  Sugar
  Cinnamon
  Ground cloves

Pastry:
- 1 teaspoon salt
- 6 tablespoons sugar
- 2 teaspoons baking powder
- 1½ cups shortening
- 8 tablespoons cold water
- 5 cups all-purpose flour
  Sugar

Filling:
Cut pumpkin in half and place on cookie sheet, cut side down. Bake at 350° until pumpkin is well done. Remove peel and seeds; chop pulp. Place pulp in a large cooking pot; mash well with potato masher, add sugar, cinnamon, and cloves to taste. Heat until flavors blend.

Pastry:
Make pastry by mixing salt and the next 5 ingredients together. Roll out as thin as possible, cut into 2-inch circles, or slightly larger. Pierce each with a fork. Place a spoonful of pumpkin mixture on one side of circle; fold pastry over, press and seal edges with a fork. Sprinkle with sugar; bake at 350° for 10 to 12 minutes, or until browned.

Cajeta may be substituted for pumpkin.

Mexican Wedding Cookies

Yield: 4 dozen cookies

- 1 cup butter
- ¼ cup sugar
- 2 cups ground pecans
- 2 cups flour, sifted
  Powdered sugar

Cream butter until softened. Add sugar, pecans, and flour. Mix well. Shape into balls using about one tablespoon of dough for each cookie. Bake at 300° for 45 minutes. Roll in powdered sugar when first taken from oven, then again when cool.

Mexican Chocolate Cake

Yield: 24 servings

Cake:
- 1 **stick unsalted butter**
- ¼ **cup unsweetened Dutch process cocoa powder**
- 1 **cup water**
- 2 **cups all-purpose flour**
- 2 **cups sugar**
- ½ **cup buttermilk, shaken well**
- 2 **large eggs**
- ½ **teaspoon baking soda**
- ½ **teaspoon baking powder**
- 2 **teaspoons vanilla extract**
- 2 **teaspoons cinnamon, rounded**
- 1 **teaspoon instant espresso coffee granules, rounded**
- ½ **teaspoon salt**
- 1½ **cups coarsely chopped walnuts or pecans (optional)**

Frosting:
- 3 **cups powdered sugar**
- 1 **stick unsalted butter, melted**
- ¼ **cup unsweetened Dutch process cocoa powder**
- ¼ **cup plus 2 tablespoons milk**
- 2 **teaspoons vanilla extract**
- 2 **teaspoons cinnamon**
- 1 **teaspoon instant espresso coffee granules**
- ¾ **cup chopped walnuts or pecans (optional)**

Cake:
Spray 13x9x2-inch cake pan with cooking spray. In small saucepan, combine butter, cocoa, and water over medium heat. Bring to boil and remove from heat. In large bowl, sift together flour and sugar, set aside. In medium bowl, whisk together buttermilk and next 7 ingredients, set aside. Add melted cocoa mixture to flour mixture using a rubber spatula to remove all mixture from saucepan. Beat with electric mixer at medium speed until well blended. Add buttermilk mixture using rubber spatula to remove all mixture from bowl. Continue beating until well blended. Batter will be very light. Fold in nuts. Pour batter into prepared pan and bake at 400° for 30 to 35 minutes or until tester inserted into center of cake comes out clean. Rotate cake twice during baking. Cake will shrink from side of pan. Place on a wire rack to cool at least 1 hour and 30 minutes. Allow cake to cool completely before frosting.

Frosting:
Combine powdered sugar, melted butter, cocoa, and milk; mix well. Stir in vanilla, cinnamon, and espresso granules. Whisk until mixture is silky smooth, add nuts if desired. Place frosting in refrigerator for

30 minutes to produce a thicker spreading consistency.

This cake can be prepared 2 days in advance, cover tightly and refrigerate. Remove cake *when needed, cut while cake is cold; bring to room temperature. Cake is best when served at room temperature.*

🌴 Capirotada (Mexican Bread Pudding)

Yield: 12 servings

20	slices whole wheat bread
3	small bananas, sliced
10	ounces grated mozzarella cheese
2½	cups water
1½	teaspoons cinnamon
1¼	cups raisins
½	cup sugar
¾	cup chopped walnuts

In each loaf pan, put a layer of bread, bananas, and cheese. Bring water to boil, add cinnamon, raisins, and sugar; remove from heat. Sprinkle bread with sugared water until it is soaked. Repeat layers until each pan is three-fourths full. Sprinkle walnuts on tops. Cut mixture into smaller pieces. Bake at 350° for 15 to 20 minutes. Serve hot or cold.

Hojarascas (Pan de Polvo)

Yield: 10 dozen cookies

10	cups flour
1	cup sugar
¼	teaspoon baking powder
1	tablespoon cinnamon
1	teaspoon salt
1½	cups pork lard
1½	cups shortening
3	eggs
1	tablespoon water
½	cup sugar
2	tablespoons cinnamon

Mix dry ingredients well. Add lard, shortening, and eggs; mix well. Add water and knead. Roll mixture into 1-inch balls. Place on ungreased cookie sheets; bake at 350° for 8 minutes. As soon as cookies are out of oven, roll in mixture of cinnamon and sugar.

Flan
(Custard with Caramel)

Yield: 12 servings

1 (14 ounce) can
   sweetened condensed
   milk
½ cup whole milk
5 eggs
2 teaspoons vanilla
   extract
1 cup sugar

Blend together condensed milk, whole milk, eggs, and vanilla. In a heavy skillet, caramelize sugar. Pour sugar into 12x9-inch glass baking dish, tipping to spread evenly. Pour in egg mixture. Place dish in larger pan, add water to larger pan to come half way up sides. Bake at 350° for 1 hour. Cool; chill thoroughly. Loosen flan with knife and invert onto serving platter.

Sopapillas
(Hot Fried Puffs)

Yield: 8 dozen

¼ cup warm water
1 package active dry yeast
1 egg
1½ cups milk
⅓ cup butter, melted
⅓ cup sugar
1 teaspoon salt
1 tablespoon cornmeal
5 cups flour
   Oil for frying
   Sugar and cinnamon
    mixture

Mix warm water and yeast with electric mixer until thoroughly mixed. Blend in remaining ingredients, except 3 cups flour. Put dough in large bowl. Cover; let stand in warm place, about 1 hour. Add remaining flour, mixing well. Knead mixture into soft dough. Cover, let rise until double in bulk. Punch down dough and store in plastic bag in refrigerator until needed. (Dough may be refrigerated for up to 2 weeks). Roll out thick; cut into triangles or squares. Heat oil in deep fryer until 400°. Fry dough until golden in color. Sprinkle with sugar and cinnamon.

Dip in butter or honey.

Index

Beneath the Palms

Index

Beneath the Palms

Beneath the Palms

Beneath the Palms

Beneath the Palms

Index

Beneath the Palms

Beneath the Palms

Brownsville Junior Service League, Inc.
P.O. Box 3151 • Brownsville, TX 78523-3151

Please send ___ copy(ies) of *Beneath The Palms* @ $18.95 each $ _____

Shipping and Handling   @ $ 3.00 each $ _____

Texas residents add sales tax   @ $ 1.56 each $ _____

                                                      Total $ _____

Ship To:

Name _____

Address _____

City _____ State _____ Zip Code_____

Method of Payment _____ Check _____ Credit Card

Please make checks payable to BJSL, Inc.

Visa / MasterCard Number

_____

Expiration Date

_____

Credit card orders may be placed by calling 1-888-992-BJSL (2575)
Proceeds from the sale of this book support the many projects of
the Brownsville Junior Service League, Inc.